PUTTING
PHILOSOPHY
TO WORK

PUTTING
PHILOSOPHY
TO WORK

ESSAYS ON SCIENCE, RELIGION, LAW, LITERATURE, AND LIFE

INQUIRY AND ITS
PLACE IN CULTURE

SUSAN HAACK

Susan Haack
2/12/09

Prometheus Books

59 John Glenn Drive
Amherst, New York 14228-2119

Published 2008 by Prometheus Books

Inquiries should be addressed to
Prometheus Books
59 John Glenn Drive
Amherst, New York 14228–2197
VOICE: 716–691–0133, ext. 207
FAX: 716–564–2711
WWW.PROMETHEUSBOOKS.COM

12 11 10 09 08   5 4 3 2 1

Library of Congress Cataloging-in-Publication Data

Haack, Susan.
    Putting philosophy to work : inquiry and its place in culture : essays on science, religion, law, literature, and life / Susan Haack.
        p. cm.
    Includes bibliographical references and index.
    ISBN: 978–1–59102–528–3
    1. Philosophy. I. Title.

B72.H22 2007
100—dc22

                                                                        2007022225

Printed in the United States of America on acid-free paper

dedicated to the memory of

Robert L. Heilbroner (1919–2005)

Louise M. Rosenblatt (1904–2005)

Peter Strawson (1919–2006)

The aim of philosophy . . . is to understand how things in the broadest possible sense of the term hang together in the broadest possible sense of the term.

—Wilfrid Sellars

CONTENTS

ACKNOWLEDGMENTS

"Staying for an Answer" was first presented, in 1998, in the School of Architecture at Virginia Tech, under its original title, "A Cannibal Among the Missionaries." It first appeared, under its present title, in *The Times Literary Supplement*, July 9, 1999, 12–14. It has been reprinted in Cassandra Pinnick, Noretta Koertge, and Robert Almeder, eds., *Scrutinizing Feminist Epistemology* (New Brunswick, NJ: Rutgers University Press, 2003), pp. 234–52; in Daphne Patai and Will Corrall, eds., *Theory's Empire: An Anthology of Dissent* (New York: Columbia University Press, 2005), pp. 552–62; and, abridged, in *Think* (2002). It has also appeared in Portuguese (2000) and Spanish (2001) translations.

"The Same, Only Different" was presented in 2001 at a colloquium, "Beginning With the Humanities," held at the Whitney Humanities Center to celebrate the 300th anniversary of the founding of Yale University. It first appeared in the *Journal of Aesthetic Education* 36, no. 3 (2002): 34–39; and was pirated, the same month, in the *Internationale Zeitschrift für Philosophie* 1 (2002): 18–22 (I still don't know how this came about). This essay has also appeared, in Swedish translation, in the humanities journal of the Swedish Research Council, *Tvärsnitt* (2005).

"The Unity of Truth and the Plurality of Truths," which began life under the title "One Truth, or Many Truths? Yes, and Yes," was first presented at a conference on Pluralism at Vanderbilt University in 2003. It was subsequently presented in the philosophy departments at Peking University, Nankei University, South China Normal University, and the University of Haifa, and at an international conference on relativism in Göteborg, Sweden (2004); in the philosophy departments at the University of California, Davis, and the University of Bologna, and at an international conference on epistemology and philosophy of science in Florianópolis, Brazil (2005). After being "preprinted" in a volume of papers from the Göteborg conference, it appeared in *Principia* 9, no. 1–2 (2005): 87–100.

"Coherence, Consistency, Cogency, Congruity, Cohesiveness, &c.: Remain Calm! Don't Go Overboard!" was written in response to an invitation from the associate editor of *New Literary History*. (His reaction to my paper—which opens by poking a little gentle fun at this invitation—was remarkably good-natured: "I've never been quoted so extensively in my life.") This piece was my Bugbee Lecture at the University of Montana (2003), and was also presented in the philosophy departments at Simon Fraser University (2003) and Georgetown (2004). It first appeared in *New Literary History* 35 (2004): 167–83; and, abridged, under the title "Coherence & Co.," in *The Philosopher's Magazine* 6, no. 2 (2004): 33–35.

"Not Cynicism, but Synechism: Lessons from Classical Pragmatism" was presented in 2004 at a conference on "Peirce-pectives on Metaphysics and Philosophy of Science" organized by Rosa Mayorga in the department of philosophy at Virginia Tech. This essay first appeared in *Transactions of the Charles S. Peirce Society* XLI, no. 2 (2005): 239–53; and then in the (long-delayed) volume for which it had originally been written, *A Companion to Pragmatism*, eds. John Shook and Joseph Margolis (Oxford: Blackwell, 2006), pp. 141–53.

"Science, Economics, 'Vision'" appeared in a special issue of *Social Research* in honor of Robert Heilbroner (71, no. 2 [2004]; 167–83), for which it was written at the invitation of the editor. It was subsequently presented at the annual conference of the Association for the History of Economics held at the University of Puget Sound, WA, in June 2005.

"The Integrity of Science: What It Means, Why It Matters," was my inaugural lecture at the annual meeting of the National Council for Ethics in the Life Sciences (Portugal), held in Porto in November 2006. It appeared in *Ética e Investigacão nas Ciências da Vida—Actas do 10⁰ Seminario do Conshelho Nacional de Éticas para as Ciências da Vida*, 2006: 9–28; and in Spanish translation (2007).

"Scientific Secrecy and 'Spin': The Sad, Sleazy Saga of the Trials of Remune," was first presented in 2004 at the Coronado II Conference organized by the Project on Scientific Knowledge and Public Policy, and subsequently at the College of Law, Arizona State University (2006). It first appeared, after strenuous tussles over a copy-editor's egregious intrusions, in *Law and Contemporary*

Problems 69, no. 3 (2006): 47–67; shortly after which I learned that it was among the top ten papers downloaded from the SSRN [Social Science Research Network] "Evidence" list.

"Truth and Justice, Inquiry and Advocacy, Science and Law," was my plenary lecture at the XXIst conference of the International Association for Legal and Social Philosophy, held in Lund, Sweden, in August 2003. It was subsequently presented in the School of Politics and Law at South China Normal University, at the Institute of Medicine, National Academies of Science, and at the Georgetown Law Center (2004); and then in the School of Law at the University of Missouri, Kansas City (2005) and the College of Law at Arizona State University (2006). After being "preprinted" in *Associations: Journal for Legal and Social Theory* (2003), it appeared in *Ratio Juris* 17, no. 1 (2004): 15–26.

"Trial and Error: The Supreme Court's Philosophy of Science," was first presented in 2003 at the Coronado I conference of the Project on Scientific Knowledge and Public Policy. It was subsequently presented at law school colloquia at the University of Montana (2003), at George Mason University, the University of Pennsylvania, and University College, London (2004), and at the University of Florida (2005). It first appeared in the *American Journal of Public Health* 95 (2005): S66–73, and was reprinted in the *International Society of Barristers Quarterly* 41, no. 2 (2006): 376–91. It has also appeared in Italian translation (2006).

"An Epistemologist Among the Epidemiologists" appeared in *Epidemiology* 15, no. 5 (2004): 521–22, for which it was written at the invitation of the editor.

"Fallibilism and Faith, Naturalism and the Supernatural, Science and Religion," was first presented in 2004 at a conference on God and the Laws of Nature organized by the department of Plasma Physics at the University of Milan. It was subsequently presented at the annual conference of the Center for Inquiry, Florida (2005) and the Center for Inquiry International (2007). It first appeared in *Dio, la natura e la legge*, eds. Stefano Moriggi and Elio Sindoni (Milan: Angelicum/Mundo X, 2005), pp. 143–54.

"The Ideal of Intellectual Integrity, in Life and Literature," was my keynote lecture at a conference on Virtue Epistemology organized by the department of philosophy at the University of Stirling, Scotland, in November 2004. The following year it was presented in the departments of philosophy at the University of South Florida and at the University of Houston. (Though this is a deeply serious paper, I was delighted when a graduate student in Houston commented that it made him laugh so hard, his face hurt!) This paper was to have been published, with the other papers from the Stirling conference, in *Philosophical Studies*, but had to be withdrawn when Springer refused to honor a prior agreement giving me control of copyright; so it first appeared in *New Literary History* 36, no. 3 (2005): 359–73.

"After My Own Heart: Dorothy Sayers's Feminism," was written for a symposium on women philosophers organized by John Lachs at the Eastern Division meeting of the American Philosophical Association in December 2000. I was on the fourth joke before any of the audience realized it was OK to laugh; so instead of submitting the paper to a philosophy journal I sent it to the *New Criterion*, where it appeared in 2001; it was reprinted in Almeder, Pinnick, and Koertge, *Scrutinizing Feminist Epistemology* (2003), pp. 244–52.

"Worthwhile Lives" appeared in *Free Inquiry* (winter 2001–2002): 50–51, for which it was written at the invitation of the editor.

"Why I Am Not an Oxymoron" was written at the invitation of the editors of a glossy British art magazine called *Wideshut*. A year after I had submitted my essay, I learned that the magazine had run out of money, and folded; so the paper appears here for the first time.

"Formal Philosophy?—A Plea for Pluralism" was written at the invitation of the editors of a volume on formal methods in philosophy; who, like the editor at *New Literary History*—though without his exquisite sense of irony—took my disavowal of the false presuppositions of their "questionnaire" in good part. This essay first appeared in *Formal Philosophy*, eds. John Symons and Vincent Hendricks (New York: Automatic Press/VIP, 2005), pp. 77–98.

I have edited the essays to unify the style of endnotes, to avoid unnecessary repetition, and to update where updating was needed; I have also, here and there, restored my original wording where copy-editors had overridden my judgment. (The acute reader will notice in these acknowledgments an undercurrent of muted protest about the present, disastrous condition of academic publishing.) I am grateful to the staff in the library at the University of Miami School of Law, and to my Faculty Assistant, Beth Hanson, for skilled and good-natured help of many kinds; and, as always, to a whole army of correspondents and audience members for helpful comments, to Mark Migotti for thoughtful criticisms and suggestions on many raw, half-baked, and almost-finished drafts, and to Howard Burdick for keeping me sane.

Introduction

PUTTING PHILOSOPHY TO WORK

Philosophy is at once the most sublime and the most trivial of pursuits. It works in the minutest crannies and it opens out the widest vistas. . . . [R]epugnant as its manners, its doubting and challenging, its quibbling and dialectics, often are to common people, no one of us can get along without the far-flashing beams of light it sends over the world's perspectives.

—William James, "The Present Dilemma in Philosophy"[1]

James's lecture, "The Present Dilemma in Philosophy," from which these words are taken, was published a century ago; but it is still relevant today. What we need, James wrote, is "a philosophy that will not only exercise your power of intellectual abstraction, but that will make some positive connexion with the actual world of finite human lives";[2] as I might put it now, what we need is a philosophy that will track underlying patterns and principles without losing sight of particulars, and that will engage with key issues of our culture without sacrificing clarity or rigor.

This is a tall order. Rigor, clarity, scope, depth, pertinence, are none of them easily achieved; and combining them is exponentially harder, for the desiderata of rigor and clarity, depth and scope are apt to pull against each other. Of course, not every piece of philosophical work, or every philosopher, must do it all. Some worthwhile philosophical work is specialized, technical, or closely scholarly;

some is broad and speculative. Some focuses on topics quite distant from public issues of the day; some tackles such issues directly. Some offers clean, rigorous abstraction; some provides subtly detailed description. Some is presented in a dry, explicit, emotionally neutral way; some in a vivid, resonant, engaged, and engaging style. Still, it's hardly surprising—since the ideal is at once so attractive and so demanding—that philosophers sometimes succumb to high-toned generalities that dissolve under close scrutiny into banality or falsehood, or to technicalities that dissolve under close scrutiny into pedantry or busywork.

Nor is it surprising—though it is much to be regretted—that today so much work in philosophy seems to fall into one or the other of these traps. Radical neo-pragmatist, feminist, and post-colonialist philosophers aspire to speak to important cultural issues (as do radical sociologists and rhetoricians of science). Sometimes their extravagances contain a grain of truth; but too often they generate more heat than light. Neo-analytic philosophers of the mainstream aspire to high standards of professionalism and rigor. Sometimes their internecine disputes illuminate the "minute crannies" of which James writes; but too often they fail to engage with larger concerns, let alone to "open out the widest vistas."

In short, philosophy is in bad shape: more and more estranged from its own history; more and more aloof from other fields of intellectual endeavor; more and more distant from "finite human lives." A decade ago, I wrote in "Preposterism and Its Consequences" that "I don't think philosophy is at present in a particularly desirable condition";[3] by now, that sounds to me like classic British understatement, and the friend who recently commented that our profession is "in a nose-dive" seems closer to the mark. Hunger for prestige, anxiety about those wretched rankings, a circling of the neo-analytic wagons against the would-be philosophers of the literature departments—whatever the reasons, philosophers now seem ever less tolerant of real intellectual diversity, or of the genuinely independent thinker.

It's a great shame; for philosophical analysis informed by the insights both of the great philosophical thinkers of the past and of neighboring disciplines has much to offer. Or so I have come to believe as, trying to figure out more clearly "how things hang together," I have found my interest drawn to questions about continuities and discontinuities between philosophy and other kinds of inquiry, and between the natural and the social sciences; about the role of science in the law; the effects of the industrial sponsorship of scientific research; the tensions between science and religion; the philosophical lessons to be learned from works of literature; and even about the meaning of life.

Though these questions have often taken me quite far from the professional mainstream, I have been encouraged and sustained along the way by the writings of the older pragmatists. Readers familiar with this tradition will notice many themes from Peirce, James, Dewey, and Mead; and may even see, as I do, an affinity between this book of mine and John Dewey's *Philosophy and Civilization*. Of course, the social issues that concern me are somewhat different from those that concerned Dewey, and my philosophical bent is more thoroughly epistemological, less political, than his; but my sub-title, *Inquiry and Its Place in Culture*, signals our shared hope of a genuinely engaged philosophy, and our shared belief in the ability of well-conceived philosophical analysis to shed light on cultural questions.

We humans are not the only animals to explore the world around us; but the human capacity for representation, for language and other symbol systems, enables us not only to explore but to inquire. We humans are not the only social animals, or even the only animals able to pass on skills to others of our kind; but without the distinctive human capacity for inquiry and articulation, culture as we know it would hardly be possible.

In recent decades, however, there have been many who have come to believe, or at least to profess to believe, that the supposed ideal of honest, unbiased inquiry is nothing but a rhetorical smoke-screen disguising the covert operation of power, politics, and rhetoric. In the first essay included here, "Staying for an Answer," I argue that these cynics' supposedly sophisticated disillusionment is really a quite crude, and an entirely factitious, despair. The ideal of honest inquiry is a robust one, well worth aspiring to. Granted, finding things out can be enormously difficult. Evidence can be hard to come by and, when we get it, may be overwhelmingly complex or seductively misleading. Moreover, our fragile will to find things out is only too easily undermined, only too readily diverted into pseudo-inquiry, self-deception, self-indulgent fantasy, or complacent confidence. But there is no need to give up on the objectivity of truth or evidence, or on the possibility of finding things out. What we need, rather, is to articulate a realistic understanding of the scope, limitations, and defects of the capacity for inquiry that all normal human beings share, and of the special capacities and quirks of individual minds—an understanding both of the possibilities and of the pitfalls of human beings' ability to inquire, to figure things out.

Among those pitfalls are jumping to conclusions—rushing to judgment on inadequate evidence; and wishful thinking—inducing yourself to believe what you would like to be true. As a result—as those radical feminists, neo-pragmatists, sociologists of science, and others, never tire of pointing out—false claims conveniently serving the purposes of the powerful have only too often been taken for known truths well-supported by strong evidence. It obviously doesn't follow,

however, as the cynics conclude, that the ideal of honest inquiry, and even the
very ideas of truth or evidence, are inherently racist or sexist. Far from it: the
capacity for inquiry is one of the most admirable talents of the human race—one
might almost say, echoing Francis Bacon, "the sovereign good of human
nature."[4] Only by honest inquiry, moreover, can we find out that racist or sexist
stereotypes *are* stereotypes, not truths.

The purpose of the next, short essay, "The Same, Only Different," is to articulate how inquiry differs from other human activities, from dancing or cookery
to storytelling or advocacy; to explore what the many and various kinds of
inquiry—in the natural sciences, the social sciences, legal or literary scholarship,
history, philosophy, forensic investigation, and so on—have in common, and
how these various kinds of inquiry differ from each other; and finally to disentangle what is true from what is false in the recently fashionable idea that all
inquiry is in some sense "interpretive." All inquiry involves obtaining and
appraising evidence, and insofar as you appraise the worth of evidence, you must
interpret it; social-scientific inquiry often involves understanding people's beliefs
and goals, and hence interpreting what they say and do; and of course literary
inquiry involves the interpretation of texts—as, subject to rather different constraints, does legal inquiry.

Issues about the meaning and the objectivity of truth, touched on only briefly
in the first two papers, are tackled head-on in the third, "The Unity of Truth and
the Plurality of Truths." There is one truth, I argue, one unambiguous, non-
relative truth-concept; and to say that a claim is true is to say (not that anyone,
or everyone, believes it, or that it follows from this or that theory, or that there is
good evidence for it, but) simply that things are as it says. But of course there are
many truths, of many different kinds, in many different vocabularies—empirical,
logical, mathematical, historical, legal, literary, . . . and so on. Isn't this, you may
wonder, too obvious to need saying? No. For only by gradually unravelling first
the densely tangled arguments that have persuaded some philosophers that there
are many truth-concepts, and others that there is no viable truth-concept at all,
and then the densely tangled arguments that have persuaded some philosophers
that there are no truths, or that only The Whole Truth About Absolutely Everything is really-and-truly true, can we appreciate both the simplicity of the idea of
truth, and its subtleties.

The playful title of the next piece, "Coherence, Consistency, Cogency, Congruity, Cohesiveness, &c.: Remain Calm! Don't Go Overboard!" reflects its
origin in the extraordinary list of questions posed by a letter of invitation from
New Literary History: "[D]oes coherence name a totalized state or an organizing
tendency? . . . Can theories of chaos bring their object to order without thereby

eliminating it? . . . In cognitive or cultural processes, is total structure an inference from perception or its enabling precondition? . . . What is the status of coherence in advanced scholarly argumentation? . . . How does [the concept of coherence] foster on the one hand an ethics of solidarity and community, on the other an imperial or totalitarian politics? How do the economics of globalization inflect coherentism today? . . . ," etc., etc. But my tongue-in-cheek deconstruction of this well-intentioned but mind-boggling invitation serves only as a prelude to a serious examination of the many meanings of "coherent" and its kin; and then to new reflections on where and why coherence is indispensable, and where and why an insistence on consistency is, rather, undesirable rigidity of mind or inflexibility of practice.

It was only after long reflection on the continuities between inquiry in the sciences and in everyday life and between inquiry in the natural and in the social sciences, and on the ways in which philosophical inquiry is like scientific inquiry and the ways in which it is different, that I saw the relevance of the regulative ideal C. S. Peirce called "synechism": an in-principle preference for hypotheses that posit continuities over those that posit sharp lines of demarcation. "Not Cynicism, but Synechism," the next, and most historical, of the essays reprinted here, is my attempt to articulate what Peirce meant by synechism, why he thought it important, and how it plays out in his metaphysics, theory of inquiry, philosophy of science, and philosophy of mind. This enables me to articulate what I now recognize as the many synechist themes in my own work.

Next, in "Science, Economics, 'Vision,'" I pursue the theme of the continuity of the social with the natural sciences, tracing the ways in which inquiry in economics is like inquiry in the natural sciences, and the ways in which it is different; and then I can sort out what is defensible in Robert Heilbroner's critique of the "scientific" aspirations of economics from what is not. There can be no economy, Heilbroner writes, and hence no economics, except in the capitalist context of markets, prices, etc. The "scientific" economics that presently predominates, he continues, is a "desiccated residue," a mathematically preoccupied and deeply unsatisfying enterprise. Falsely claiming objectivity, it risks assimilating the behavior of people to the "behavior" of atoms, and the "laws" of the market to the laws of nature.

Heilbroner's conception of economics as possible only in the context of capitalism, I argue (wryly recalling my undergraduate course on "The Soviet Economy") is unduly narrow; and his critique of contemporary economics-as-science is an overreaction to the physics-envy of which some economists are, doubtless, guilty. Nevertheless, there is something right about Heilbroner's concern that a too-exclusive emphasis on economics-as-science may crowd out the "visionary" economics for which he hankers: his implicit recognition of the dangers of confusing inquiry and advocacy, and of making local, contingent economic arrangements seem inevitable, and his explicit insistence that we need to think about the benefits and drawbacks of different possible ways of ordering the production and distribution of goods and services. You will notice that Heilbroner's explicit concern that a too-exclusively technical and mathematized economics is losing touch with the big questions about the production and distribution of resources that preoccupied some of the greatest economic thinkers of the past closely parallels my own fear that neo-analytic philosophy is in danger of crowding out the important issues that preoccupied the greatest philosophical thinkers of the past.

You will also notice that issues about the shading of inquiry into advocacy "research," not just in economics but in the sciences generally, are close to the heart of my next essay, "The Integrity of Science: What It Means, Why It Matters." In 1918, Oswald Spengler wrote in *The Decline of the West* that by the year 2000 science would have come to an end, "fall[ing] upon its own keen sword."[5] He was spectacularly wrong; the sciences have been, and continue to be, among the most remarkably successful of human cognitive enterprises. And the gradual integration of different sciences and branches of science with one another, bringing ever-firmer interlocking of disparate kinds of evidence—whether of evolutionary theory with geology and genetics, of biology with physics, or of the social with the natural sciences—continues to enhance the warrant of the most firmly inked-in entries in the vast crossword puzzle of science. But though I have great admiration for the achievements of the sciences, I also see the danger of complacency; for, as the scale and the expense of scientific work has grown, the fragile internal social mechanisms that have thus far succeeded in keeping most scientists more or less honest have come under considerable strain.

Focusing now not on explanatory integration but on integrity in the sense of "firm adherence to values," I argue that the key values of the scientific enterprise are honesty in seeking out, assessing, and reporting evidence, and willingness to share evidence with others in the field. When things go well, these values are instilled in young scientists in the course of their long apprenticeship; reinforced by the incentives of recognition for good work and loss of reputation for cheating; monitored by conscientious peer review at journals and grant-giving bodies; and honored in the culture of the universities. But there is always the danger that competing values in the larger society in which scientific work takes place—the political values of government sponsors of science, for example, or the commercial values of industrial sponsors—may erode commitment to these core ideals.

And as the potential for scientists to profit from their work has grown, along with the entanglement of the universities with industry, the pressure to get grants and to publish, the strains on the peer-review process and on the journals, etc., this danger has grown ever more severe. There is disturbing evidence that scientists' commitment to sharing data and to reporting it honestly is suffering a kind of creeping erosion; especially, it seems, in the medical sciences. The story of Merck's blockbuster arthritis drug, Vioxx—first marketed in 1999, withdrawn from the market in 2004 because of serious cardiovascular risks, and by the end of 2006 the subject of around 27,200 lawsuits against the manufacturer—is a vivid illustration of the many ways things can go wrong.

Evidence sharing contrasts with secrecy or the withholding of evidence; honesty contrasts with misreporting results or giving unpalatable data a more favorable spin. The next essay, "Scientific Secrecy and 'Spin,'" tells "The Sad, Sleazy Saga of the Trials of Remune." A drug company funds a large-scale clinical trial of a new AIDS therapy, to be led by a medical scientist at the University of California, San Francisco; when the study is halted because the data suggest the drug is ineffective, the company takes legal action, trying to prevent publication of the results; when the scientists concerned publish anyway, the company sues for millions of dollars in damages; the same year, stockholders file a multiparty suit alleging that the company manipulated its stock price by misleading the public about the effectiveness of the drug; four years later, with this suit still pending and the drug still not approved by the FDA, the company website affirms that the results of previous clinical trials "demonstrate" that Remune "has the potential to slow the progression of HIV."

"Trials" in the title of this paper refers, of course, both to the clinical trials of the drug, and to the legal proceedings in which the company was embroiled. The following pair of essays, turning specifically to the role of science in the law, focus primarily on how the US legal system handles the scientific testimony now so often crucial to a case. The first of these, "Truth and Justice, Inquiry and Advocacy, Science and Law," opens by articulating the connection between substantive justice and factual truth, and sketching the ever-increasing dependence of the legal system on the expert testimony of scientific witnesses in determining factual issues. Lawyers, legal scholars, and scientists themselves have long expressed concern about the expert witness system—the legal faction complaining that venal and incompetent scientists will testify to whatever the party that hires them requires, while the scientific faction complains that judges, jurors, and attorneys are hopelessly ignorant and deplorably gullible where science is concerned. But, I argue, the problem lies deeper than either side realizes, in serious tensions between science and the legal culture.

Because of the tension between the investigational character of the scientific enterprise, and the adversarial character of the US legal culture, the law often gets less from science than science could give; because of the tension between the in-principle revisability of even the best established scientific claims, and the concern of the legal system for promptness and finality, the legal system often asks more of science than science can give. These tensions underlie legal efforts to domesticate scientific evidence by means of the ever-evolving tests for the admissibility of expert testimony: from the old "*Frye* Rule" through the Federal Rules of Evidence to the most recent standards set by *Daubert v. Merrell Dow Pharmaceuticals* (1993) and subsequent Supreme Court rulings on the issue. They also underlie recent modifications of the legal culture, such as extended statutes of limitations and John Doe warrants specifying the perpetrator's DNA (small but significant compromises of the concern for promptness and finality), and increased use of court-appointed experts (a small but significant compromise of the commitment to adversarialism).

The second essay of this pair, "Trial and Error: The Supreme Court's Philosophy of Science," focuses primarily on *Daubert*, the US Supreme Court's first-ever ruling on the standards of admissibility of scientific testimony. Writing for the majority, Justice Blackmun makes a remarkable foray into philosophy of science. Apparently confusing the question of whether expert testimony is reliable with the question of whether it is genuinely scientific, looking for a test to discriminate scientific, and hence reliable, from unscientific, and hence unreliable, testimony, he runs together elements from Karl Popper's and Carl Hempel's incompatible conceptions of science. But the task is misconceived, for not all, and not only, scientific testimony is reliable. Since 1993, the Supreme Court has quietly backed away from *Daubert*'s muddled philosophy of science, but not from federal judges' responsibility for screening expert testimony. The legal system is still fumbling to find how best to use scientific expertise.

The next, very short piece, "An Epistemologist Among the Epidemiologists," takes up issues about "weight of evidence methodology" that surfaced in *G.E. v. Joiner*. Mr. Joiner had alleged that his lung cancer was promoted by exposure to PCBs (polychlorinated biphenals) in the oil insulating the electric transformers on which he worked. His experts appealed to the combined "weight of evidence" of toxicological studies, studies on animals, and small statistical studies. G.E.'s attorneys argued in reply that this "methodology" is nothing but a fallacy, a pathetic pretence of making a strong case for causation by piling up a lot of weak or marginally relevant evidence. It's true, of course, that additional evidence of other kinds can't magically transform a poor statistical study into a good one. Nevertheless, I argue, *some* congeries of evidence of different kinds *can* constitute a strong case: when statistical evidence of even a weak correlation between risk-factor F and disease D interlocks with toxicological evidence of the physiological ill-effects of F and with studies showing an increased occurrence of D in animals exposed to F, it can support the conclusion that F causes elevated risk of D more strongly than any component piece of evidence by itself could do.

The following essay, "Fallibilism and Faith, Naturalism and the Supernatural, Science and Religion," turns from the relations between science and law to the relations between science and religion. Religion is a human activity of a quite different kind from science; it isn't, and doesn't purport to be, inquiry of any kind. Theology, however, does claim to be a branch of inquiry; and natural theology purports to be continuous with inquiry in the sciences. Here, however, I see important *dis*continuities: between the reliance of the sciences on the evidence of the senses, and theological appeals to a supposedly distinctive and scientifically inaccessible "religious experience"; between the natural explanations sought by scientists, and the supernatural explanations sought by theologians; and between the fallibilism of the sciences, and religious dogma and appeals to faith.

All the same, there is something right in the idea—found in the reflections of thoughtful scientists like Michael Polanyi and Percy Bridgman—that the demands and satisfactions of scientific work, especially the self-transcendence required of all serious inquirers, can be genuinely uplifting to the human spirit. "The Ideal of Intellectual Integrity, in Life and Literature" pursues a theme closely related to this last point—but from a very different angle. The strengths of intellectual character that distinguish the honest inquirer from the dishonest and the responsible inquirer from the irresponsible develop, in those who have them, by a process no less complex, no less subtle, and no less individual than the development of every other aspect of a person's character; and it is in the work of novelists such as George Eliot, Samuel Butler, and Sinclair Lewis that we find the subtlest and most finely detailed imaginative pictures of the development of intellectual character.

A particularly fine case in point is Samuel Butler's semi-autobiographical *Bildungsroman, The Way of All Flesh.* Butler tells the story of Ernest Pontifex's zigzag path from timid child to callow youth to half-baked curate and finally to intellectual adult. Through painful and humiliating experience Ernest comes to realize how hopelessly self-deceived he had been, and how horribly miseducated; and he begins to get a glimmering of the difference between really trying to figure something out and merely going through the motions, and the difference between really believing something and merely mouthing the words to oneself. Ernest's story poignantly illustrates vital aspects of the life of the mind largely ignored by contemporary epistemologists—though not by Peirce, who wrote illuminatingly about the difference between genuine inquiry and the sham, or by Bridgman, who wrote illuminatingly about what is at stake, for the individual and for society, in "the struggle for intellectual integrity."

The following piece, "After My Own Heart: Dorothy Sayers's Feminism," again mixes philosophical business with literary pleasure. Sayers's *Gaudy Night* is a detective story set in an Oxford women's college, Shrewsbury, of which Harriet Vane, professional detective-novelist and part-time sleuth, is a graduate, and Miss de Vine, to whom allegiance to the fact is "a powerful spiritual call," is the history tutor. It is also a detective story that explores important issues both about the relation of epistemological and ethical values, and—the focus of this essay of mine—about the place of women in the life of the mind. In one of her refreshingly old-fashioned essays on feminism, Sayers observes that "women are more like men than anything else on earth." Resonating with my conviction that the capacity for inquiry is a *human* thing, this splendid line informs my argument here: a refusal to acknowledge women's full humanity, and a correlative inability to appreciate each woman's full individuality, really does lie at the heart of sexism (and, sad to say, at the heart of too much "feminist epistemology").

"What is the meaning of life?", presupposing as it does that there is some one thing for the right answer to identify, is a really bad question. In "Worthwhile Lives"—once again citing Sayers's keen observations about how much human beings have in common, and yet how multifarious the differences among individuals are—I ask instead which of the vast variety of purposes and projects that may give shape and meaning to a person's life are really satisfying, and which really good. Reflecting that, flexible and adaptable as we are, circumstances inevitably limit our ability to follow the projects that best suit our taste and talents, and musing on my good fortune in having been born at a time and in a place where educational and other opportunities were not closed to women, I end with some reflections about the satisfactions, and the frustrations, of a life in philosophy.

Hence the two essays that complete the book—two very different pieces of intellectual autobiography. The first is my reply to those critics who claimed to have detected a contradiction in the title of an earlier collection of my essays, *Manifesto of a Passionate Moderate*.[6] Explaining "Why I Am Not an Oxymoron," I point out that strong feelings don't always or inevitably cloud your judgment; they may be just what's needed to motivate the hard work of figuring something out. For me, the awful suffocating feeling of being trapped in a false dichotomy is a very powerful incentive to think my way to habitable middle ground.

The last essay, "Formal Philosophy? A Plea for Pluralism," was written in response to a questionnaire from the editors of a volume on formal methods in philosophy—another invitation I soon found myself happily deconstructing, for every one of their questions turned out to rest on false presuppositions. *For certain philosophical purposes*, formal methods are precisely what is needed; not, however, for all. So, declining to identify myself as a "formal philosopher," I try instead to articulate the many and various questions within the purview of philosophy, the many and various talents useful to a philosopher, and the many and various methods and tools useful to philosophical analysis. And, declining the editors' invitation to identify "*the* most neglected topics" or "*the* most important open problems" in philosophy today, instead I conclude this essay—and now this book—with a "small specimen of philosophical questions which press for industrious and solid investigation."

NOTES

1. William James, "The Present Dilemma in Philosophy," in *Pragmatism* (1907: ed. Frederick H. Burkhardt, Fredson Bowers, and Ignas K. Skrupskelis [Cambridge: Harvard University Press, 1975]), pp. 9–26, p. 10.

2. James, "The Present Dilemma in Philosophy" (n. 1), p. 17.

3. "Preposterism and Its Consequences" (1996), in Susan Haack, *Manifesto of a Passionate Moderate: Unfashionable Essays* (Chicago: University of Chicago Press, 1998), pp. 188–208, p. 188.

4. Francis Bacon, "Of Truth" (1625), in *Francis Bacon's Essays*, ed. Oliphant Smeaton (London: Dent, and New York: Dutton; Everyman's Library, 1906), pp. 1–3, p. 2.

5. Oswald Spengler, *The Decline of the West* (1918–22), trans. Charles Francis Atkinson (New York: Knopf, 1926–28), vol. 1, p. 424.

6. Haack, *Manifesto of a Passionate Moderate* (n. 3).

1

STAYING FOR AN ANSWER

The Untidy Process of Groping for Truth

Some years ago now, I heard my then-dean, a physicist by training, express his unease at the suggestion that the mission statement for the College of Arts and Sciences include the phrase, "concern for truth." The word makes people nervous, he warned, and they're bound to ask, "whose 'truth'?" A sociologist colleague, seconding the dean's reservations, remarked that, while of course his research advances knowledge, he isn't concerned with "truth." A couple of us pointed out that, unless your conclusions are true, they aren't really knowledge, only purported knowledge; and I did my best to explain that it doesn't follow from the fact that people disagree about what is true that truth is relative to perspective. But in due course a Strategic Plan for the college specified curricular innovations required by the "fundamental questions" that have been raised "about the presumed universality and objectivity of 'truth.'"[1]

Probably most of you have heard, not exactly this story, but other stories essentially similar, only set in other places and with different characters; for the ideas my dean had picked up are by now almost an orthodoxy in academia, taken in some quarters—admittedly, more often in the humanities and the social sciences than in the physics department!—as indications of intellectual sophistication and moral rectitude.

Naturally, proponents of this new almost-orthodoxy—the "Higher Dismissiveness," as Anthony Gottlieb calls it, or in my terminology, the "New Cynicism"—differ among themselves on the finer points. But they agree that the supposed ideal of honest inquiry, respect for evidence, concern for truth, is a kind of illusion, a smoke-screen disguising the operations of power, politics, and rhetoric; and that those of us who think it matters whether you care about the truth, who feel no need for precautionary scare quotes when we write of fact, knowledge, evidence, etc., are hopelessly naive. As if this weren't bad enough, the feminists and multiculturalists among them suggest that in our naiveté we are complicit in sexism and racism, and the sociologists and rhetoricians of science among them suspect us of reactionary conformism with the military-industrial complex.

Faced with such an intimidating double accusation of naiveté and moral backwardness, many take the ostrich attitude, apparently hoping that if they ignore the New Cynicism hard enough, it will go away. But an old-fashioned prig like myself begins to feel—well, rather like the proverbial cannibal among the missionaries.

A thoughtful cannibal will notice, at the heart of the New Cynicism, a profound intolerance of uncertainty and a deep unwillingness to accept that the less than perfect is a lot better than nothing at all. And so again and again true, fallibilist premises are transmuted into false, cynical conclusions: what is accepted as known fact is often enough no such thing, *therefore*, the concept of known fact is ideological humbug; one's judgment of the worth of evidence depends on one's background beliefs, *therefore*, there are no objective standards of evidential quality; science isn't sacred, *therefore*, it must be a kind of confidence trick; and so on.

But there's really no need to give up on the objectivity of truth, evidence, etc., provided you're fallibilist enough. What is most urgently needed is a realistic understanding of our epistemic situation, of how complicated evidence can get and how difficult serious inquiry can be. Of course, this will be only the beginning of the work, for then there will be the questions of the place of the sciences within inquiry generally, of the differences between science and literature, of the roots of relativism, and of the claim of the New Cynicism to represent the interests of the oppressed and marginalized.

Evidence is complex and ramifying, often confusing, ambiguous, or misleading. Think of the controversy over that four-billion-year-old meteorite discovered in 1984 Antarctica, thought to have come from Mars about eleven thousand years ago, and containing what might possibly be fossilized bacteria droppings. Some space scientists thought this was evidence of bacterial life on Mars; others thought the bacterial traces might have been picked while the meteorite was in Antarctica; and others again believed that what look like fossilized bacteria droppings might be merely artifacts of the instrumentation. How did they know that giving off these gases when heated indicates that the meteorite comes from Mars? that the meteorite is about four billion years old? that this is what fossilized bacteria droppings look like?—like crossword entries, reasons ramify in all directions.

How reasonable a crossword entry is depends on how well it is supported by its clue and any already completed intersecting entries; how reasonable those other entries are, independent of the entry in question; and how much of the crossword has been completed. How justified a belief is, similarly, depends on how well it is supported by experiential evidence and by reasons, i.e., background beliefs; how justified those background beliefs are, independent of the belief in question; and how much of the relevant evidence the evidence includes.

The quality of the evidence for a claim is objective, depending on how supportive it is of the claim in question, how comprehensive, and how independently secure. A person's judgments of the quality of evidence, however, are perspectival, depending on his background beliefs. Suppose you and I are working on the same crossword puzzle, but have filled in some long, much-intersected entry differently; you think a correct intersecting entry must have an "F" in the middle, while I think it must have a "D" there. Suppose you and I are on the same appointments committee, but you believe in graphology, while I think it's bunk; you think how the candidate writes his gs is relevant to whether he can be trusted, while I scoff at your "evidence." Or, to take a real example: in 1944, when Oswald Avery published his results, even he hedged over the conclusion to which they pointed, that DNA is the genetic material; for the then-accepted wisdom was that DNA is composed of the four nucleotides in regular order, and so is too stupid, too monotonous, a molecule to carry the necessary information. But by 1952, when Hershey and Chase published their results, the tetranucleotide hypothesis had been discredited; and then it could be seen that Avery already had good evidence in 1944 that DNA, not protein, is the genetic material.

Inquiry can be difficult and demanding, and we very often go wrong. Sometimes the obstacle is a failure of will; we don't really want to know the answer badly enough to go to all the trouble of finding out, or we really *don't* want to know, and go to a lot of trouble *not* to find out. I think of the detective who doesn't really want to know who committed the crime, just to collect enough evidence to get a conviction, of the academic who cares less about discovering the causes of racial disharmony than about getting a large grant to investigate the matter—and of my own disinclination to rush to the library to check out the article that might oblige me to redo months of work.

Other things being equal, inquiry goes better when the will and the intellect, instead of pulling in different directions, work together; that's why intellectual integrity is valuable. But even with the best will in the world, even when we really want to find out, we often fail. Our senses, imaginations, and intellects are limited; we can't always see, or guess, or reason, well enough. With ingenuity, we can devise ways of overcoming our natural limitations, from cupping our ears to hear better, through tying knots in rope or cutting notches in sticks to keep count, to highly sophisticated electron microscopes and techniques of computer modelling. Of course, our ingenuity is limited too.

Everyone who looks into how some part or aspect of the world is—the physicist and the detective, the historian and the entomologist, the quantum chemist and the investigative journalist, the literary scholar and the X-ray crystallographer—works on part of a part of the same vast crossword. Since they all investigate the same world, sometimes their entries intersect: a medical researcher relies on an amateur historian's family tree in his search for the defective gene responsible for a rare hereditary form of pancreatitis; ancient historians use a technique devised for the detection of breast cancer to decipher traces on the lead "postcards" on which Roman soldiers wrote home.

So successful have the natural sciences been that the words "science" and "scientific" are often used honorifically, as all-purpose terms of epistemic praise. (To make sure we get the point, the television actors who promise that new, scientific, Wizzo will get our clothes cleaner wear white coats.) Unfortunately, this honorific usage disguises the otherwise obvious fact that not all, or only, scientists are good, honest, thorough, imaginative inquirers. Some scientists are lazy, some incompetent, some unlucky, a few crooked; and plenty of historians, journalists, detectives, etc., are good inquirers.

Science is neither sacred nor a confidence trick. Standards of stronger and weaker evidence, better and worse conducted inquiry, are not internal to the sciences; and there is no mode of inference, no "scientific method," exclusive to the sciences and guaranteed to produce true, or probably true, or more nearly true, or more empirically adequate results. Nevertheless, as human cognitive enterprises go, the natural sciences have been remarkably successful; not because they use a uniquely rational method of inquiry, unavailable to other inquirers, but in part because of the many and various "helps" they have devised to overcome natural human limitations. Instruments of observation extend sensory reach; models and metaphors stretch imaginative powers; techniques of mathematical and statistical modelling enable complex reasoning; and the cooperative and competitive engagement of many people in a great mesh of subcommunities within and across generations not only permits division of labor and pooling of evidence but also—though very fallibly and imperfectly, to be sure—has helped keep most scientists, most of the time, reasonably honest.

Science, like literature, requires imagination. Scientists, like writers of literature, stretch and amplify the language they inherit: a non-proteinous substance in the nucleus of cells is dubbed "nuclein," and later comes to be known as "nucleic acid"; then we have "deoxyribose nucleic acid"; then "ribonucleic acid," subsequently acknowledged to be "ribonucleic acids," in the plural; and then—almost a century after "nuclein" was coined—"transfer RNA," "messenger RNA," and so on. Scientists, like writers of literature, rely on metaphors: the chaperone molecule, the Spaghetti Hypothesis, the uncles-and-aunts experiments, parental investment, and so forth. But it doesn't follow, and it isn't true, that science is indistinguishable from fiction. The distinction between the imaginative and the imaginary is key.

Scientists engage in writing, and writers of literature engage in inquiry; but the word "literature" picks out a bunch of kinds of writing, while the word "science" picks out a bunch of kinds of inquiry. A scientist dreams of structures, classifications, and laws that, if he is successful, are real, and explanations that, if he is successful, are true. Imagination, and imaginative exploration of imagined explanations, comes first; but to go beyond mere speculation, appraisal of the likely truth of the imagined conjecture, itself often requiring imagination in the design of experiments, instruments, etc., must come after. And this requires that serious scientific metaphors, those that are not just picturesque speech but working intellectual tools, eventually be spelled out in literal detail: what, literally, is invested in reproduction? what constitutes maximizing return?

Progress in the sciences is ragged and uneven, and each step, like each crossword entry, is fallible and revisable. But each genuine advance potentially enables others, as a robust crossword entry does; "nothing succeeds like success" is the phrase that comes to mind. Think of Watson and Crick checking their model of DNA using only a ruler and a plumb line, and then of Max Perutz,[2] years later, checking his structure for the far more complicated hemoglobin molecule using a complex computer program; or of how, starting with the (relatively) simple X-ray, eventually we had the PET-scan, the CAT-scan, MRI.

Just about every inquirer, in the most mundane of everyday inquiries, depends on others; otherwise, each would have to start on his part of the crossword alone and from scratch. Natural-scientific inquiry is no exception; in fact, it is more so—the work, cooperative and competitive, of a vast intergenerational community of inquirers, a deeply and unavoidably social enterprise. But it doesn't follow, and it isn't true, that scientific inquiry is nothing more than a process of social negotiation in which scientists trade their theoretical loyalties for prestige, or that the entities postulated in scientific theories are nothing more than social constructions.

It is true, however, that both the internal organization of science and its external environment can affect how well or how poorly scientific work gets done. As ever more elaborate equipment is needed to make ever more recherché observations, scientific work tends to get more expensive. When only governments and large industrial concerns can afford to support science, when some scientists are tempted to go prematurely to the press, some find it possible to make fortunes from their work, the expert witness business booms, there is no guarantee that mechanisms that have thus far proven more or less adequate to sustain intellectual integrity will continue to do so. There are no grounds for complacency.

Some of the knowledge the natural sciences have achieved has the potential to cause grave harm—knowledge brings power, and power can be abused. Of course it doesn't follow, as some proponents of the New Cynicism are tempted to conclude, that the natural sciences haven't achieved genuine knowledge after all. But difficult moral and political questions about the distribution of resources, the applications of scientific knowledge, etc., cannot responsibly be left to scientists alone to settle. Again, there are no grounds for complacency.[3]

In scientific inquiry, and in inquiry of every kind, what we take to be legitimate questions sometimes turn out to be flawed. Questions about the properties of phlogiston, for example, turn out to rest on a false presupposition, and so have no true answer; some texts turn out to be ambiguous in ways of which the author is unaware, and so have no uniquely correct interpretation; and so on. None of this has any tendency to undermine the objectivity of truth. Sometimes, speaking carelessly, we say that something is true for you, but not for me. But this has no tendency to undermine the objectivity of truth either; what we mean is only that the something— liking chocolate chip cookie ice cream, say, or being over six feet tall—is true of you but not of me; or else that you believe whatever-it-is, but I don't.

A statement or belief is true just in case things are as it represents them to be; so everyone who believes anything, or who asks any question, implicitly acknowledges—even if he explicitly denies it—that there is such a thing as truth. Truth is not relative to perspective; and there can't be incompatible truths (this is a tautology, since "incompatible" means "can't be jointly true"). But there are many different truths—different but compatible truths—that must somehow fit together. It doesn't follow that all the truths about the world must be unified in the logical positivists' strong sense of that term, that they must be reducible to a privileged class expressed in a privileged vocabulary; nor, in particular, that all the truths about the world must be expressible in the language of physics. Rather, physics supplies a contour map on which the social sciences, history, etc., super- impose a road map—the superimposed maps each representing, in its own "vocabulary," the same one, real world.

Though what is true is not relative to perspective, what is accepted as true is; though incompatible statements can't be jointly true, incompatible claims are frequently made. But a dreadful argument ubiquitous in the New Cynicism con- fuses what is accepted as true, what passes for truth, with what is true. From the true, fallibilist premise that what passes for truth, known fact, strong evidence, well-conducted inquiry, etc., is sometimes no such thing, but only what the pow- erful have managed to get accepted as such, the Passes-for Fallacy moves to the false, cynical conclusion that the concepts of truth, fact, evidence, etc., are ideo- logical humbug.

Ruth Bleier, for example, complains that the claim by some neurophysiol- ogists that there are differences in brain structure corresponding to the sex- related differences in cognitive ability (Bleier adds, the supposed differences), rests on "sloppy methods, inconclusive findings and unwarranted interpreta- tions," not to mention "unacknowledged ideological commitments."[4] Perhaps she is right. But if so, the reasonable conclusion would be: supposing, after care- fully re-examining its presuppositions, we determine that the question is a legiti- mate one, we need better investigation using rigorous methods, seeking more conclusive findings based on warranted interpretations and free of ideological commitments. Bleier, however, commits the Passes-for Fallacy, and draws the cynical conclusion: bias is everywhere, objectivity is impossible, and the "social production of knowledge" is inextricably conditioned by "gender, class, race, and ethnicity."

When it is stated plainly, the Passes-for Fallacy is not only obviously invalid, but also in obvious danger of undermining itself; for if, as the conclusion says, the concepts of truth, evidence, honest inquiry, etc., are ideological humbug, then the premise couldn't be really-and-truly true, nor could we have objectively good evidence, obtained by honest inquiry, that it is so. Usually, how- ever, as shorthand for what is accepted as knowledge, what passes for truth, etc., the cynics write of "truth," i.e., so-called "truth," of "knowledge," i.e., so-called "knowledge," etc. The effect of the scare quotes is to neutralize the implication of success normally carried by these words; truth must be so, but "truth" needn't be; knowledge must be true, but "knowledge" needn't be. As the scare quotes become ubiquitous, the difference between truth and "truth," knowledge and "knowledge," facts and "facts," begins to blur; and what used to be success words pick up that characteristic sneering tone: "known fact"—yeah, right!

As the distinction is blurred between truth and "truth," known facts and "known facts," etc., the Passes-for Fallacy begins to look like a valid argument; the idea that there can be incompatible truths begins to sound plausible; and certain forms of relativism begin to look inevitable. It makes sense to talk of what is taken for true, what is accepted as good evidence, what passes for known fact, only relative to some person or group of people. So, if you don't distinguish what is true from what is taken for true, etc., it will seem that truth, etc., must be subjective or relative.

Proponents of the New Cynicism aren't always or unambiguously relativist, however; often they shift up and back between relativism and tribalism: between denying that it makes sense to think of epistemic standards as objectively better or worse, and claiming that *their* (non-white, non-Western, non-masculinist, non-scientific, etc.) standards are superior. Shielded by this strategic ambiguity, they can duck accusations that their relativism is self-undermining, and at the same time evade the necessity of explaining what makes their, tribalist epistemic standards better.

Among the most accomplished practitioners of this ducking and weaving is Richard Rorty, who evades accusations of epistemic relativism by shifting to a kind of tribalism according to which a belief is justified just in case it is defensible by *our*, Western, epistemic standards. And it is thanks to Rorty that the New Cynicism has come to be associated with pragmatism. This, however, is very peculiar; for classical pragmatism was fallibilist, not cynical. Here is C. S. Peirce, the founder of pragmatism: "Out of a contrite fallibilism, combined with a high faith in the reality of knowledge, all my philosophy has always seemed to grow";[5] and William James, who made pragmatism known: "[W]hen . . . we give up the quest for certitude do not thereby give up the quest or hope of truth itself."[6]

But Rorty, who writes that "the pragmatist view is of . . . 'true' as a word which applies to those beliefs on which we are able to agree,"[7] and that "truth is entirely a matter of solidarity,"[8] offers an essentially opposite message. I won't even *mention* such self-styled neo-pragmatists as Stephen Stich, who writes that "once we have a clear view of the matter, most of us . . . will not see any value in having true beliefs"[9]; or Louis Menand, who writes that pragmatism is the view that "the whole force of a philosophical account of anything . . . lies in the advertised [*sic*] consequences of believing it."[10]

Thanks to such other influential proponents as Sandra Harding, the New Cynicism has also come to be associated with feminism. This is no less peculiar than the kidnapping of "pragmatism"; and even more disturbing. The old feminism, emphasizing the common humanity of women and men, focused on equality, justice, opportunity. "The fundamental thing is that women are more like men than anything else on earth," wrote Dorothy Sayers, "they are human beings"; and went on to warn against the "error of insisting that there is an aggressively 'feminist point of view' about everything."[11] Winifred Holtby declared her allegiance to a style of feminism committed, not to pressing the claims of a supposed "woman's point of view," but to "the primary importance of the human being."[12]

But contemporary academic feminism, turning the sexist stereotypes that old-fashioned feminists used to deplore into new-fangled "women's ways of knowing," or demanding "politically adequate research and scholarship" instead of honest inquiry, offers an essentially opposite message. And in a closely parallel elision, multiculturalism has transmuted from commitment to the admirable goal of mutual learning from cultural diversity into a flabby relativism or an arbitrary tribalism. As radical feminists and multiculturalists have jumped on the bandwagon of the New Cynicism, it has come to be thought that to suppose that there is such a thing as truth, that it is possible to discover the truth by investigation, or that the natural sciences have made many true discoveries, must be to harbor regressive political tendencies. This is an idea as tragic as it is bizarre.

Yes, excessive confidence that what you take to be true, *is* true—the "blight of cocksureness," in Peirce's phrase—can be a tool of oppression, and has sometimes served the purposes of sexism and racism. This reminds us that respect for evidence requires not only a disposition to give up a belief in the face of contrary evidence and to proportion the degree of your belief to the strength of the evidence, but also a willingness to envisage the possibility that you have been going about a question in the wrong way altogether, or that it isn't a legitimate question after all—and to acknowledge when you just plain don't know.

And yes, as we inquire, people's feelings will sometimes be hurt. As we fumble our way to the truth, incomplete evidence will sometimes mislead us into accepting hurtful falsehoods; and some of the truths we discover will be painful, unpalatable, not what we would have wished to be the case. But unless it is possible to find out how things really are, it is not possible to discover that racist and sexist stereotypes *are* stereotypes, not truths; nor to trace the roots of racist or sexist prejudices or figure out how to overcome them; nor to know what changes really would make society better.

Not all the reasons for the fashionable disenchantment with truth, evidence, etc., are intellectual; part of the explanation is sociological. Putting the last first and the first last, Jacques Barzun observes, "valuing knowledge, we preposterize the idea, and say: 'everyone must produce written research in order to live, and it shall be deemed a knowledge explosion.'"[13] As preposterism has become the way of academic life, conceptions of "productivity" and "efficiency" more appropriate to a manufacturing plant than to the pursuit of knowledge have become firmly entrenched. The effect, inevitably, is a gradual erosion of intellectual integrity.

We are overwhelmed by bloated publishers' catalogues filled with glowingly incredible endorsements, by a bombardment of books and journals and a clamor of conferences and meetings in which it is close to impossible, except by sheer luck, to find the good stuff. No wonder, then, that many take the easy way out, conforming to whatever party line will best advance their career, or that many lose their grip on the demands of real inquiry, forgetting that you may work for years on what turns out to be a dead end, and that it is part of the meaning of the word "research" that you don't know how things will turn out.

Pseudo-inquiry is ubiquitous: both sham reasoning, making a case for a conclusion to which you are already unbudgeably committed at the outset, and, especially, fake reasoning, making a case for a conclusion to the truth-value of which you are indifferent. Long ago, Peirce predicted that when this happens, we will "come to look upon reasoning as mainly decorative. The result of this state of things is of course a rapid deterioration of intellectual vigor. . . . Man loses his conceptions of truth and of reasoning"[14] (woman too, I am sorry to say). When pseudo-inquiry is ubiquitous, people are uncomfortably aware, or half-aware, that reputations are made as often by a clever defense of the indefensible or the incomprehensible as by real work, and become increasingly skeptical of what they hear and read. Soon those wretched sneer quotes, and the Passes-for Fallacy, are everywhere. And many, afraid of being duped or of being thought naive, manage to persuade themselves that honest inquiry isn't really possible or desirable anyway.

How has this factitious despair come to be thought to represent the interests of the oppressed and marginalized? In part because, as universities have tried to welcome women and blacks as full participants in the life of the intellect, we have allowed ourselves to be distracted from the entirely admirable goal of making a person's race or sex matter less to our judgment of the quality of her or her mind, and begun looking for ways in which a person's sex or race might itself be a qualification for intellectual work. As the stress on the interests of this or that class or category of person has waxed, our sense of our common humanity and our appreciation of individual differences has waned, until we are in danger of forgetting that fallible inquiry—the ragged, untidy process of groping for, and sometimes grasping, something of how the world is—is a *human* thing, not a white male thing.

This is very sad. For "Howsoever these things are . . . in men's depraved judgements and affections, yet . . . the inquiry of truth, which is the love-making or wooing of it, the knowledge of truth, which is the presence of it, and the belief of truth, which is the enjoying of it, is the sovereign good of human nature." Thus Francis Bacon, who warned us that "factitious despair" of the possibility of finding things out "cuts the sinews and spurs of industry"; and, as he continued, "all for the miserable vainglory of having it believed that whatever has not yet been invented or discovered will never be invented or discovered hereafter."

NOTES

1. This was several years, and several deans, ago (for some reason, deans of the college don't last very long); and this Strategic Plan has, so far as I know, been forgotten.

2. Max Perutz (1914–2002) won the 1962 Nobel Prize in chemistry for solving the structure of hemoglobin (jointly with John Kendrew who solved the structure of myoglobin).

3. Many of the issues and examples discussed in this section were developed in more detail in my *Defending Science—Within Reason: Between Scientism and Cynicism* (Amherst, NY: Prometheus Books, 2003); recent developments on the question of early Martian life are sketched in the new preface to the paperback edition (2007).

4. Ruth Bleier, "*Science* and the Construction of Meanings in the Neurosciences," in Sue V. Rosser, ed., *Feminism Within the Science and Health Care Professions: Overcoming Resistance* (Oxford: Pergamon, 1988), pp. 91–104, p. 92.

5. C. S. Peirce, *Collected Papers*, eds. Charles Hartshorne, Paul Weiss, and (vols. 7 and 8) Arthur Burks (Cambridge: Harvard University Press, 1931–58), 1.14.

6. William James, "The Will to Believe," in *The Will to Believe and Other Essays* (1897) (New York: Dover, 1956), p. 17.

7. Richard Rorty, "Science as Solidarity," in John S. Nelson, Allan Megill, and Donald M. McCloskey, eds., *The Rhetoric of the Human Sciences* (Madison: University of Wisconsin Press, 1987), pp. 38–52, p. 45.

8. Richard Rorty, *Objectivity, Relativism and Truth* (Cambridge: Cambridge University Press, 1991), p. 32.

9. Stephen P. Stich, *The Fragmentation of Reason: Preface to a Pragmatic Theory of Cognitive Evaluation* (Cambridge: MIT Press, Bradford Books, 1990), p. 101.

10. Louis Menand, editor's introduction to *Pragmatism: A Reader* (New York: Vintage, 1997).

11. Dorothy L. Sayers, "The Human-not-Quite Human," in Sayers, *Unpopular*

Opinions: Twenty-One Essays (New York: Harcourt, Brace and Company, 1947), pp. 142–49, p. 142. See also "After My Own Heart: Dorothy Sayers's Feminism," pp. 209–16 in this volume.

12. Winifred Holtby, cited in Rosalind Delmar, "Afterword" to Vera Brittan, *Testament of Friendship* (1945) (London: Virago, 1980), pp. 443–53, p. 450.

13. Jacques Barzun, *The American University* (New York: Harper and Row, 1968), p. 221.

14. Peirce, *Collected Papers* (n. 5), 1.57–8.

15. Francis Bacon, "Of Truth" (1625) in *Francis Bacon's Essays* (1625), ed. Oliphant Smeaton (London: Dent and New York: Dutton, 1906), pp. 1–3, p. 3.

16. Francis Bacon, *The New Organon* (1620), Book I, Aphorism LXXXVIII.

2

THE SAME, ONLY DIFFERENT

I want to talk about what is common to inquiry of every kind, and how different kinds of inquiry differ from each other; about what the element of truth is in the idea that all inquiry is interpretive, and the different senses in which different kinds of inquiry involve interpretation. So I have borrowed as my title a phrase my grandmother used when she explained a new idea to me: "You know such-and-such? Well, this is the same, only different."

Unlike such other activities as composing a symphony, cooking dinner, writing a novel, or pleading a case in court, inquiry is an attempt to discover the truth of some question or questions—though sometimes the upshot is not an answer, but a realization that the question was in some way misconceived; and quite often, once you have answered one question, you find yourself facing a whole slew of new ones. In the academy, in politics—everywhere, in fact—pseudo-inquiry is ubiquitous: sham reasoning, making a case for some proposition to the truth of which one is already unbudgeably committed; and fake reasoning, making a case for some proposition to the truth of which one is indifferent, but advancing which one believes will benefit oneself. Genuine inquiry, however, is a good-faith effort to arrive at the truth of the matter in question, whatever the color of that truth may be.

There are many different kinds of inquiry, as there are different kinds of question—legal and literary, historical and histological, genetic and geographical, etc., etc. Nevertheless, every kind of empirical inquiry, from the simplest everyday puzzling over the causes of delayed buses or spoiled food to the most complex investigations of detectives, historians, and scientists, involves seeking out, and assessing the relevance and weight of, evidence—experiential evidence, and reasons ramifying in all directions. All empirical inquirers—molecular biologists and musicologists, entomologists and etymologists, sociologists and string theorists, investigative journalists and immunologists—work on some part of the same vast crossword puzzle; literally, they all investigate some part or aspect of the one real world.

Understandably enough, given the extraordinary explanatory successes the natural sciences have achieved, "science" and "scientific" have become honorifics: university catalogues offer "Management Science," "Library Science," "Military Science," even "Mortuary Science"; Christian fundamentalists demand equal time for "creation science"; and so on. But not all and not only scientists are good, honest, thorough inquirers; and the evidence with respect to scientific claims is not always good, strong, or reliable.

Natural-scientific inquiry is like everyday empirical inquiry, only different. Standards of good evidence and well-conducted inquiry are not internal to the sciences. Rather, to borrow a fine phrase of Gustav Bergmann's, the natural sciences represent the long arm of common sense; amplifying and extending the senses by means of specialized instruments, stretching the imagination by means of metaphors and analogies, improving reasoning power by means of intellectual and physical tools, and evolving a social organization that enables cooperation and competition, and allows each scientist to take up the crossword where others have left off.

Many have hoped to explain the success of natural-scientific inquiry by appeal to a supposedly uniquely rational "scientific method," but they never could agree on what that method *is*. They were looking at things wrong: rather, as Percy Bridgman put it, "the method of science, insofar as it is a method, is doing one's damnedest with one's mind, no holds barred."[1] Scientists make informed guesses about the explanation of some puzzling event or phenomenon, figure out the consequences of their conjecture's being true, and check how well those consequences stand up to the evidence—as all empirical inquirers do. But the natural sciences have developed a vast range of tools and techniques to extend their evidential reach and stiffen and refine their respect for evidence— "helps" to inquiry, in Francis Bacon's memorable phrase.

Astronomers devise ever more sophisticated telescopes, chemists ever more sophisticated techniques of analysis, and medical scientists ever more sophisticated methods of imaging internal states and processes. Scientists learn as they go along what control is needed to block a potential source of experimental error, what statistical technique to rule out a merely coincidental correlation. So scientific helps are local and evolving; but they are not *mere* "folkways," not *just* "local practices" like religious rituals, initiation ceremonies, or culinary traditions. They rely on previous scientific work, and may go wrong; but when they go right they enable scientists to get more evidence, and judge its purport more accurately.

Social-scientific inquiry is—well, it's like natural-scientific inquiry, only different. In fact, the most important line of demarcation runs, not exactly between the natural and the social sciences, but between those areas of scientific inquiry that take human beings' beliefs, intentions, etc., as part of their subject matter, and those that don't. Intentional science, as we might call it, thus includes medical scientists' investigations of psychosomatic illness and the placebo effect, but excludes physical geography, physical anthropology, and psychologists' investigations of non- or pre-representational creatures.

Methodological monists insist that the social sciences must use "the scientific method," just as physics and chemistry do. Their opponents maintain that the method of social science is *sui generis*, a matter not of causal explanation but of "understanding" ("a policy of deep breathing followed by free association," in Richard Braithwaite's splendidly scathing phrase).[2] But really, intentional science relies on experience and reasoning, as all empirical inquiry does; only, since it aims to understand people's behavior by coming up with explanatory hypotheses about their beliefs, goals, etc., it requires, not microscopes or telescopes, but well-designed questionnaires, double-blinding, tests of statistical significance, and so forth.

Inquirers in one area sometimes find it useful to borrow helps from another: for example, General Motors used statistical techniques developed by the Centers for Disease Control to track potential "epidemics" of defects in their cars and trucks. But sometimes, in hopes of looking as much as possible like their colleagues in the more prestigious natural sciences, psychologists, criminologists, sociologists, etc., borrowing inappropriate natural-scientific helps, have preferred symbolic formulae and technical jargon to real precision, real conceptual clarity, real insight into human nature.

All of us, in the most ordinary of everyday inquiry, sometimes conjecture about others' motives, goals, truthfulness, and so on; and—long before there were social scientists—historians, novelists, playwrights, witch doctors, lawyers, politicians, etc., pondered over human nature and society. No wonder, then, that sometimes psychologists, sociologists, etc., seem only to be telling us familiar truths in a pointlessly forbidding jargon. However, even as we note that physics-envy has been a serious handicap to intentional social science, and even as we recognize that writers and playwrights engage in inquiry as a means to the end of writing illuminating, entertaining, edifying, etc., novels and plays, we should not forget that fiction, unlike history or intentional social science, is not itself a form of inquiry.

It is a question how far, and in what ways, human social behavior is biolog-ically determined; what is universal human nature, what its local and contingent manifestations; what is natural, what is socially constructed. Everywhere, for example, human beings form hierarchies; but only in some places and at some times are there pharaohs or kings, and in even fewer are there democratic elections. Though they are brought into being by human activity, and even con-stituted in part by peoples' beliefs, social institutions, roles, and rules are nonetheless real. So intentional social science—forgive my changing metaphors mid-stream!—superimposes a road map on the contour map drawn by the natural sciences. Sometimes we need a dual-purpose map to find our way: when we try to figure out why AIDS has spread so fast in sub-Saharan Africa, for example, and why many more women than men are affected, we need to understand both the mechanism of infection, and the disruption of social and sexual mores that provides the virus with its opportunity.

Sometimes it is said that all inquiry involves an element of interpretation. And it is true. But, as John Stuart Mill observed, the worst kind of ambiguity arises, not with terms like "file" or "box," which have two or more quite different meanings, but with words like "is," which have several closely related meanings. "Interpretive," if we don't get it under control, threatens ambiguity of the most dangerous kind.

All empirical inquiry involves the interpretation of evidence. A letter is found that seems to show that Marilyn Monroe blackmailed President Kennedy; but the address includes a zip code, and the letter is typed using correction ribbon, neither of which existed at the time the letter is dated. A meteorite is found that may show that there was once bacterial life on Mars; but what look like fossilized bacteria droppings may be artifacts of the instrumentation, or per-haps were picked up while the meteorite was in Antarctica. A tightly woven mesh of evidence, well anchored in experience, can be very strong, but when experi-ential anchoring is shaky or explanatory integration weak, evidence can be ambiguous, confusing, or misleading; and empirical evidence is always, to some degree, incomplete or otherwise imperfect.

Evidential interpretation is different from textual interpretation, as natural signs like clouds or a rash are different from conventional signs like words or maps—as different as the world is from a book. (A seventeenth-century philosopher who thought of the scientist as deciphering God's Book of Nature, or a twentieth-century philosopher who has persuaded himself that everything is textual, would disagree; but they would be mistaken.) However, like any kind of jointly undertaken inquiry, natural-scientific inquiry is also interpretive in a second, textual sense; to share evidential resources, scientists must interpret each others' reports of their observations, experiments, and theorizing. While textual interpretation is the primary business of a literary scholar, in the sciences it is secondary, a means to the end of discovering truths about the world; nevertheless, it is a crucial means, without which the sciences could not have succeeded as well as they have.

The interpretation of scientific papers and articles, however, is as different from the interpretation of works of literature as scientific texts are from literary texts. There is, to be sure, an element of convention in the blandly impersonal "style of no style" of official scientific papers; nevertheless, the author of a scientific text normally aims to convey information as explicitly and precisely as he can, and the reader to carry away as much of that information as possible. All interpretation is a cooperative effort between writer and reader; but a scientific writer normally does his best to close his text to any but the intended reading, minimizing the constructive role required of the reader.

The author of a literary text, however, may intend not only to evoke emotional resonance, not only to please with verbal elegance or fun, but also to allow a creative role for the reader, an openness to new thematic interpretations, some better and some worse. Then there are legal texts—the watertight contract, the sloppily drafted will, the Uniform Commercial Code, US Supreme Court rulings, the Constitution, and so forth—offering some less, some more constructive scope to an interpreter, but subject to different constraints and desiderata than the literary.

Intentional social science involves interpreting peoples' beliefs, desires, intentions, etc., usually on the basis of what they do, say, or write, and, often but not always, of our knowledge of the meanings of words in their language. The enterprise is somewhat akin to textual interpretation—only, of course, different: calling on information about the meaning of what a person says or writes to conjecture what his beliefs and intentions may be, rather than calling on information about an author's intentions and beliefs to help interpret a text.

Though the intentional sciences all include people's beliefs, goals, etc., in their purview, each does so in its own distinctive way: the psychologist investigating the role of expectation in perceptual error, the economist calculating the mutual interactions of consumer confidence and interest rates, the sociologist estimating what increment of cognitive performance can be attributed to charter schools, or the anthropologist trying to understand the significance of this ritual dance in the life of the tribe. Our anthropologist, however, may have to solve simultaneous equations: investigating the beliefs and motives of the people he studies at the same time as he figures out how to translate their language—interpretation in yet another sense.

Feeling themselves the poor relations in the present culture of higher education, and perhaps hoping to make themselves seem indispensable, scholars in the humanities are sometimes tempted to indulge in loose talk about the ubiquity of the interpretive. But if we grasp what is common to inquiry of every kind and what is distinctive about different kinds of inquiry, if we grasp the sense in which all inquiry is interpretive and the senses in which some kinds of inquiry are distinctively so, we begin to glimpse a richer, more realistic, and more encouraging picture both of what unites us as colleagues in the life of the mind, and of the remarkably various ways and means of our different disciplines.

NOTES

1. Percy Bridgman, "The Prospect for Intelligence" (1945), in Bridgman, *Reflections of a Physicist* (New York: Philosophical Library, 1950; 2d. ed. 1955), pp. 526–52, p. 535.

2. Richard Braithwaite, *Scientific Explanation: A Study of the Function of Theory, Probability and Law in Science* (Cambridge: Cambridge University Press, 1953), p. 272.

3

THE UNITY OF TRUTH AND THE PLURALITY OF TRUTHS

The ordinary man knows only one kind of truth, in the ordinary sense of the word. He cannot imagine what a higher or a highest truth may be. Truth seems to him no more capable of comparative degrees than death. . . . Perhaps you will think as I do that he is right in this.
  —Sigmund Freud, *New Introductory Lectures on Psychoanalysis*, 1930[1]

"**T**rue" has a large extended family of uses. Polonius's advice to Laertes, "To thine own self be true. . . . Thou canst not then be false to any man,"[2] reminds us that the root of our word "true," the Old English "treowe," meant "faithful." In some uses, "true" retains this older meaning still: when you apply for a British passport, your unflattering photograph must be endorsed by some responsible person—a doctor, clergyman, schoolteacher, or whatever—in these words: "I certify that this is a true likeness of . . ."; and we speak not only of true likenesses but of true friends, true followers, and true believers. Then again, we say that the frog is "not a true reptile," or describe a joint or beam as "out of true." But I shall set these uses aside to focus, as philosophers do, on truth as it applies to propositions, statements, beliefs, etc., when they are, as the *Oxford English Dictionary* puts it, "in accordance with fact or reality, not false or erroneous."

My thesis, with respect to this use, will be that *there is one truth, but many*

---

truths: i.e., one unambiguous, non-relative truth-concept, but many and various propositions, etc., that are true. One truth-concept: to say that a claim is true is to say (not that anyone, or everyone, believes it, or that it follows from this or that theory, or that there is good evidence for it, but) simply that things are as it says. But many truths: particular empirical claims; scientific theories; historical propositions; mathematical theorems; logical principles; textual interpretations; statements about what a person wants or believes or intends; statements about grammatical, social, or legal roles and rules; and etc. Put like this, my thesis sounds almost embarrassingly simple, even naive. Still—as Frank Ramsey said in a closely related context—"there is no platitude so obvious that eminent philosophers have not denied it";[3] and as soon as you ask why anyone would deny that there is one truth-concept, or that there are many true propositions, it becomes apparent that my initial, simple formulation disguises many complexities.

Someone might deny that there is one truth-concept either because he thinks that there is more than one such concept, or else because he thinks that there is none. In the first category (those who hold that there is more than one truth-concept) are those who think that "true" must have different meanings as applied to different kinds of proposition, the empirical and the mathematical or the ethical, for example, or the scientific and the literary or the theological; those who think that truth is relative to the individual, or to culture, community, theory, or conceptual scheme; and Alfred Tarski and those who follow him in proposing a hierarchy of language-relative truth-predicates. In the second category (those who hold that there is no truth-concept) are those who believe, or profess to, that the concept of truth is nothing but rhetorical or ideological humbug.

Someone might deny that there are many true propositions either because he thinks that there are no true propositions, or else because he thinks that there is only one. Those who deny that there is any legitimate truth-concept would, or should, also deny that there are any true propositions; and F. H. Bradley, maintaining that no actual judgment is better than partially true, seems to have thought that nothing short of The Whole Truth About Everything is really-and-truly true. Most often, though, those who apparently deny that there are many truths are really maintaining that there is only one *kind* of true proposition; perhaps because (like Bradley) they are committed to an idealist picture according to which the only genuine truth is about the Reality behind the Appearances, or perhaps because they are committed to a strong reductionism according to which the only ultimate truths are the truths of physics, or, etc.

By exploring these arguments against it and articulating where they go wrong, I hope gradually to bring out the subtleties of my deceptively simple-sounding thesis, and in the process to begin building a robust defense.

1. THE UNITY OF TRUTH

Let me start, then, with the arguments for a plurality of truth-concepts: first for multiple senses of "true," and then for the relativity of truth to culture, community, theory, conceptual scheme, or language.

The way we ascertain that it is true that $7 + 5 = 12$ seems very different from the way we ascertain that it is true that DNA is a double-helical, backbone-out macromolecule with like-with-unlike base pairs. What makes it true that there are marsupial mice in Australia, or that, for every planet, the square of its period of revolution around the sun divided by the third power of its mean distance from the sun is a constant, seems very different from what makes it true that an unlawful homicide occurring in the commission or attempted commission of a felony constitutes first-degree murder, or from what makes it true that Daniel Deronda was brought up in ignorance of his Jewish descent. So perhaps it is no wonder that it has sometimes been supposed that true propositions are *so* varied and *so* heterogeneous that there can't be just one concept of truth, but must be many—mathematical truth, scientific truth, legal truth, literary truth, and so forth. But the heterogeneity of true propositions doesn't require a plurality of truth-concepts.

Any plausible definition of truth must take for granted the Aristotelian insight that "to say of what is that it is, or of what is not that it is not, is true":[4] the various correspondence theories, which turn that emphatic adverb for which we reach when we say that p is true just in case *really, in fact, p*, into serious metaphysics; Tarski's semantic theory; and Ramsey's "redundancy" theory and its present-day minimalist, deflationist, and disquotationalist descendants. Of these, Ramsey's seems to be the simplest and most direct: "[my] definition that a belief is true if it is 'a belief that p' and p, but false if it is 'a belief that p' and $-p$ is . . . substantially that of Aristotle . . . a belief that Smith is either a liar or a fool is true if Smith is either a liar or a fool, and not otherwise." Or again: "the most certain thing about truth is that 'p is true' and 'p,' if not identical, are equivalent"; truth is "when a man believes that A is B and A *is* B."[5]

However, the old label "redundancy theory"[6] is misleading: though Ramsey held that "true" is eliminable from direct truth attributions like "it is true that Caesar crossed the Rubicon," he realized that it is indispensable for indirect truth ascriptions like "he is always right." Since the newer labels "disquotationalism," "minimalism," and "deflationism" seem rather vague and variable in their reference, I prefer a term coined by Dr. Kiriake Xerohemona: "laconicism"; for Ramsey's account is undeniably "terse, concise," and as the etymology of "laconicist" suggests, Spartan.

Ramsey's laconicism is incomplete; most significantly, explaining those indirect truth-attributions requires an account of propositional quantifiers that doesn't itself depend on the concept of truth.[7] Moreover, laconicism obviously doesn't give us a criterion of truth; and it leaves many issues about representation and reality open. But this, at least, is hardly surprising; for Ramsey aspires precisely to capture the core meaning of "true"—to articulate the highest common factor of the truth-concept in all its many applications. Whatever kind of proposition is said to be true, what is said of it is the same: that it is the proposition that *p*, and *p*; or, as I put it earlier, that things are as it says. However, what the relevant things are depends on the proposition in question: which is why what makes a proposition of one kind true can be very different from what makes a proposition of another kind true, and why, depending on what kind of a proposition it is the truth-value of which we want to ascertain, we may set out to find a proof, or send a team to Australia to catalogue the wildlife of the bush, or, etc.

The case of truth in literature is special enough to deserve its own paragraph. Sometimes talk of "literary truth" refers to the truth of claims about fictional characters—such as Daniel Deronda, who wasn't a real person, but a central character in George Eliot's novel of the same name. To say that it is true that Daniel Deronda was brought up in ignorance of his Jewish descent is, I take it, simply to say that, *according to the novel*, Deronda was brought up in ignorance of his Jewish descent (of course, the meaning of "according to the novel" isn't perfectly transparent; but this is not the place to try to spell it out). Sometimes, however, talk of "literary truth" refers to the truths about real human beings and real human doings that are conveyed by a fictional narrative, such as the truths about the power of ignorance conveyed in this novel of Eliot's.[8] These are regular truths about real human beings and real human doings; they aren't special, superfine literary truths. What is special and superfine is the skill and subtlety with which Eliot conveys the truth that ignorance can be a powerful force in a person's life, and in the lives of those around him or her; but the truth that is conveyed is true in just the usual sense.

Sometimes we say that something is "true for you, but not for me"; but this is just a careless way of saying either that you believe whatever-it-is, but I don't, or else that whatever-it-is is true *of* you, but not of me. The example, simple as it is, points to two main sources of the idea that truth is subjective or relative, and hence that there is no one truth, simpliciter, but only truth-for-you and truth-for-me, or only truth-for-this-culture and truth-for-that-culture: a confusion of truth with belief, and a confusion of truth with truth-of.

Students sometimes write, meaning that Descartes believed that the mind and the body are distinct substances, that "for Descartes, the mind and the body are distinct substances"; and this unhappy way of putting it sometimes tempts them into a kind of subjectivism about truth. But this confusion can be dispelled by pointing out that belief and truth are distinct concepts, and that what some person believes, and what is true, may be quite different things. To be sure, it's a tautology that to believe that p is to hold p true. Nevertheless, we understand that other people sometimes hold false beliefs; that we ourselves have held false beliefs in the past; and that in due course we may well discover that some of our present beliefs—although we can't, of course, presently say which ones—are false. And it obviously doesn't follow from the fact that in different cultures or at different times different propositions are believed to be true, that truth is culturally or temporally relative.

Many social or cultural institutions, roles, and rules—monarchy, money, monasteries, marching bands, etc.—are found in only some cultures, or in different forms in different societies; so claims about them are capable of truth or falsity only when completed by reference to a place and a time. For example, claims to the effect that the law is thus and so can be true or false only with respect to some legal system or systems—"the law of the land"—and to a time. "Novel scientific evidence is admissible only if it is generally accepted in the field to which it belongs" (the "*Frye* rule") is false in federal courts, where the requirement is that admissible expert testimony, including scientific testimony, be relevant and reliable; but it is true in state courts in Florida—or at least, it *was* true in state courts in Florida until 2001, when the Florida Supreme Court's ruling in *Ramirez* unclarified the situation.[9] Rather as "the front door is red" doesn't make it to true or false until a particular front door, and a time, are specified, "the law requires such-and-such" doesn't make it to true or false until a particular legal system, and a time, are specified; but once they're given, no further relativization is required. You might put this by saying that the truth of a legal claim is relative to a legal system and a time; but it obviously doesn't follow that truth itself is.[10]

Sometimes it is suggested that truth is relative, not to culture or community, but to theory. Ordinarily, "p is true in theory T" means "according to theory T, it is true that p," i.e., "theory T implies that p"; which, like "true in the novel," poses no problem for my thesis. The issue is whether it makes sense to describe propositions as true or false without reference to any theory. I think it does. It is true in the phlogiston theory, for example, that phlogiston is given off during combustion; but the phlogiston theory is false, and so is the proposition that phlogiston is given off during combustion.

Some philosophers of science have had doubts about the appropriateness of describing scientific theories as true or false. Concerned that, if theoretical "statements" were really statements, they would have to be deemed empirically meaningless by the standards of the Verification Principle, the instrumentalist wing of Logical Positivism maintained that theories are just intellectual instruments for deriving observational predictions. The newer manifestation of the instrumentalist impulse, constructive empiricism—even though it maintains that the goal of science is empirical adequacy, not truth—allows that theories are either true or false. But the recently fashionable idea that theories are best construed as "models" is taken by some proponents as denying this.[11] *None* of these, however, entail that truth is theory-relative. And neither does the "meaning-variance thesis" proposed by Paul Feyerabend and Thomas Kuhn; that theoretical and even observational terms may have different meanings in different theories, and one and the same sentence express different propositions, perhaps one true and the other false, so far from implying that the propositions expressed are not true, or false, period, implies that they are.[12]

Sometimes it is suggested that truth is relative, not to culture or community, not to theory or paradigm, but to conceptual scheme. In *Renewing Philosophy*, Hilary Putnam writes that there are no descriptions of reality independent of perspective, and that it is impossible to divide our language into two parts, a part that describes how the world is anyway, and a part that describes our conceptual contribution. This, he tells us, "simply means that you can't describe the world without describing it"; nevertheless, he continues, it is a point of real philosophical importance, for it reveals that there can be many different descriptions of the world in many different vocabularies, all of them *"equally 'true'."*[13] This is quite a tangle; but since I have done my best to disentangle it elsewhere,[14] I hope you will forgive me if I'm brisk here. It's certainly true that you can't describe the world without describing it; in fact, it's a tautology. But it's certainly false that incompatible descriptions of the world can be true; in fact, it's a contradiction. What is true and not tautologous is that there are many different but compatible truths, expressible in different vocabularies. But this is just the second of my themes, that there are many truths—which requires no relativization or fragmentation of the truth-concept.

Tarski's thesis that we need, not just the one truth predicate, but a whole hierarchy of language-relative truth predicates, suffers no such ambiguities as Putnam's "conceptual relativity"; and it is the conclusion of seemingly straightforward arguments in semantic theory.

There has been some confusion, however, about the relation of Tarski's semantic theory of truth to theories of the minimalist/deflationist/disquotationalist family. Tarski himself says that you might think of his theory as explicating Aristotle's dictum in a precise way which, unlike correspondence theories, requires no appeal to such notions as fact or correspondence—which in their traditional philosophical senses Tarski regards as irredeemably obscure.[15] So far, fair enough. Recently, however, Tarski is sometimes classified as a disquotationalist;[16] when in fact he holds that expressions within quotation marks are not semantically part of the expression as a whole.[17] More consequentially for present purposes, Tarski's T-schema has also been described as a paradigm of deflationism,[18] when in fact his approach differs very significantly from Ramsey's laconicism.[19]

Tarski proposes a Material Adequacy Condition that fixes the extension of the truth-predicate by requiring that any acceptable definition of truth have as consequences all instances of the T-schema, "S is true iff p" (where "S," on the left, names the sentence on the right). He emphasizes, however, that though each instance constitutes a partial definition, the T-schema is not itself a definition of truth.[20] The definition Tarski gives, and then shows to be materially adequate, applies not to propositions but to the closed well-formed formulae (wffs) of certain formal languages; for unlike propositions, wffs have a definite syntactic structure, and Tarski's definition exploits this structure to get a grip on all the infinitely many wffs of the language. However, closed formulae may be constructed out of open formulae, which are not true or false, but rather satisfied, or not, by sequences of objects; so Tarski first gives a recursive definition of "satisfies," and then defines "true": "satisfied by all infinite sequences of objects."

Tarski's first argument for the relativity of truth to language derives from his choice of truth-bearer: one and the same string of symbols might be a sentence or wff in more than one language, true in one, but false or meaningless in the other. (As I explain to my students, "the department of philosophy at the University of Miami is on the seventh floor of the Ashe Building" is true-in-American-English, but false-in-British-English, which counts floors "ground, first, second, . . .") A staunch proponent of propositions as the sole or primary truth-bearers would reply that Tarski's insistence on "true-in-L_1," "true-in-L_2," etc., is a mistake; what's needed is simply to acknowledge that "the philosophy department is on the seventh floor" expresses different propositions in the two languages—one true, and one false. I would put it another way: it isn't necessary to resort to "true-in-American-English" and "true-in-British-English"; it suffices to say that "the philosophy department is on the seventh floor," *qua* sentence of American English, is true, and "the philosophy department is on the seventh floor," *qua* sentence of British English, is false.

But Tarski's main argument for a hierarchy of truth-predicates derives from his solution to the Liar Paradox: distinguishing the object-language (the language *for* which truth is defined) from the meta-language (the language *in* which truth is defined), he requires that the metalinguistic predicate "true" be relativized to the object-language; and thus transmutes the offending sentence, "this sentence is false," into "this sentence is false-in-O"—which, since it is a sentence not of the object-language but of the meta-language, is not paradoxical but harmlessly false. So in his theory Liar-type paradoxes cannot even be expressed, and *a fortiori* cannot be derived as theorems. The reason semantic paradoxes arise in natural languages, Tarski suggests, is that these languages include unstratified concepts of truth and falsity that can be applied to sentences of the language itself. Some critics, however, have felt that his diagnosis is too sweeping, and his cure too drastic. I agree, at least, that Tarski doesn't give us a really satisfying explanation of what goes wrong in that very specific, very small class of sentences that give rise to trouble, such as "this is true," "this is false," "this is not true"; and that his stratification of languages and corresponding multiplication of truth-concepts is at best artificial.

Tarski's (demonstrably materially adequate) definition of truth is undeniably an impressive technical achievement; but there is a peculiar doubleness about his approach that makes it less than satisfying philosophically. His definition applies to wffs of formally specifiable logical and mathematical languages, but not (so Tarski himself maintained, and I believe he was right) to the sentences of natural languages like Polish or English; and his response to the Liar is to devise a hierarchy of formal languages in which the paradoxical formulae are ill-formed. Insofar as Tarski has anything to say about the concept of truth in natural languages, he seems to suspect that it is irredeemable: "*the very possibility of a consistent use of the expression 'true sentence' which is in harmony with the laws of logic and the spirit of everyday language seems to be very questionable*";[21] yet his project of defining truth for formal languages seems to make sense only against the background of the ordinary concept of truth, the concept we apply to sentences of natural languages, to people's beliefs, etc.

This doubleness comes to the surface in Tarski's reply to the objection that he hasn't given the "real meaning" of "true." He doesn't claim, he writes, that his is the "right" or the "only possible" conception of truth—whatever that means, he adds; he wouldn't be upset should some future world congress of truth-theorists vote to reserve "true" for other, non-classical, conceptions, and give him the word "frue" instead. But implicit in this apparently concessive response is the claim that his definition is (a modernized version of) the "classical conception"; moreover, Tarski immediately adds that he can't imagine how anyone could argue that the semantic conception is "wrong."[22] So he isn't claiming that the semantic conception is "right," but can't imagine how anyone could argue that it's "wrong"; hmmm.

Anyway, there are responses to the Liar that *don't* require fragmenting the truth-concept. Ramsey's solution—which he gave in the context, not of his discussions of truth, but of his proposed modification of Russell's Theory of Types—required stratification of propositions, but no multiplicity of truth predicates.[23] A number of contemporary deflationists have adopted some form of the solution proposed by Saul Kripke, which admits just one (albeit only partially defined) truth predicate.[24] However, Ramsey's laconicism seems most hospitable to an approach which, instead of treating "true" and "false" as predicates expressing properties, treats them, as Ramsey says, as "prosentences" like "yes" and "no," functioning as placeholders for a proposition or propositions being indirectly affirmed or denied. This suggests that the reason the Truth-teller leaves the semantic wheels spinning idly is that there's nothing to be affirmed except that this is being affirmed; and the reason the Liar jams the semantic machinery is that there's nothing to be denied except what is being affirmed.[25]

Now let me turn to the considerations that have led some to think that there is *no* truth-concept, that the idea of truth is somehow illegitimate or misconceived— mostly, nowadays, very different from the considerations that pulled Tarski at least partway to this conclusion. The fact that contemporary cynics often refuse even to use the word "true" without hedging it with precautionary scare quotes provides an important clue to what is going on.

The effect of scare quotes is to turn an expression meaning "X" into an expression meaning "supposed X, so-called 'X.'" So scare-quotes "truths," as opposed to truths, are propositions, beliefs, etc. that are *taken to be* truths—many of which are not really truths at all. We humans, after all, are thoroughly fallible creatures: even with the best will in the world, finding out the truth can be hard work; and we are often willing, even eager, to *avoid* discovering, or to cover up, unpalatable truths. The rhetoric of truth, moreover, can be used in nefarious ways. Hence the idea that truth is nothing more than a rhetorical device for the promotion of claims that it would serve the interests of the powerful to have believed: the seductive but crashingly invalid argument I have dubbed the "Passes-for Fallacy."[26]

What passes for truth, the argument goes, is often no such thing, but only what the powerful have managed to get accepted as such; *therefore* the concept of truth is nothing but ideological humbug. The premise is true; but, stated plainly, this argument is not only obviously invalid, but also in obvious danger of undermining itself. If, however, you don't distinguish truth from scare-quotes "truth," or truths from scare-quotes "truths," it can seem irresistible; which is partly why, despite its crashing invalidity, the Passes-for Fallacy now seems ubiquitous. The fallacy is encouraged by regimes of propaganda and, in our times, by an overwhelming flood of information, and misinformation, which promotes first credulity and then cynicism, as people realize they have been fooled. For when it becomes notorious that what are presented as truths are not really truths at all—that *Pravda* is full of lies and propaganda,[27] that the scientific breakthrough or miracle drug trumpeted in the press was no such thing—people become understandably distrustful of truth claims, and increasingly reluctant to speak of truth without indicating their distrust by means of neutralizing quotation marks; until they lose confidence in the very idea of truth, and those formerly precautionary scare quotes cease merely to warn and begin to sneer: "'Truth'? Yeah, right!"

Still, the Passes-for Fallacy isn't the only source of cynicism about truth; there is no shortage of philosophers armed with apparently more sophisticated arguments against the legitimacy of the concept. Richard Rorty, for one, conducts a kind of guerilla warfare; disguising himself in a stained and tattered uniform apparently taken from a Davidsonian prisoner, he taunts the foot-soldiers of the analytic army—"you like arguments, right? OK: here you go!"—and lobs one confusing argumentative grenade after another. In *Philosophy and the Mirror of Nature* he avers that there are two senses of "true": "the homely and shopworn sense . . . that Tarski and [Donald] Davidson are attending to," in which "true" just means "what you can defend against all comers," and a "specifically philosophical sense . . . designed precisely to stand for the Unconditioned." The second being clearly unacceptable, he suggests, we must accept the first; i.e., in effect, give up truth, and acknowledge only scare-quotes "truth." And in later writings, describing the intellectual history of the West as "an attempt to substitute a love of Truth for a love of God," Rorty avers: "I do not have much use for notions like . . . 'objective truth.'" To call a statement true, he tells us, is just to give it a "rhetorical pat on the back"; "'true' [is] a word which applies to those beliefs upon which we are able to agree"; "[t]ruth is entirely a matter of solidarity."[28]

Of course, the suggestion that Tarski, or Davidson, thinks that truth is whatever you can defend against conversational objections is bizarre, and the supposed philosophical use of "true" is mysterious, to put it mildly. In any case, the dichotomy on which Rorty's argument by elimination rests is startlingly false. And his proposed reduction of truth to here-and-now agreement—apparently the result of stripping C. S. Peirce's definition of truth, as the Final Opinion on which inquirers would agree were scientific inquiry to continue indefinitely, of everything that anchors it to the world—clearly won't do. Yes, sometimes "true" is used as an expression of agreement; yes, to say that we agree that *p* is to say that we agree that *p* is true. But we may agree that *p* when *p* is *not* true, and we may not agree that *p* when *p* *is* true.

The proposed demotion of "true" to a mere rhetorical device—apparently a nod to Ramsey, misconstrued as urging that "true" is redundant save for its rhetorical usefulness—is no better. "True" is, indeed, rhetorically useful; but its rhetorical usefulness depends on its having the semantic role it does. Certainly *Pravda* was called *Pravda* (as the University of Miami newspaper is called *Veritas*) for propaganda purposes; but the names wouldn't serve those propaganda purposes so well if "*pravda*" and "*veritas*" were *mere* expressions of approval, like "huzzah!" or "yippedydoodah!"[29] As for Rorty's hints that concern for truth is a kind of superstition, and his boast that truth isn't something about which *he* gives a damn, Peirce long ago made the appropriate response: "You certainly agree that there is such a thing as Truth. Otherwise, reasoning and thought would be without a purpose. . . . Every man is fully satisfied that there is such a thing as truth, or he would not ask any question."[30]

As my earlier allusions to instrumentalism, constructivism, and "modelism" in philosophy of science revealed, even among those who are "fully satisfied that there is such a thing as truth," some doubt that the concept is of any relevance to understanding science. I disagree: "science," as I understand it, refers to a loose federation of kinds of inquiry; and the goal of inquiry is to discover true answers to the questions into which you are inquiring. Were the point crucial to the argument of this paper, I would need to add that this is not to say that scientists seek THE TRUTH, as distinct from true answers to their questions, and neither is it to deny that scientists very often, and reasonably, claim only that their answers are probably, or possibly, true; but since these issues aren't essential here, I will set them aside.[31]

2. THE PLURALITY OF TRUTHS

Now let me turn—much more briefly, you will be relieved to hear—to the arguments against a plurality of truths.

If there were no legitimate truth concept, there would *a fortiori* be no genuine, bona fide truths. But then, as Peirce says, reasoning really would be without a purpose; for inquiry, assertion, belief, argument, question-and-answer, etc., are all intimately dependent on the concept of truth. This is why Rorty is reduced to reducing inquiry to "carrying on the conversation," and justified belief to "whatever can overcome all conversational objections," and to dismissing four hundred years of successful scientific investigation as just "a model of human solidarity." But it is also why, in asserting that to call a statement true is just to give it a rhetorical pat on the back, he undermines what he asserts; for to assert that p—which Peirce likens to swearing an affidavit or taking an oath that p[32]—is precisely to commit yourself (not to the scare-quotes "truth," but) to the truth of p.

Bradley doesn't deny the legitimacy of the truth-concept; but he holds that "truth is . . . always imperfect." Every judgment is "conditional," he writes, meaning that it is incomplete, expressing less than the whole truth; there can be no truth that is entirely true, he continues, and no error that is entirely false, i.e., contains no grain of truth: "[o]ur judgements . . . can never reach as far as perfect truth, and must be content merely to enjoy more or less of *Validity*." However, "p is only part of the truth" doesn't imply "p is only partially true." This point seems sometimes to elude historians, who—observing, correctly, that any account of a past event will inevitably omit or play down some aspects while it includes or highlights others—are tempted to conclude that no historical account can be true, but at best scare-quotes "true." A straightforward acknowledgment of incompleteness and selectivity would be preferable.

In my initial statement of my thesis I said that there are "many *and various* propositions that are true"; and I meant it. But there have been many who have held that all real truths, or perhaps all ultimate truths, are of just one kind. The idea that the world of appearances is mere illusion, and an ideal or spiritual realm the real reality, has been a recurring theme in the history of philosophy, and of the world religions: from Plato's claim that the Forms are really real, with sensible particulars hovering somewhere "between being and non-being," to religious conceptions of this world as illusory, the next world as truly real, or of a holy text as the source of all real truths. In our times, however, the tables have been turned by ambitious scientific reductionists maintaining that all truths can be derived from scientific laws, and ultimately from the laws of physics. These days, religious believers are more likely to feel the need to argue, defensively, not that theirs is the only real truth there is, but that there really are spiritual, as well as scientific, truths.

Fortunately perhaps, it is hardly feasible for me to undertake a comprehensive discussion of reductionism here. But I will venture to say that, in view of their large historical element, it seems very doubtful even that the biological sciences are wholly reducible to physics; and that—despite the significant parallels between human beings' social behavior and that of other animals, and despite the undeniable biological constraints on our social interactions—it also seems very doubtful that the intentional social sciences are wholly reducible to biology. For the intentional social sciences appeal to people's beliefs, hopes, etc.; and though these are neurophysiologically realized, the relevant families of neurophysiological configurations have to be identified, not by their neurophysiological characteristics, but by reference to patterns of verbal behavior in a person's linguistic community, to denotation and meaning, and to the things in the world that those beliefs, etc., are about.

This isn't to say, and I don't believe, that there is non-physical mind- or soul-stuff; it's all physical, all right, even if it isn't all physics. Neither is it to say, and I don't believe either, that the intentional social sciences are wholly disjoint from the natural sciences. The social sciences, though not reducible to the natural sciences, are integrated with them. The natural sciences draw the contour map of the biological roots of human nature and the biological constraints on human culture; the social sciences superimpose a road map of local and cultural specifics: marriage customs in New Guinea, the failures of the Soviet economy, the rise of modern science in seventeenth-century Europe, etc.

This doesn't yet speak to the question of the relation of the sciences to inquiry more generally. I don't believe the sciences are the only sources of truth, or the only legitimate kinds of inquiry; nor do I believe the sciences can explain everything. There are many scientific questions as yet unanswered, not to mention those that can't as yet even be asked; and there are many questions (legal and literary, culinary and commercial, ethical and epistemological, . . . , etc.) beyond the scope of the sciences. However, it doesn't follow that there are sources of knowledge over and above what Peirce called the "method of experience and reasoning"—the method of everyday empirical inquiries into the causes of delayed buses and spoiled food, and the method refined and amplified by the sciences. Asking, "Can science explain everything?" in the challenging tone of a question-expecting-the-answer-no, religious believers sometimes suggest that a negative answer clinches the matter in their favor. But obviously it *doesn't* clinch the matter; and I for one am skeptical of supernatural explanations, and of the supposed deliverances of "religious experience"—as I am of the supposed special "ways of knowing" sometimes claimed for women, or Native Americans, or, etc.[33]

There are truths of many kinds; but not of any and every kind anyone has ever imagined. And of course there aren't rival, incompatible truths or "knowledges." The title of Pope John Paul II's 1996 address acknowledging the theory of evolution as "more than a hypothesis"—"Truth Cannot Contradict Truth"—makes the point with admirable clarity.[34] However, it isn't always easy to know whether this claim and that are compatible; even formal consistency or inconsistency may not be easy to determine, and compatibility or incompatibility, depending also on subtleties of meaning, is apt to be harder yet. We humans are susceptible to both ignorance and error, on both empirical and logical questions. This doesn't mean that there are really no truths, or that it's not possible to discover some of them; it does mean that we had better be willing to revise what we believe should the evidence turn out against it.

If A believes that p, and B believes that not p, one of them must be mistaken. Though this is a tautology, some apparently find it unacceptably harsh. Perhaps they feel it is a breach of civility, disrespectful even, to suggest that those who disagree with you are mistaken;[35] perhaps they hope that concepts of etiquette, like politeness, collegiality, etc., could stand in for logical or epistemological concepts. No doubt they are motivated by a kindly tolerance and open-mindedness; but the interrelations of the concepts of respect and disagreement are far subtler than they acknowledge, and the hope that "discourse ethics" will suffice to serve our epistemological needs is vain. The issues here are very complex; but I shall have to confine myself to a couple of rather simple paragraphs.

First: If I have reason to respect your intelligence, and you disagree with me about whether p, I should think again; maybe I'm mistaken, confused, or missing something. On the other hand, if I discover that you believe something silly, this will lower my opinion of you; and if it's something *really* silly (and I have no reason to think you are trapped in a pocket of misleading evidence) I may lose my respect for your intelligence, or perhaps for your integrity. Of course, I may be wrong in thinking that what you believe is silly; and, even more importantly from a practical point of view, even if I'm right this doesn't entitle me to lock you up, burn down your house of worship, or indoctrinate you or your children with beliefs I think more reasonable.

Second: Successful inquiry often requires cooperation, and often depends crucially on communication among individuals; but the epistemologically desirable kind of communication isn't merely a matter of following the norms of good conversational conduct, as those norms are ordinarily understood. Donald McCloskey writes of listening, of paying attention, of not raising one's voice.[36] But as Francis Crick observed of his working relationship with James Watson, successful collaboration requires that "you must be very candid, one might almost say rude, to the person you are working with"; if "politeness creeps in . . . this is the end of good collaboration in science."[37] This unwillingness to waste time and energy making nice, is, indeed, a mark of respect for each other's seriousness as an investigator.

There is one truth-concept, but many true propositions; whether a proposition is true or false (or neither) is an objective matter; our efforts to discover truths about the world are fallible—the conclusions here are simple enough, in a way. But the arguments needed to reach these conclusions, far from being simple and one-dimensional, are complex and twisting, sometimes technical, sometimes subtle. So perhaps it is appropriate to end with a reminder—not from a philosopher but from a novelist—about just how complex truth can be:

> The truth [is] not a line from here to there, and not ever-widening circles like the rings on a sawn log, but rather trails of oscillating overlapping liquids that poured forth but then assumed a shape and life of their own, that circled back around in spirals and fluctuations to touch and color all truths that came out after that one.[38]

NOTES

1. Sigmund Freud, "A *Weltanschauung*," *New Introductory Lectures on Psychoanalysis* (1933). My source is John Gross, *The Oxford Book of Aphorisms* (Oxford: Oxford University Press, 1983), p. 227.

2. Shakespeare, *Hamlet* (ca. 1600), Act I, Scene 3, lines 78–80.

3. F. P. Ramsey, *On Truth*, eds. Nicholas Rescher and Ulrich Majer (Dordrecht, The Netherlands: Kluwer, 1992), p. 12.

4. Aristotle, *Metaphysics*, trans. Christopher Kirwan (Oxford: Oxford University Press, 1971), Book Gamma, Chapter. 7, 1011b2.

5. Ramsey, *On Truth* (n. 3); the quotations come, in order of appearance, from pp. 11–12, xviii n. 5, and 9.

6. The label—which I used myself in *Philosophy of Logics* (Cambridge: Cambridge University Press, 1978)—seemed appropriate when only Ramsey's "Facts and Propositions" (1927), in *The Foundations of Mathematics*, ed. Richard Braithwaite (London: Routledge and Kegan Paul, 1931), pp. 138–55, was available. But since Ramsey's manuscripts of 1921–29 were published in 1992 (*On Truth*, n. 3), it has become apparent that the term is misleading.

7. This poses significant difficulties: on an objectual interpretation of the quantifiers, sentential variables stand in for the names of sentences, and so, e.g., "for all p, if he says that p, then p" would amount to "for all p, if he says that p, then 'p' is true"; while on a substitutional interpretation, it would amount to "every substitution-instance of 'if he says that p, then p' is true." For ways of avoiding circularity, drawing on the work of Arthur Prior and C. J. F. Williams, see María-José Frápolli, "The Logical Enquiry Into Truth," *History and Philosophy of Logic* 17 (1996): 179–97.

8. George Eliot, *Daniel Deronda* (1876; Harmondsworth, Middlesex, UK: Penguin Books, 1987). At the beginning of chapter 21, Eliot interrupts her narrative with a powerful paragraph on the damage ignorance can wreak.

9. While officially reaffirming Florida's adherence to *Frye*, the Florida Supreme Court screened for reliability as an indicator of general acceptance. *Ramirez v. State*, 8120 S.2d 836 (Fla. 2001). See also "Trial and Error: The [US] Supreme Court's Philosophy of Science," pp. 161–77 in the present volume.

10. See also Haack, "Truth, Truths, 'Truth' and 'Truths' in the Law," *Harvard Journal of Law and Public Policy* 26, no. 1 (2003): 17–21.

11. See for example Ronald Giere, *Science Without Laws* (Chicago: University of Chicago Press, 1999). My views on instrumentalism, constructive empiricism, and "modelism" may be found in *Defending Science Within Reason: Between Scientism and Cynicism* (Amherst, NY: Prometheus Books, 2003), pp. 124–48.

12. On "meaning variance" (and its many meanings) see Haack, "'Realism,'" *Synthese* 73, no. 2 (1988): 275–98.

13. Hilary Putnam, *Renewing Philosophy* (Cambridge: Harvard University Press, 1992), pp. 122–23.

14. Haack, "Reflections on Relativism: From Momentous Tautology to Seductive Contradiction" (1996), in Haack, *Manifesto of a Passionate Moderate: Unfashionable Essays* (Chicago: University of Chicago Press, 1998), pp. 149–66.

15. Alfred Tarski, "The Semantic Concept of Truth" (1944), in *Readings in Philosophical Analysis*, eds. Herbert Feigl and Wilfrid Sellars (New York: Appleton-Century Crofts, 1949), pp. 52–84, pp. 53–54, and pp. 69–70.

16. As Quine suggests in *Quiddities* (Cambridge: Harvard University Press, 1987), p. 213.

17. Alfred Tarski, "The Concept of Truth in Formalized Languages" (1933), in *Logic, Semantics, Metamathematics*, trans. J. H. Woodger (Oxford: Clarendon Press, 1958), 152–278, pp. 159ff.

18. Scott Soames, *Understanding Truth* (Princeton, NJ: Princeton University Press, 1999), p. 218.

19. In "the Semantic Concept of Truth (n. 15), pp. 68–70, Tarski replies to the anticipated objection that "true" is redundant (though he doesn't mention Ramsey). Despite Tarski's clear repudiation of an account like Ramsey's, however, Rescher and Majer (the editors of Ramsey, *On Truth*) describe Ramsey as having come remarkably close to anticipating Tarski.

20. Tarski, "The Semantic Concept of Truth" (n. 15), p. 55.

21. Tarski, "The Concept of Truth in Formalized Languages" (n. 17), p. 165.

22. Tarski, "The Semantic Concept of Truth" (n. 15), pp. 65–66.

23. F. P. Ramsey, "The Foundations of Mathematics" in *The Foundations of Mathematics and Other Logical Essays*, ed. R. B. Braithwaite (London: Routledge and Kegan Paul, 1931), pp. 1–61, p. 48.

24. Saul Kripke, "Outline of a Theory of Truth," *Journal of Philosophy* 72 (1975): 698–716. Kripke relies in part on the concept of groundedness introduced by Hans

Herzberger in "Paradoxes on Grounding in Semantics," *Journal of Philosophy* 17 (1976): 145–67. Scott Soames, *Understanding Truth* (n. 18), pp. 163–200. Hartry Field, "A Revenge-Immune Solution to the Semantic Paradoxes," *Journal of Philosophical Logic* 32, no. 2 (2003): 138–77.

25. The approach at which I gesture metaphorically here has some affinity with the account developed in detail in Dorothy Grover, *A Prosentential Theory of Truth* (Princeton, NJ: Princeton University Press, 1992), pp. 212–36.

26. See Haack, "Knowledge and Propaganda: Reflections of an Old Feminist" (1993) in Haack, *Manifesto of a Passionate Moderate* (n. 14 above), pp. 123–36, and "Staying for an Answer" (1999), this volume, pp. 25–36. The *locus classicus* on the deceptive power of scare quotes is David Stove, *Popper and After: Four Modern Irrationalists* (1982), reprinted under the title *Anything Goes: Origins of the Cult of Scientific Irrationalism* (Paddington, Australia: Macleay Press, 1988), chapter 1.

27. From 1918 *Pravda* ("*The Truth*") was a leading Soviet newspaper and an official organ of the Communist Party; it was closed, by decree of President Yeltsin, in 1991.

28. The quotations come, in order of appearance, from Richard Rorty, *Philosophy and the Mirror of Nature* (Princeton, NJ: Princeton University Press, 1979), pp. 308–309; *Contingency, Irony and Solidarity* (Cambridge: Cambridge University Press, 1989), p. 22; "Trotsky and the Wild Orchids," *Common Knowledge* 3, no. 1 (1992): 140–53, p. 141; *Consequences of Pragmatism* (Hassocks, Sussex, UK: Harvester Press, 1982), p. xvii; "Science as Solidarity," in John S. Nelson, Alan Megill, and Donald M. McCloskey, eds., *The Rhetoric of the Human Sciences* (Madison, WI: University of Wisconsin Press, 1987), pp. 38–52, p. 43; *Objectivity, Relativism and Truth* (Cambridge: Cambridge University Press, 1992), p. 32.

29. See also Haack, *Evidence and Inquiry: Towards Reconstruction in Epistemology* (Oxford: Blackwell, 1993), pp. 183–94; "Confessions of an Old-Fashioned Prig," in *Manifesto of a Passionate Moderate* (n. 26), 7–30, pp. 18–21.

30. C. S. Peirce, *Collected Papers*, eds. Charles Hartshorne, Paul Weiss, and (vols. 7 and 8) Arthur Burks (Cambridge: Harvard University Press, 1931–58), 2.138 and 5.211. [References are by volume and paragraph number.]

31. But see Haack, *Defending Science—Within Reason* (n. 11), chapter 5.

32. Peirce, *Collected Papers* (n. 30), 2.252.

33. See also Haack, *Defending Science* (n. 11), pp. 154–61 (on the relation of the social to the natural sciences), and pp. 96–98 (on the continuity of scientific with everyday empirical inquiry); and "Fallibilism and Faith, Naturalism and the Supernatural, Science and Religion," pp. 183–94 in the present volume.

34. Pope John Paul II, "Message to the Pontifical Academy of Sciences," *Acta Apostolica Sedia* 88 (1998). Islamic philosopher Ibn Rushd (1126–1198) is reported to have said that "truth does not oppose truth"; see Peter J. King, *One Hundred Philosophers: The Life and Work of the World's Greatest Thinkers* (London: Quarto and New York: Barron's, 2004), p. 62.

35. A curious phenomenon, this, explored in more detail in Jonathan Rauch, *Kindly Inquisitors: The New Attacks on Free Thought* (Chicago: University of Chicago Press, 1993).

36. Donald M. McCloskey, *Knowledge and Persuasion in Economics* (Cambridge: Cambridge University Press, 1993), pp. 99ff.

37. Francis Crick, *What Mad Purusit: A Personal View of Scientific Discovery* (New York: Basic Books, 1988), p. 13.

38. Jeffrey Lent, *After the Fall* (New York: Vintage, 2000), pp. 253–54.

4

COHERENCE, CONSISTENCY, COGENCY, CONGRUITY, COHESIVENESS, &C.

Remain Calm! Don't Go Overboard!

In the tumultuous business of cutting in and attending to a whale, there is much running backwards and forwards among the crew. Now hands are wanted here, and then again, hands are wanted there. There is no staying in any one place, for at one and the same time everything has to be done everywhere. It is much the same with him who endeavors the description of the scene.
—Herman Melville, *Moby-Dick*[1]

A nd it is much the same when you're faced with the "leading questions" in our editor's letter of invitation:[2] "As a matter of science or philosophy, does coherence name a totalized state or an organizing tendency? Do synchronic and diachronic modes of coherence reinforce or interfere with each other? Can theories of chaos bring their object to order without thereby eliminating it? Does the chaos-theory paradox have analogues in the human or social sciences? In cognitive or cultural processes, is total structure an inference from perception or its enabling precondition? Is incoherence a sustainable option for visual, musical, or literary art? Is coherence a property that methods of inquiry discover, or one that they produce? When historicist or cultural studies—often expressly disavowing coherentism—appeal from a local correspondence to an overarching totality, what grounds that appeal? What is the status of coherence in advanced scholarly argumentation? In rhetoric and composition teaching? Is the concept of coherence value-neutral or value-laden? How does it foster on the one hand an ethics of solidarity and community, on the other an imperial or totalitarian politics? How do the economics of globalization inflect coherentism today? Can one think of coherences in the plural, or is there something in the logic of the concept that overrides differences and assimilates its instances to itself?"

Goodness! Now hands are wanted in epistemology, now in philosophy of science, now in aesthetics, now in cultural studies, and now in economics and political theory; and "at one and the same time everything has to be done everywhere."

I can offer only my reflections on some of the many roles played by some of the many concepts of the coherence family. "Concepts," in the plural; for "coherence" has a whole raft of meanings, distinct though sometimes subtly interrelated, and is applied to a whole range of very different things: what a logician means by speaking of the consistency of an axiomatic system, for example, is not what a literary critic means by speaking of the consistency of a fictional character or the congruity of this sub-plot with the overall theme of a novel; what an epistemologist means by speaking of the coherence of a set of beliefs or a scientist of the consilience of the physical with the social sciences is not what a sociologist or political theorist means by speaking of the cohesiveness of this society or the solidarity among the members of that trade union. So my first task, in what follows, will be simply to disentangle some of the multiple meanings and multiple objects of "coherent"; then, looking more closely at a field where coherence concepts have sometimes been asked to play a central role, I shall offer my assessment of "coherentism" in epistemology; and finally, by way of conclusion, I will suggest answers to at least some of the questions on our editor's extraordinary list.

———————— ◆ ————————

Besides being used to describe the texture of batter or cement, "consistency" denotes one dimension of logical appraisal. A set of propositions is formally, or logically, inconsistent just in case a contradiction—the conjunction of a formula and its negation, "p and not-p"—can be derived from it; otherwise, it is logically consistent. Inconsistent formulae can't be jointly true; hence the importance of consistency proofs, meta-logical demonstrations that this or that formal logical system does not allow the derivation of a contradiction.[3] The need for such proofs became vividly clear early in the history of modern logic, when Gottlob Frege's pioneering articulation of the unified propositional and predicate calculus turned out *not* to be consistent: Russell's Paradox ("the set of all sets which are not members of themselves is a member of itself if and only if it is not a member of itself") was derivable as a theorem.[4]

Outside formal-logical contexts, "consistent" is often used, not in this strict sense, but as a broader term connoting the mutual compatibility of a set of propositions. In this usage, "consistent" takes into account not only logical form but also the meanings of words (e.g., given the meaning of "bachelor," "Tom is a bachelor" and "Tom is married" are mutually incompatible, though not formally inconsistent). Of course, mutually incompatible propositions can no more be jointly true than formally inconsistent formulae can; there can't be incompatible truths or "knowledges." Yes, there are many *different* truths; but not incompatible ones. Yes, incompatible propositions can be *accepted* as true; but they can't all *be* true. And yes, sometimes we say that something is "true for you but not for me"; but this is just a misleadingly elliptical way of saying that you believe whatever-it-is (that tax cuts will stimulate the economy, that life on earth was seeded from other planets) but I don't, or else that whatever-it-is (liking Wagner, or having red hair) is true *of* you but not of me.

Since mutual compatibility is a necessary condition for the truth of a set of propositions, some philosophers have hoped, by adding to simple consistency or mutual compatibility such further requirements as comprehensiveness or mutual entailment, to devise a concept of coherence that would constitute both a necessary and a sufficient condition of truth. F. H. Bradley wrote that "[t]ruth is an ideal expression of the Universe, at once coherent and comprehensive";[5] and various versions of the coherence theory of truth were defended by other Idealists and sympathizers, among them H. H. Joachim, Brand Blanshard, Bernard Bosanquet, and A. C. Ewing. Even among the Logical Positivists, though most, like Moritz Schlick and Rudolf Carnap, favored some kind of correspondence theory, Otto Neurath defended a coherence approach.[6] Sometimes, as in Blanshard, coherence was held to constitute, not just the criterion, but the nature or definition of truth; but often, interest in coherence was really more epistemological than metaphysical. In 1973 Nicholas Rescher defended "the coherence theory of truth" in his book of the same title. What he proposed, however, was not that coherence could constitute a definition, or even a "guaranteeing" criterion, but only that it is an "authorizing" criterion, i.e., a fallible indication, of truth.

And it is in epistemology—the philosophical theory of knowledge, where at least since Plato one central concern has been to understand the difference between really *knowing* something, and merely believing something that happens to be true—that coherence concepts have of late played their most prominent philosophical role. One main focus has been on what makes a belief justified, what constitutes good or adequate grounds, reasons, or evidence; and coherentism, with its traditional rival, foundationalism, is one of the standard theories in this domain. Taking justification to require anchoring in the world, foundationalist theories explain justified empirical belief as belief either directly justified by the subject's sensory and/or introspective experience, or else supported by beliefs which are so justified, or supported by beliefs which are supported by beliefs which are so justified, ... or, etc. Taking justification to be a relation exclusively among beliefs, coherence theories explain justified empirical belief as belief that coheres with the subject's other beliefs.

Epistemological justification is a synchronic concept, assessing a person's epistemic status with respect to some belief at a time. Some have hoped that the concept of coherence, in some epistemological, consistency-plus sense, could serve as the basis for an account of rational belief-*change*, proposing that rational revisions of belief should maintain, or if necessary restore, coherence. At least construed as proposing a necessary but not a sufficient condition for rational belief change, this seems on its face both more modest and more plausible than a coherence theory of justified belief.

Perhaps it also gestures, at least, towards a deeper idea. Sometimes we speak of a "tension" between this idea and that; usually when, though they are not exactly incompatible, they pull strongly in opposite directions—as if one more step in the direction of either would land us in a contradiction (as a taut rope would break, or a taut sail tear, if subjected to even a little more strain). "Tension" is just the word that comes to mind when, for example, you think about the relation between the scientific and the religious world-pictures: no scientific theory says that there is no God, or that God did not create the universe, or, etc.; still, Stephen Hawking observes, "We are such insignificant creatures on a minor planet of a very average star in the outer suburbs of one of a hundred thousand million galaxies. So it is difficult to believe in a God that would care about us."[7] Tension can be fruitful, in more ways than one. Even outright inconsistency can be an important incentive to renewed intellectual effort, as with the many and various developments of set theory after Frege. The effort to accommodate potentially conflicting desiderata is often the spur to intellectual advance; e.g., the need to acknowledge both that the world is independent of our beliefs about it, and that we can sometimes manage to acquire knowledge of it, which underlies much recent debate over the various forms of realism and their rivals.[8] And the effort to express contrasting moods or competing values, as we shall see, can be artistically fruitful.

Sometimes we appraise, not sets of propositions or theories, not people's beliefs, but people's thinking, speech, and writing for coherence.

What counts as thinking coherently depends on the context: a physician checks whether a patient in shock knows his own name, what day it is, who is currently president, and so forth; but the academic I describe as "not thinking coherently" can pass *that* test all right—the complaint is, rather, that his thinking is muddled, fuzzy, scrambled, or even outright contradictory. Of course, it's normal for one's first thoughts about a difficult question to be inchoate, and to shift up and back between one conclusion and its opposite; there's nothing wrong with that. Sometimes, though, rather than working through this frustratingly fuzzy initial stage, people seize on a confused or half-baked idea and rely on it in all their thinking on some subject, heedless of its inability to carry the burdens placed on it. As Peirce observed, the consequences can be disastrous: "It is terrible to see how a single unclear idea, a single formula without meaning, lurking in a young man's head, will sometimes act like an obstruction of inert matter in an artery, hindering the nutrition of the brain, and condemning its victim to pine away in the fullness of his intellectual vigor and in the midst of intellectual plenty."[9]

Sets of propositions can be inconsistent; situations or states of affairs can't, but they can be chaotic or confused. And, just as there can be a sober description of a drunken man, or an orderly description of "the tumultuous business of cutting in and attending to a whale," there can be a consistent description of an inconsistent set of propositions: the description I gave earlier of Frege's inconsistent logic, for example, or a detective's report of the inconsistency between witness A's testimony and witness B's. But often, when we speak of the coherence of a person's speech or writing, we have in mind, not consistency in the logical or quasi-logical sense, but something more pragmatic: as when we praise a colleague's or student's paper or presentation for its cogency, or complain that it is lazy, muddy, jumbled, hard to follow; or when we describe the speech of someone drunk, drugged, or mentally disturbed, or of an academic undone by too much Theory, as "incoherent"—i.e., disordered, rambling, garbled, glossogonous word-salad or high-toned gobbledygook.

"Incoherent" is sometimes used, again of someone's speech or writing, in the rather more specialized philosophical sense of "self-undermining": as I might say that when a philosopher claims that truth is relative to culture, or that there are no beliefs—though neither the proposition that truth is relative to culture nor the proposition that there are no beliefs contains any hidden contradiction—*his asserting this* undermines what he asserts; for one who sincerely makes a categorical assertion expresses his belief, and makes a non-relative claim to truth.

When it is actions that are being appraised, "consistent" means something like "behaving in the same way in similar circumstances"; and so applies not to a single action, but to a person's (or sometimes an institution's) practices or actions over time. The desirability or otherwise of consistency, so understood, depends on whether you are consistently following ill-considered ways of behaving for no better reason than that this is how you behaved in the past, or consistently following a well-considered policy of action—precisely the point of that famous observation of Ralph Waldo Emerson's, that "a foolish consistency is the hobgoblin of little minds, adored by little statesmen and philosophers and divines." Emerson rightly scorns the mental rigidity of one who refuses to change his beliefs in the face of new evidence, or who obsessively insists on doing things as he has always done them, regardless of the success or failure of those past actions: "He may as well conform himself with his shadow on the wall."[10] But the distinction between a wise consistency and a foolish, often forgotten when Emerson's observation is quoted only in part, is essential.

There's nothing objectionable about the concern for consistency shown by the copy editor who spots your two spellings of "judg[e]ment," or asks you please to decide whether "prima facie" should be in italic or roman type, and stick to it; but there *is* something objectionable about the concern for consistency shown by the copy editor who officiously imposes a dismal and pointless conformity of style or usage. Jacques Barzun reports a classic encounter with an icily polite young person who challenged his use of capitals to distinguish "Liberal," as in "Gladstone, the Liberal prime minister" from "liberal," as in "Edward VII, who was also liberal—toward his mistresses"; apparently, Barzun comments, the young man believed that "the firm's readers (the author's don't exist) will compare several of their books and exclaim, 'My, what inconsistent capitalization!'"[11]

However, since fairness demands that people similarly situated be similarly dealt with, consistency in practice is sometimes a legitimate, even an essential, concern—felt by the conscientious teacher grading papers, or the jurist looking to precedent (the concern expressed in the legal principle of *stare decisis*, standing by what was decided). But here too the desirability of consistency depends on the wisdom of the practice being consistently applied: it would be worse than foolish of me to continue adding up the marks for each question wrong, in order to maintain consistency with the mistake I made the first time; and, though we want the law to provide stability and predictability, we don't want it to stagnate, to be totally unresponsive to social change.

Cognitive psychologists have their own word for a kind of incoherence that especially interests them, the tensions between a person's beliefs and his actions and preferences: Leon Festinger's "cognitive dissonance." This is the concept explored in his theoretical writings and in his case studies of millennial sects whose members react to the failure of their prophecies of the end of the world, not by acknowledging that they were mistaken, but by reinterpreting their prophecy and proselytizing more energetically; it is also the theme of Alison

Lurie's wickedly funny fictional variations on these real quirks of human nature in *Imaginary Friends*.[12]

As the example suggests, our appraisals of coherence and incoherence extend not only to theories, and not only to the speech, writing, beliefs, attitudes, and actions of real people, but also to literary texts and fictional characters. Occasionally, when we use "consistent" and "inconsistent" of works of literature, it is in much the same sense as when we appraise a theory, or someone's beliefs, for consistency. I once heard Peter Geach argue, against the proposal that we understand what a possible world is by analogy with a novel, that there are sometimes inconsistencies in novels—e.g., geographical inconsistencies in *War and Peace*; he meant "inconsistent," obviously, in the quasi-logical sense. (Though these inconsistencies are significant for Geach's logical point, they are of no real importance to our assessment of the novel; but one can easily imagine inconsistencies in a detective story, say, making nonsense of the plot.) More often, though, in literary contexts the point is not the consistency or otherwise of the chronological, geographical, forensic, or other, details of a fictional work, but the consistent or inconsistent behavior of its characters, the congruence or incongruity of its themes, or the unity or disunity of its mode of presentation or its language.

In *The Way of All Flesh* Samuel Butler writes that his friends used to say of Ernest Pontifex (whose zigzag path to maturity the book chronicles) that "when he rose he flew like a snipe, darting several times in various directions before he settled down to a steady, straight flight," but that "once he had got into this he would keep to it."[13] This sent me first to my bird book, and then back to Aristotle's observation that characters should be consistent, but "[i]f the model for the representation is somebody inconsistent, and such a character is intended, even so it should be consistently inconsistent."[14] Here "consistent" is used in the same sense in which it applies to the behavior of real people, now extended to fictional characters. In *Daniel Deronda* there is a satisfying congruity of intertwined narratives, unified by George Eliot's theme of the power of ignorance: Deronda, originally unaware of his origins, and no less prejudiced against Jews than those around him, discovers that he is Jewish himself, and explores what that means to him. Gwendolen Harleth, too blithely and self-confidently ignorant to realize how ignorant she really is, makes a disastrous marriage in a desperate effort to save herself when her family faces financial ruin.[15] Here "congruous" means something like "illustrating the same theme."

But in a work of literature not only such congruities, but also, sometimes, the well-chosen *in*congruity may be pleasing. We enjoy not only narrative parallels but also contrasting intertwined plots and skillfully sliced and spliced narratives; we appreciate the well-chosen anachronism of the modern-dress production of a Shakespeare play that successfully conveys its lessons for our time; and we find the well-chosen grammatical incongruity not only a rich source of verbal humor, but also, sometimes, a wonderfully effective literary device: as with the pleasant shock of the opening line of chapter 5 of Ursula Le Guin's *The Left Hand of Darkness*: "My landlady was a voluble man"[16]—a startling verbal incongruity that is exactly right given her cast of hermaphrodite, but otherwise very human, characters.

Like "consistent," "cohesive" suggests physical as well as abstract sticking together: as a cookbook might instruct you to add water until the dough is cohesive in consistency. But, unlike "consistent," "cohesive" is often used of social groups, such as a tribe or society or church whose members are united by shared beliefs, attitudes, and goals. Some political thinkers, Plato among them, have placed a very high value on social cohesiveness, far outweighing their concern for citizens' freedom or happiness; others see social cohesiveness as sometimes benign, but sometimes a dangerous expression of tribalism. Here I'm with the others: admirable as we might find the solidarity of the British as they pulled together, temporarily overcoming barriers of class and accent, in the fight against Hitler, we should never forget that "solidarity" has another, frightening face: the grim conformity of totalitarian states, the rigidly closed ranks and long-held grudges of Mafia families, and so on.

Now it is time, narrowing the focus somewhat, to look more closely at the role played by coherence concepts in epistemology, and specifically at the debates between foundationalist and coherentist theories of epistemological justification.

Coherentists believe that foundationalism is unable to acknowledge the pervasive mutual support among beliefs, and that it has no plausible account of how, exactly, experience is supposed to contribute to justification. But foundationalists believe that coherentism is unable to acknowledge the relevance of experience to empirical justification, and that its reliance on interrelations among beliefs only thinly disguises a vicious circularity of reasons. So the issues that have been most to the fore have been the role, if any, of a person's sensory and introspective experience in the justification of his empirical beliefs, and the legitimacy, or otherwise, of mutual support among beliefs.

How could I be justified in believing there's a blue-jay in the bougainvillaea, unless I see the thing, or hear it, or rely on the report of someone who sees or hears it, or, etc.? On the face of it, the relevance of experience to empirical justification, the need for a person's beliefs about the world to be anchored in his interactions with the world, seems undeniable; yet coherentism seems to deny it. Many coherentists have tried to accommodate experience obliquely: by granting a distinguished status to perceptual beliefs, by introducing an additional requirement supposed to guarantee experiential input, or, etc. But the results have not been encouraging.

It is arbitrary to grant a distinguished initial status to perceptual beliefs, or experiential beliefs generally, without some reason for privileging these particular kinds of belief rather than other kinds; but it is impossible to give the obvious reason—that experiential beliefs are justified at least in part not by the subject's other beliefs, but by his experience—without sacrificing coherentism. It is much the same with additional requirements to the effect that a coherent belief-set must be sensitive to experiential input, such as Laurence BonJour's "Observation Requirement," which turns out to be ambiguous. On one interpretation (the subject must believe that his belief-set includes highly reliable cognitively spontaneous, i.e., non-inferential, beliefs), it is coherentist, all right, but it doesn't guarantee experiential input; on the other (the subject's belief-set must actually include highly reliable cognitively spontaneous beliefs) it guarantees experiential input, all right, but is no longer coherentist.[17]

In epistemological contexts coherence is usually construed, as it was in the older coherence theories of truth, as requiring something more than simple consistency, even in the broader, quasi-logical sense: comprehensiveness, proposed by Bradley and, in the logically sophisticated form of "maximal consistency," by Rescher; explanatory coherence, suggested by Wilfrid Sellars;[18] probabilistic consistency, understood sometimes simply as requiring that the probabilities a person assigns to various propositions should be compatible with the axioms of the mathematical calculus of probabilities, but sometimes as identifying probabilities with degrees of belief, and recasting the whole epistemological picture in terms of the theory of probability. For all these elaborations of coherence, however, coherentists have mostly had surprisingly little to say about how, exactly, the mutual support they take to justify a person's beliefs differs from a vicious circle of reasons, beyond averring that there *is* a difference.[19] The standard foundationalist objections to coherentism, in short, seem to stick.

But so do the standard coherentist objections to foundationalism. Older foundationalists sometimes held that basic beliefs are fully justified by the subject's experience; more recently, most have held only that basic beliefs are justified by experience to some degree. Some older foundationalists eschewed mutual support altogether; but recently most have acknowledged that mutual support among derived beliefs may raise their degree of justification. Once you've gone this far, however, it is arbitrary to deny that the degree of justification of "basic" beliefs may also be raised, or lowered, by their relations to other beliefs; but to grant this is to give up the distinction of basic versus derived beliefs altogether.

And foundationalists have had surprisingly little to say about how a proposition a person believes—that there's a bird in the bush, say—can be justified by his seeing the thing; when his seeing the bird is an event, not a proposition capable of standing in logical or quasi-logical relations to other propositions. The most apparently promising approach is to try to tie the relevance of experience to the fact that we learn certain words, the "observational" ones, ostensively, i.e., by direct association with this or that sensory experience; but this approach has come to seem less promising as doubts have grown about the viability of a sharp distinction between observational words and others.

In short, coherentism won't do; but foundationalism doesn't seem to be a viable option either.

The foundherentist theory I proposed in *Evidence and Inquiry* combined the strongest points of coherentism and foundationalism, while avoiding their weaknesses.[20] According to this theory, the structure of evidence is neither linear nor one-dimensional. What determines how justified a person is in believing something is how supportive his evidence is of the belief in question; how secure his reasons are; independent of that belief; and how much of the relevant evidence his evidence includes.

Supportiveness of evidence is explained in terms of explanatory integration. This is close kin to the older idea of consilience, meaning etymologically "jumping together," and introduced into philosophical discourse by the nineteenth-century philosopher of science William Whewell, who referred to the "consilience of inductions" when an explanatory conjecture made to account for one phenomenon turns out also to account for other, different, phenomena as well.[21] It is also close kin to the more recent concept of explanatory coherence or mutual explanatoriness among beliefs. But the role of explanatory integration in the foundherentist theory is more modest than the role of explanatory coherence in the coherence theory; for in the foundherentist account supportiveness is only one of the several dimensions of evidential quality.

The foundherentist theory distinguishes legitimate mutual support among beliefs from a vicious circle of reasons: the degree to which a belief is justified depends in part on how justified the beliefs that support it are, *independent of any support they themselves get from the belief in question*. And the foundherentist theory does this without leaving us with a whole mesh of mutually supportive beliefs hanging in midair; for, though it requires no privileged class of basic beliefs, it allows the relevance of experience: experiential evidence—which, since it consists of perceptual events, not propositions believed, does not itself stand in need of justification—anchors the mesh to the world.[22]

At the time of *Evidence and Inquiry*, however, I had relatively little to say about exactly *how* experiential evidence anchors a person's empirical beliefs. The amplified and refined account developed in *Defending Science—Within Reason* fills this lacuna, starting from the old idea that the relevance of experience arises somehow from the way we learn language, but without requiring a sharp dichotomy of ostensive versus verbal definitions, observational versus non-observational predicates. As foundherentism says, experiential evidence and background beliefs work together, as clues and completed intersecting crossword entries do.[23] A person's experiential evidence, his seeing, hearing, smelling, or feeling this or that, though not itself propositional, can support a proposition in virtue of the association of words with experience and with other words acquired as we learned language. But that association is multilayered: e.g., a child is first introduced to the word "dog" in the presence of clearly visible dogs, but later learns "looks like a dog, but . . . ," "toy dog," etc., and realizes that not everything that looks like this falls under "dog," and not everything that falls under "dog" looks like this. This subtler conception of language-learning motivates, not a foundationalist account in which there are basic beliefs justified by experience alone, but a foundherentist account in which the support given an empirical belief by experience may be raised, or lowered, by other beliefs of his.

Since foundherentism accommodates both foundationalist and coherentist insights, it offers a better way out of the impasse of foundationalism and coherentism than the relativization of justification to context or community that is sometimes proposed. According to standard forms of contextualism,[24] epistemic justification consists in a subject's conformity to the epistemic practices of his community. Richard Rorty, who avers that "there is nothing more to be said about either truth or rationality apart from a description of the familiar procedures of justification which a given society—*ours*—uses," proposes a nonstandard variant according to which justification consists in conformity to the epistemic practices of our community.[25] Very misleadingly, Rorty sometimes describes himself as a coherentist: perhaps simply because he rejects foundationalism, perhaps because he wants to ally himself with Donald Davidson—or perhaps because he thinks of justification as agreement, not among a person's beliefs, but of one person's beliefs with other peoples'.

"The only sense in which science is exemplary is that it is a model of human solidarity,"[26] Rorty writes, thus giving social cohesiveness a starring epistemological role, and apparently assimilating the achievements of four centuries or so of scientific investigation to—what? a really good trade union? Yes, noncollusive agreement among witnesses is some indication of their truthfulness. Yes, science is a deeply social enterprise: the evidence with respect to scientific claims is usually a shared resource; and inquiry in the sciences is the work, cooperative and competitive, of generation upon generation of inquirers, who are able to complete new crossword entries in part because of the successes, or sometimes the failures, of those who have worked on the puzzle before them. And yes, consensus in the scientific community is epistemologically significant. But not in the way Rorty supposes: the fact that scientists agree on a theory doesn't warrant it; gradually killing off those who don't accept a new scientific idea, or playing a tape repeating "the earth moves" under the pillows of the holdouts while they sleep, won't make the claim in question any more likely true. No, consensus in the scientific community is epistemologically significant because—by no means always, but on the whole and in the long run, often enough—the strong evidence that warrants the theory also explains scientists' agreement.

Whether construed in the usual, relativist style, or in Rorty's more tribalist fashion, contextualism really is a desperate measure: abandoning the idea of objectively better or worse evidence, it would, among other things, knock away the essential epistemological underpinnings of the entire legal system. Fortunately, however, since foundherentism avoids the pitfalls of foundationalism and of coherentism, no such desperate measures are necessary.

Now, as I promised, back to the list of questions that started it all.

"Can one think of coherences in the plural, or is there something in the logic of the concept that overrides differences and assimilates its instances to itself?" "Coherence" has multiple meanings, and multiple objects; but it is better to say this directly, and to distinguish rather than assimilate those multiple meanings— paying due attention also to their interrelations, naturally—than to signal them obliquely by that coyly postmodern plural form, "coherences," without making the distinctions explicit.

"Do synchronic and diachronic modes of coherence reinforce or interfere with each other?" Well, the desirability of consistency in one's beliefs underlies both the concern to avoid contradiction among one's beliefs at a time, and the need to adjust one's beliefs when, over time, new evidence comes in that suggests that something you formerly believed is false. But the desirability of consistency in practice, in one's actions over time—when such consistency *is* desirable—stems not simply from the desirability of consistency in action as such, but from the desirability of a consistent practice of well-considered actions.

"Is the concept of coherence value-neutral or value-laden?" My first reaction was that, like the famous peppermint burgundy of Monty Python's "Wines of Australia" sketch, this question "should be laid down—and left." Talk of "the" concept of coherence is misleading, since there isn't just one concept in play; and "value-laden" seems to have become value-laden, a pejorative phrase that hints, without quite saying, that the concept in question covertly imposes an undesirable (usually, a politically undesirable), agenda. "Consistent," as I said, is used as a term of favorable logical appraisal, "coherent" as a term of favorable epistemological appraisal, "congruous" as a term of favorable literary appraisal, "cohesive" as a term of favorable political appraisal, and "cogent" as a favorable term of appraisal of thought, speech, and writing. Still, as I also said, inconsistency may prompt fruitful intellectual advance, coherence is only one component in an understanding of justified belief, incongruities of various kinds may be effective literary devices, social cohesiveness takes both desirable and undesirable forms, and so on. Coherence, in its various senses, has sometimes been undervalued; but it has sometimes, also, been overvalued.

This suggests a possible answer to the question of how coherence can "foster on the one hand an ethics of community or solidarity, [and] on the other an imperial or totalitarian politics": that, as the propagandists of totalitarian regimes have always understood only too well, the ameliorative use of "cohesive" (or "unified," etc.) can disguise the fact that solidarity has its dark side.

"Is incoherence a sustainable option for . . . literary art?" It depends. There's certainly a role for incongruities in narrative, inconsistencies in character, verbal adventurousness and rule-breaking—of the right kinds, and in the right contexts; but not always or everywhere. An academic paper, in particular, is rarely an ideal context for the more adventurous kinds of rule-breaking that might work elsewhere. Hence, my first response to the next question, "What is the status of coherence in advanced scholarly argumentation?": it is certainly better that an academic paper be cogent than not, and too-fancy literary forms are apt to get in the way of clear exposition; it would be much harder to explain the structure of DNA, or even the theory of poetic meter, in iambic pentameter rather than plain prose. As usual, though, my first response needs amplification and qualification.

We value cogency in thinking at least as much as cogency in speech and writing. So we shouldn't forget that sometimes, when a person stumbles, mumbles, and fumbles in presenting his ideas, it is because what he is struggling to articulate is new and difficult; perhaps his thinking is coherent enough, but he can't yet quite articulate it, or perhaps his thinking is as yet inchoate, but potentially fruitful. Nor should we forget that superficially cogent presentation sometimes only disguises shallow or poorly thought-out ideas. And we shouldn't confuse real cogency with the prissy pseudo-precision of some neo-analytic philosophers, or with the portentous pseudo-profundity of some literary scholars; nor should we fool ourselves into thinking that humor,[27] a sense of style, or a good ear for prose rhythms are somehow inappropriate to the academic *genre*, or a sign of insufficient seriousness.

"What is the status of coherence in rhetoric or composition teaching?" Analytic philosophers generally construe "rhetoric" as the art of persuasion by means of emotive language and such, by contrast with logic, the theory of good, valid arguments; and tend to look down on it. Literary scholars, on the other hand, generally construe "rhetoric" much more broadly, as the art of prose discourse, logic included; and value it quite highly. If "rhetoric" is narrowly construed, anyway, there is little question that, while incoherence of one kind or another may impede persuasion, it may, on the other hand, advance it. Gross incoherence was no obstacle to the effectiveness of Big Brother's propaganda, and it needn't be in real life, either; in fact, it can even be useful, for incoherent propaganda is sure to include something for everyone—and you really *can* fool too many of the people too much of the time.

What about coherence in composition teaching? At first blush, the answer seems easy enough: many students have had sadly limited experience of well-crafted English, and it is a real achievement to help them write workmanlike, cogent prose; not least because learning to present your ideas cogently—and to try again, and again, when you fail—is such a significant step toward acquiring the discipline of hard thinking. Unfortunately, though, real cogency is subtle and difficult, and *ersatz* cogency much easier to teach than the real thing. So perhaps I need to add that we do our students a grave disservice if we encourage them, in the name of cogency, to mimic the constipated or windy style of their professors; or if we give them the impression that it is more important to shun the generic "he," or to get their bibliographies in impeccable *Chicago Manual* style, than to have something subtle and worthwhile to say, and to take pleasure in the flexibility and power of our language as they explore how best to say it.

NOTES

1. Hermann Melville, *Moby-Dick: Or, The Whale* (1851). (New York: Signet classics, New American Library, 1998), p. 309.

2. The letter from Prof. Herbert Tucker, associate editor of *New Literary History*, in response to which I wrote this paper.

3. In classical logic, moreover, any well-formed formula whatever is derivable from a contradiction (though in some non-classical, "paraconsistent" logics the damage is contained).

4. Jean Van Heijenoort, ed., *From Frege to Gödel: A Source Book in Mathematical Logic 1879–1931* (Cambridge, MA: Harvard University Press, 1967), includes Gottlob Frege, *Begriffsschrift* (1879), on pp. 1–82; Bertrand Russell's letter to Frege about the paradox (1902), on pp. 124–25; and Frege's reply (1902), on pp. 127–28.

5. F. H. Bradley, *Essays on Truth and Reality* (Oxford: Oxford University Press, 1914), p. 223.

6. See A. C. Ewing, *Idealism: A Critical Survey* (London: Methuen, 1934); Carl G. Hempel, "On the Logical Positivists' Theory of Truth," *Analysis* 2 (1935): 49–59; Nicholas Rescher, *The Coherence Theory of Truth* (Oxford: Clarendon Press, 1973), chapter II.

7. The quotation is from a BBC television program called *Masters of the Universe*; my source is Michael Shermer, *How We Believe: The Search for God in an Age of Science* (New York: W. H. Freeman and Company, 2000), p. 102.

8. See Susan Haack, "Realisms and Their Rivals: Recovering Our Innocence," *Facta Philosophica* 4, no. 1 (2002): 67–88.

9. Charles Sanders Peirce, *Collected Papers*, eds. Charles Hartshorne, Paul Weiss, and (vols. 7 and 8) Arthur Burks (Cambridge: Harvard University Press, 1931–58), 5.393 (1878). [References to the *Collected Papers* are by volume and paragraph number.]

10. Ralph Waldo Emerson, "Self-Reliance" (1902), in *The Works of Ralph Waldo Emerson* (Roslyn, NY: Readers' Service Company, n.d.), p. 102.

11. Jacques Barzun, "Dialogue in C-Sharp," in *A Word or Two Before You Go . . .* (Middletown, CT: Wesleyan University Press, 1986), pp. 115–17, p. 117. See also his "A Copy-Editor's Anthology," pp. 85–91 in the same volume.

12. Leon Festinger, *A Theory of Cognitive Dissonance* (Evanston, IL: Row and Person, 1957); Leon Festinger, Henry W. Reicken, and Stanley Schacter, *When Prophesy Fails: A Social and Psychological Study of a Modern Group that Predicted the Destruction of the World* (1956; New York: Harper and Row, 1964). Alison Lurie, *Imaginary Friends* (New York: Henry Holt and Company, Owl Books, 1967).

13. Samuel Butler, *The Way of All Flesh* (1903; New York: Modern Library, 1998), p. 213. See also "The Ideal of Intellectual Integrity, in Life and Literature," pp. 195–208 in the present volume.

14. Aristotle, *Poetics I*, trans. Richard Janko (Indianapolis, IN: Hackett Publishing Company, 1987), p. 19.

15. George Eliot, *Daniel Deronda* (1878; Harmondsworth, Middlesex, UK: Penguin Books, 1967).

16. Ursula Le Guin, *The Left Hand of Darkness* (New York: Ace Books, 1969).

17. See e.g., Laurence BonJour, *The Structure of Empirical Knowledge* (Cambridge: Harvard University Press, 1985); Donald Davidson, "A Coherence Theory of Truth and Knowledge," in *Kant oder Hegel?* ed. Dieter Heinrich (Stuttgart: Klett-Cotta, 1983), pp. 423–38, reprinted in Alan Malachowski, ed., *Reading Rorty* (Oxford: Blackwell, 1990), pp. 120–34. Both are criticized in detail in my *Evidence and Inquiry: Towards Recon-*

struction in Epistemology (Oxford: Blackwell, 1993), chapter 3; 2nd edition, *Evidence and Inquiry: A Pragmatist Reconstruction of Epistemology* (Amherst, NY: Prometheus Books, forthcoming, 2009). (By 1997, BonJour had given up coherentism in favor of a kind of foundationalism.)

18. Wilfrid Sellars, "Some Reflections on Language-Games," in *Science, Perception and Reality* (London: Routledge and Kegan Paul, 1963), pp. 321–58.

19. In *Coherence in Thought and Action* (Cambridge: Bradford Books, MIT Press, 2000), Paul Thagard claims that his coherentism can avoid vicious circularity by providing algorithms that "effectively calculate how a whole set of elements fit together, without linear inference of p from q and of q from p" (p. 76). But his "elements" are heterogeneous and ill-defined; his "algorithms" are vitiated by their reliance on purely intuitive assignments of weight, undefined primitive terms such as "explains," etc.; and when, on p. 78, he presents a pair of diagrams to illustrate the difference between mutual support and a vicious circle, the diagram supposedly representing legitimate mutual support appears to consist of two diagrams representing vicious circles of reasons superimposed on each other!

20. See Haack, "Theories of Knowledge: An Analytic Framework," *Proceedings of the Aristotelian Society*, LXXXIII (1982–83): 143–57; *Evidence and Inquiry* (n. 17), chapter 4; and "A Foundherentist Theory of Empirical Justification," first published in *Theory of Knowledge: Classical and Contemporary Sources*, ed. Louis Pojman (Belmont, CA: Wadsworth, second edition, 1998), pp. 283–93, and reprinted (without the many mistakes introduced by Wadsworth's copy editor) in *Epistemology: An Anthology*, eds. Ernest Sosa and Jaegwon Kim (Oxford: Blackwell, 2000), pp. 226–36, in *Epistemology: Contemporary Readings*, ed. Michael Huemer (New York: Routledge, 2002), 417–34, and in Steven Luper, ed., *Essential Knowledge* (New York: Longman's, 2004), 157–67.

21. William Whewell, *Philosophy of the Inductive Sciences* (1840), in *Selected Writings on the History of Science*, ed. Yehuda Elkana (Chicago: University of Chicago Press, 1984), pp. 121–254. The term was adopted by E. O. Wilson as the title of his *Consilience: The Unity of Knowledge* (New York: Knopf, 1998).

22. In *Coherence in Thought and Action* (n. 19 above), pp. 41ff., Thagard claims that his coherentist account "subsumes" foundherentism. I believe this is a confusion; see Haack, "Once More, With Feeling: Response to Paul Thagard," in *Susan Haack: A Lady of Distinctions*, ed. Cornelis de Waal (Amherst, NY: Prometheus Books, 2006), pp. 294–97.

23. See also Haack, *Defending Science—Within Reason: Between Scientism and Cynicism* (Amherst, NY: Prometheus Books, 2003), chapter 3.

24. For a standard (early, and now unfairly neglected) statement of the contextualist position, see David Annis, "A Contextualist Theory of Epistemic Justification," *American Philosophical Quarterly* 15, no. 3 (1978): 213–19.

25. Richard Rorty, "Science as Solidarity," in *The Rhetoric of the Human Sciences*, eds. John S. Nelson, Allan Megill, and Donald M. McCloskey (Madison: University of Wisconsin Press, 1987), pp. 38–52, p. 42. Chapter 9 of my *Evidence and Inquiry* (n. 17) includes a detailed critique of Rorty's critique of epistemology.

26. Rorty, "Science as Solidarity" (n. 25), p. 46.

27. Robert Klee, editor of *Scientific Inquiry: Readings on the Philosophy of Science* (New York: Oxford University Press, 1999), feels that he must "give the reader warning" in his introduction that certain of the selections—safely corralled in sections headed "Polemical Interlude"—are written "in a somewhat witty style" (p. 4). Oh dear.

5

NOT CYNICISM, BUT SYNECHISM

Lessons from Classical Pragmatism

Probably you all know that hoary old joke about the two behaviorists meeting on the street: "Hi! You're fine, how am I?" We laugh; but sometimes another person really *can* notice something about your mental goings-on of which you're not quite aware yourself—as I realized when, in the discussion after I had given a talk on philosophy of science at Yale, Karsten Harries observed: "Oh, I *see*; you're a synechist." Up till then I had been most conscious of the influence of C. S. Peirce's stalwart defense of the "scientific attitude," a genuine desire to learn the truth; of his arguments that the very possibility of inquiry presupposes a kind of realism; of the Critical Common-sensism I had adopted, and adapted, from him; and of course of his penchant for neologisms. But as I mulled over Harries's comment I soon saw that synechism *is*, indeed, one of those pragmatist ideas that has made its way into my philosophical thinking, or perhaps another of those philosophical leanings of mine that makes pragmatism congenial; and that my Critical Common-sensism could itself be plausibly construed as synechist in spirit.

So the task I have set myself here is first to articulate the regulative principle Peirce calls "synechism," its connections with objective idealism, agapism, tychism, and logical realism, and its role in Peirce's understanding of what metaphysics is and does; and then—as my subtitle suggests—to trace (some of) the themes in my metaphysics, philosophy of science, and philosophy of mind that qualify me as a synechist, at least in a broad sense of the word.

However, though my title contrasts the synechism of the classical pragmatist tradition with the cynicism of recent self-styled neo-pragmatism—I couldn't resist the play on words!—I shan't spend long on the Vulgar Pragmatism of Richard Rorty and his admirers. But I will tell you the wonderfully ironic story of Peirce's first public presentation of synechism, when he read the nearly finished version of "The Law of Mind" at the Harvard Graduate Philosophy Club in May of 1892. Among those present were Peirce's brother Jem, Josiah Royce, Francis Ellingwood Abbot, Dickinson S. Miller, and Charles Montague Bakewell. The same day, Abbot wrote in his diary that "[Peirce] read an able paper on 'Syechism,' his new system of philosophy"; the following day, Bakewell reported in a letter to George H. Howison that he had "[h]eard Mr. Chas. Peirce read a paper last evening on Continuity, the Law of Mind, or '*Cynicism*.'" Honestly: I am not making this up.

But of course synechism has nothing whatever to do with cynicism. Introducing a paper of 1893 entitled "Immortality in the Light of Synechism," the editors of *The Essential Peirce* describe synechism as "the doctrine that everything is continuous";[1] and Peirce himself refers to synechism as a "doctrine" both in the introduction and in the conclusion of "The Law of Mind" (which, after he had presented it at Harvard, was published in the *Monist* for 1892, the third of five metaphysical papers of his that appeared between 1891 and 1893). Some years later, however, in his entry on "Synechism" for *Baldwin's Dictionary of Philosophy and Psychology*, Peirce wrote that "[s]ynechism is not an ultimate and absolute metaphysical doctrine; *it is a regulative principle of logic, prescribing what sort of hypothesis is fit to be entertained and examined*"; it is "that tendency of philosophical thought which insists upon the idea of continuity as of prime importance . . . and, in particular, upon the necessity of hypotheses involving true continuity."[2] This seems a significantly better formulation, more plausible in itself, and making better sense of Peirce's observations about the synechist's attitude to dualisms.

"[E]ven in its less stalwart forms," Peirce writes, "[s]ynechism . . . can never abide dualism, properly so called," not even dualism "in its broadest legitimate meaning," the style of philosophy that "performs its analyses with an axe, leaving, as the ultimate elements, unrelated chunks of being." However, he continues, unlike certain "philosophic cranks," the synechist "does not wish to exterminate the conception of twoness."[3] Indeed, Peirce surely doesn't mean to "exterminate" secondness, or to eschew dual distinctions; and anyway, the point about "unrelated chunks of being" surely applies no less to brute trichotomies, etc., than to brute dichotomies. The idea, as I understand it, is rather that we should look for underlying continuities, and recognize that supposedly sharp distinctions may be better conceived as lines of demarcation drawn at some point on a continuum. The comment Peirce makes in his *Logic Notebook* for 1909, on the successful execution of his experiment in triadic logic, is emblematic: "Triadic logic is universally true. Dyadic logic is not absolutely false however, it is only L [at the limit of truth and falsity]."[4]

In the terminology of our day, we might say that the synechist idea is to favor hypotheses that treat supposed differences of kind as really only significant differences of degree. But Peirce's own way of putting it—that the trouble with the axe-wielding style of philosophy is not simply that it makes binary distinctions, but that it leaves us with "unrelated chunks"—has the virtue of making it more apparent why he maintains that synechism "amounts to the principle that inexplicabilities are not to be considered as possible explanations." For continuity, he argues, is a kind of perfect generality: "[t]rue generality is . . . nothing but a rudimentary form of true continuity. Continuity is nothing but perfect generality of a law of relationship"; and generality is "the form under which alone anything can be understood." The regulative principle of synechism advises a preference for abductive hypotheses positing continuities, because "the only possible justification for so much as entertaining a hypothesis is that it affords an explanation of the phenomena"; and hypotheses that break reality into unrelated components "set up a barrier across the road" of science.[5]

In the introductory paragraph of "The Law of Mind" Peirce describes himself as having attempted to develop the synechist idea, "a good many years ago," in his anti-Cartesian papers in the *Journal of Speculative Philosophy* for 1868; presumably alluding to the ideas about the continuity of cognition in "Questions Concerning Certain Faculties Claimed for Man"—which, indeed, are with hindsight clearly no less synechist (though he didn't use this word at that time) than "How to Make Our Ideas Clear" is pragmatist (though he didn't use that word either). I would add that, in virtue of its awareness of the continuities between human learning and other animals' exploration of their environment, and between inquiry and other means of settling opinion, "The Fixation of Belief" (1877) seems no less synechist in spirit.[6]

In the concluding paragraph of "The Law of Mind," Peirce writes that synechism carries along with it "a logical realism of a most pronounced type; . . . objective idealism; [and] tychism, with its . . . thorough-going evolutionism."[7] In

"Immortality in the Light of Synechism," he writes that, though it is not itself religion but a [meta-]hypothesis of scientific metaphysics, synechism "may play a part in the onement of religion and science," by envisaging the possibility of a continuity of carnal and spiritual consciousness.[8] And in just a few pages at the beginning of "The Logic of Continuity"[9] he presents a stunning metaphysical panorama in which the idea of continuity is the organizing principle linking agapism, tychism, and the categories.

This is Peirce the metaphysician at his most philosophically fertile, his most mathematically imaginative, his most scientifically sweeping, and his most cosmologically prescient; but also his most darkly Cimmerian.[10] Nevertheless, it behooves me to try to articulate what Peirce sees as key synechistic hypotheses —objective idealism; agapism; tychism; logical realism—as clearly as I can.

Sometimes Peirce presents his objective idealism by contrast with Cartesian dualism: as we saw earlier, in "Immortality in the Light of Synechism"; and in "The Architecture of Theories," where he writes that "[t]he old dualistic notion of mind and matter . . . as two radically distinct kinds of substance, will hardly find any defenders today." This means, he continues, that we are obliged to accept some form of "hylopathy, otherwise called monism," of which he distinguishes three: neutralism, materialism, and idealism. Neutralism, he argues, since it makes inward and outward aspects of substance both primordial, violates Ockham's razor. Materialism, he continues, is "quite as repugnant to scientific logic as to common sense; since it requires . . . that a certain kind of mechanism will feel . . . [as] an ultimate, inexplicable regularity." "The one intelligible theory of the universe," he concludes, "is . . . objective idealism," which acknowledges "the physical law as derived and special, the psychical alone as primordial," and "matter [as] effete mind, inveterate habits becoming physical laws."[11]

However, objective idealism is not, it seems, really opposed to materialism in every sense of the word: indeed, in "Notes for a Book, to be entitled 'A Guess at the Riddle,'" Peirce had written that "[f]aith requires us to be materialists without flinching." Nor does objective idealism really flatly deny that matter can feel; in fact, Peirce speculates very suggestively about how it can: "feeling, or immediate consciousness, arises in an active state of nerve-cells"; "[t]here is no doubt that this slime-mould, or this amoeba, or at any rate some similar mass of protoplasm, feels . . . when it is in its excited condition." And in "Man's Glassy Essence," Peirce reaffirms that "[p]rotoplasm certainly does feel"; but now he continues, this "can never be explained, unless we admit that physical events are but degraded or undeveloped forms of psychical events." Once it is acknowledged that matter is just mind informed by inveterate habits, the only further explanation needed is why in protoplasm these habits are "to some slight extent broken up. " Peirce acknowledges the dependence of mind on matter, but denies that mental phenomena are controlled by sheer physical law.[12]

But what does it mean to say that matter is just effete mind, or that physical events are only undeveloped forms of psychical events? Peirce writes that "[t]hought is not necessarily connected with a brain. It appears in the work of bees, of crystals, and throughout the purely physical world";[13] it is "in the organic world," he continues, and develops there. This suggests that we should take "thought" and "mind" to refer *both* to the particular minds of particular organisms, *and* to the intelligible patterns, the Platonic Ideas, found in the formation of crystals or the hexagonal cells of a honeycomb. So Mind, with a capital "M," is the capacity of the universe for forming patterns, its *logos* if you like; while minds, with a small "m," are very specialized, plastic, adaptable arrangements of matter.

Agapism, the "doctrine of evolutionary love," hypothesizes an evolution from an initial chaos into order. Peirce summarizes the idea in the first of the papers in the *Monist* series, "The Architecture of Theories":

> . . . in the beginning—infinitely remote—there was a chaos of unpersonalized feeling, which being without connection or regularity would properly be without existence. This feeling, sporting here and there in pure arbitrariness, would have started the germ of a generalizing tendency. Its other sportings would be evanescent, but this would have a growing virtue. Thus, the tendency to habit would be started; and from this, with the other principles of evolution, all the regularities of the universe would be evolved.[14]

Elsewhere Peirce observes that this is not just an evolution of the existing universe, but "a process by which the very Platonic forms themselves . . . are becoming developed" out of initial vague potentialities. And it is not mere "tychastic evolution," evolution by sporting or fortuitous variation, nor mere "anancastic evolution," evolution by mechanical necessity; it is "agapastic evolution," evolution "by creative love," by affinity—of which tychastic and anancastic evolution are merely degenerate forms.[15]

The key mechanism of agapastic evolution is "The Law of Mind" to which the title of Peirce's first explicitly synechist paper refers, and which he states as follows: "ideas tend to spread continuously and to affect certain others which stand to them in a peculiar relation of affectibility."[16] I construe this as a hypothesis both about the evolution of Mind, i.e., the orderliness of the universe, and about the evolution of minds, i.e., how an understanding of the world in possible for us. "Every attempt to understand anything . . . supposes, or at least *hopes*, that the very objects of study themselves are subject to a logic more or less identical with that which we employ," Peirce writes;[17] suggesting a gradual evolution of thought toward harmony with its object, minds with Mind, destined to culminate in the Final Opinion. This, I believe, is the "logical realism of the most pronounced type" that Peirce associates with synechism.

But now let me return to Peirce's summary of agapism, which continues: "At any time, however, an element of pure chance . . . will remain." This is tychism, the doctrine that absolute chance is a factor of the universe, that not everything is determined by law. Today, because of its apparent anticipation of the indeterminism of quantum mechanics, tychism is probably the best known of Peirce's metaphysical ideas. For Peirce himself, however, it was not preeminent. He would not object if his metaphysical system as a whole were to be called "synechism," he says; but to call it "tychism" would be unacceptable: "[f]or although tychism does enter into it, it only enters as subsidiary to that which is really . . . the characteristic of my doctrine, namely, that I chiefly insist upon continuity, or Thirdness." For the element of chance is a remnant of the original disorder, which will remain only "until the world becomes an absolutely perfect, rational and symmetrical system in which mind is at last crystallized in the infinitely distant future,"[18] at which point it will be finally superseded, *aufgehoben*.

But this summary of synechistic themes in Peirce's philosophy remains seriously incomplete; for it omits to mention his thoroughly synechistic conception of metaphysics itself, its objects and its methods.

Peirce acknowledges the affinity of pragmatism with the earlier positivism of Auguste Comte. Moreover, he writes that historically metaphysics has been the arena of "ceaseless and trivial disputation"; it "is in a deplorably backward condition," "a puny, rickety, and scrofulous science."[19] But by now it should be entirely unnecessary for me to say that, far from taking the blithely dismissive attitude of which Rorty boasts—"the pragmatist . . . does not think of himself as *any* kind of metaphysician"[20]—Peirce is a metaphysician of remarkable depth and breadth.

Unlike indiscriminately anti-metaphysical positivist philosophies, Peirce's pragmat[ic]ism is a prope-positivism which envisages the possibility of a reformed, scientific metaphysics:

> [The Pragmatic Maxim] will serve to show that almost every proposition of ontological metaphysics is either meaningless gibberish—one word being defined by other words, and they by still others, without any real conception ever being reached—or else is downright absurd; so that, all such rubbish being swept away, what will remain of philosophy will be a series of problems capable of investigation by the observational methods of the true sciences. . . . So, instead of

merely jeering at metaphysics, . . . the pragmaticist extracts from it a precious essence, which will serve to give life and light to cosmology and physics.[21]

The reformed metaphysics Peirce envisages will be, not "seminary philosophy," but "laboratory philosophy,"[22] scientific both in its motive and in its method. It will be undertaken with the "scientific attitude," out of a genuine desire to discover the truth; and it will use, not the A Priori Method of "what is agreeable to reason," but the scientific method, i.e., the method of experience and reasoning.

Peirce ties these two points together: he insists that the reason for its deplorable condition is *not* that there is any peculiar difficulty in the subject-matter of metaphysics, and not, in particular, that its objects are beyond the reach of experience; rather, he maintains, the reason metaphysics is in such a bad way is that it has fallen into the hands of theologians, who are by profession committed to protect and defend religious doctrine, and so—lacking the true desire to learn—cannot possibly undertake their work with the scientific attitude. Elsewhere, he notes that theologians and moralists tend to insist on sharp dichotomies (the saved versus the damned, good versus evil); and observes "how helpless such minds are in attempting to deal with continuity . . . the leading conception of science."[23]

The "common opinion . . . that Metaphysics is backward because it is intrinsically beyond the reach of human cognition," Peirce writes, "is a complete mistake"; as is the idea that metaphysics "is inscrutable because its objects are not open to observation."[24] Metaphysics does, and must, rest on observable phenomena. If we fail to realize this, it is because the observations on which metaphysics depends are so familiar that we ordinarily pay no attention to them—in fact, they are far more readily available than the observations needed by the special sciences; for they require, not expensive or specialized instruments, but only careful attention to our everyday experience. Philosophy "does not undertake to make any special observations or to obtain any perceptions of a novel description. Microscopes and telescopes, voyages and exhumations . . . are substantially superfluous. . . . It contents itself with a more attentive scrutiny and comparison of the facts of everyday life. . . ."[25]

Like the special sciences, scientific metaphysics will rely on all three modes of reasoning—abductive, deductive, and inductive; and, differing from the special sciences not in kind but in degree of generality, sometimes "welds itself" with them.[26] Nevertheless, scientific metaphysics is neither reducible to the special sciences nor subordinate to them. For since metaphysics investigates the most general aspects of reality, it is the discipline to which it falls to supply key presuppositions of the special sciences; which are, therefore, based on—though not derivable from—the underlying metaphysics. This thought is implicit when Peirce writes that the immature condition of metaphysics has greatly hindered progress both in the physical sciences and in the "Moral or Psychical" sciences of psychology, linguistics, anthropology, and sociology.[27] It is explicit when he writes that the "principal utility" of philosophy is "to furnish a *Weltanschauung*, or conception of the universe, as a basis for the special sciences";[28] and that the "special sciences are obliged to take for granted a number of most important propositions, because their ways of working afford no means of bringing these propositions to the test. In short, they always rest upon metaphysics."[29]

Peirce hopes that "by proceeding modestly, recognizing in metaphysics an observational science, . . . without caring one straw what kind of conclusions we reach . . . but just honestly applying induction and hypothesis . . . the disputes and obscurities of the subject may at last disappear."[30] But as I understand him, he recognizes that even scientific metaphysics may be poorly conducted; i.e., there is no guarantee against *bad* good metaphysics—metaphysics of the right kind, but nevertheless mistaken.

Peirce says, not that objective idealism, agapism, tychism, logical realism, etc., are implied or required by synechism, but that synechism "carries [these ideas] along" with it; meaning that these hypotheses, being *of the type* that synechism *qua* regulative principle recommends, have the merit of being at least potentially explanatory. But their synechistic character does not guarantee their truth; and they are not the only hypotheses of the desirable, synechistic type. I surely am, as Harries realized, a kind of prope-synechist, i.e., a synechist in a broad sense; but I don't endorse all, or only, the synechist hypotheses that Peirce himself proposes.

However, among the recognizably synechist themes in my philosophical thinking, one of the first that comes to mind is an understanding of the nature and the task of metaphysics very close to Peirce's. But because, nowadays, theologians constitute a lesser threat to the health of the philosophical enterprise than literary postmodernists and their ilk, I have been inclined to put what are essentially the same ideas in a somewhat different way. First, if it is to be worth anything, philosophy must be a kind of inquiry, an effort to discover the truth of the questions within its scope. If, as Rorty urges, it were to give up this aspiration and become just "a kind of writing," it's not clear that philosophy *would* be worth much.[31] This is not to deny that some works of philosophy, like some works of history, etc., qualify as "literary" in the aesthetically honorific sense of the word: as Plato's dialogues surely do, and Francis Bacon's *Essays*, and many others; nor is it to deny that some works of imaginative literature convey philosophical truths: as George Eliot's *Daniel Deronda* surely does, and George Orwell's *Nineteen*

Eighty-Four, and many others. It is only to place philosophy on a continuum (the continuum of kinds of inquiry) to which the sciences, history, etc., also belong.

This conception requires, second, that there be a class of questions characteristic of philosophical inquiry, and capable of true or false answers. Rorty—who suggests that the idea of a specifically epistemological class of questions arose only in the context of a distinction between science and philosophy implicit in Descartes and Hobbes, but was not made explicit until Locke and Kant—maintains that there is really no such class. I think there *is* a characteristically philosophical type of question; not, however, that the class of such questions is set in stone. Not all or only the questions on the agenda of the philosophers of ancient Greece were still to be found on Descartes's agenda, nor are all or only Descartes's questions to be found on, say, Quine's or Derrida's. We may be sure that Heraclitus didn't concern himself with the "Gettier problem," and I don't suppose Edmund Gettier has been much concerned with the cosmic-*logos* problem.

The evolution of new questions and the displacement of old ones is simply one of the ways in which any healthy discipline develops. It is a familiar fact that over time the questions tackled by the sciences have shifted and changed; e.g., Friedrich Miescher (the man who first identified the stuff, which he called "nuclein") couldn't even have conceived the question about the structure of DNA that Watson and Crick were later to become famous for answering; for the concept of macromolecule, and the idea that stereochemical structure as well as chemical composition matters, came only later. The fact that, in philosophy as in the sciences, new theories and new concepts raise new questions and displace older ones doesn't mean there are no characteristically philosophical questions.

In the course of its long history, however, metaphysics has only too often been focused on questions that were eventually displaced as they turned out to rest on false presuppositions. (The appropriate response to such questions is obvious, if laborious: trace their roots until you find the falsehood, the wrong answer, among the assumptions on which they depend.) In fact, I see this long history of misconceived questions based on wrong answers to earlier questions as the chief source of the idea that there must be something just inherently wrong with the metaphysical enterprise as such—an idea which, in my opinion as in Peirce's, is "a complete mistake."

Like Peirce, I take the fundamental questions of metaphysics to be about the world, albeit questions characterized by a peculiar kind of abstraction and generality (a point Quine makes vivid when he writes that, while the question of how many and what kinds of beetle there are is characteristic of zoology, the question of how many and what kinds of thing or stuff there are is characteristic of metaphysics). This isn't to deny that answering metaphysical questions often requires strenuous efforts at conceptual clarification: Peirce's articulation of his realism, for example, led him to adopt, and adapt, Duns Scotus's conception of reality; and after the very first sentence of my statement of Innocent Realism—"there is one real world"—I too faced the obligation to clarify what I mean by "real," and to say what there being one world, rather than none or more than one, precludes.[32] Nevertheless, my Innocent Realism, like Peirce's "scholastic realism of a somewhat extreme stripe" is—as metaphysical theories ought to be—about the world, not just about conceptual schemes or linguistic frameworks.

This means, third, that metaphysics cannot be conducted purely *a priori*, but must, as Peirce said, use the method of experience and reasoning. Not, as Peirce also said, that metaphysicians need to conduct experiments or set off on expeditions; for metaphysical abductions and meta-abductions can be expected to be at the highest level of generality, and the evidence by which they stand or fall, again as Peirce said, can be expected to be more commonplace than recherché. If we are wondering whether there are uniformities in nature, no fancy equipment or skillful experiment will help; nevertheless, the common experience that we can successfully predict how animals, or people, or stuff will behave *is* apropos.

This approach enables us to steer clear on the one hand of apriorism, represented in our times by the "descriptive metaphysics" that Peter Strawson defended in the wake of the Logical Positivist (post-Humean, post-Comtean) critique of the legitimacy of the metaphysical enterprise, and even more strikingly by Saul Kripke's appeals to the synthetic *a priori* and David Lewis's quasi-Leibnizian modal realism; and on the other hand of a Quinean scientism that would make metaphysics secondary to, dependent on, current scientific theorizing,[33] Peirce's synechist conception of metaphysics was far ahead not only of his own time, but also of ours.

A second synechist theme of mine, the continuity of inquiry in the sciences with everyday empirical inquiry, is also present in Peirce; but it is somewhat disguised by his use of "science" equivalently to "genuine, good-faith inquiry," "the scientific attitude," equivalently to "the genuine desire to discover the truth," and "the scientific method" equivalently to "the procedures of good-faith inquiry." It is expressed less obliquely by John Dewey, who writes that "scientific subject-matter and procedures grow out of the direct problems and methods of common sense";[34] and by Sidney Hook, who writes that "scientific method is the refinement of the canons of rationality and intelligibility exhibited by the techniques of behavior and habits of inference involved in the arts and crafts of men; its pattern is everywhere discernible even when overlaid with myth and ritual."[35]

In our times, "science," "scientific," etc., are often used as vague, all-purpose terms of epistemic praise. This is quite at odds with Peirce's inclusive usage, which accommodates all good-faith inquiry under the rubric "science"; for, covertly suggesting that only the work of scientists is good inquiry, it is exclusive in spirit. This modern, honorific use of "science" has contributed to the presumption that there must be a criterion of demarcation distinguishing real science, the genuine article, both from lesser intellectual enterprises and from pseudo-scientific mumbo jumbo, and a uniquely rational method of inquiry that explains the successes of the sciences. But in place of this axe-wielding demarcationist approach, I have proposed a Critical Common-sensist account that acknowledges epistemological, methodological, and metaphysical continuities between inquiry in the sciences and everyday empirical inquiry.[36]

That honorific use of "scientific evidence" notwithstanding, the evidence with respect to scientific claims, like the evidence with respect to empirical claims generally, includes both experiential evidence and reasons, working together. But the experiential evidence relevant to scientific claims usually depends on instruments of observation that themselves depend on previous scientific theorizing; the mesh of reasons supporting scientific claims is even more complex and ramifying; and, almost always, scientific evidence is a shared resource. In the notes to their first paper proposing the double-helical structure of DNA, for example, Watson and Crick cite twenty-three other papers; and this is only the tip of an enormous iceberg, for they also depend implicitly on a vast body of what could by that time be simply taken for granted as background knowledge.

At least in the sense in which that phrase is often understood, there is no "scientific method": i.e., no mode of inference or procedure of inquiry unique to the sciences and guaranteed to produce true, or more probable, or more nearly true, or more empirically adequate, etc., results. There are the procedures and modes of inference of all empirical inquiry; but these are not used *only* by scientists. And there are the many and various helps to inquiry that have been devised by generation upon generation of scientists, constantly evolving, and often local to this or that area of science; but these are not used by *all* scientists.

Of course, scientists investigate the same world—the one real world—as historians, investigative journalists, detectives, legal and literary scholars, auto mechanics, and the rest of us do; a scientist trying to solve the structure of the hemoglobin molecule, for example, a detective checking blood traces left at a crime scene, and a housewife trying to figure out how to get bloodstains out of the laundry are all investigating the same stuff. Successful scientific inquiry, like successful empirical inquiry of any kind, is possible only because we, and the world, are a certain way: we have sense organs competent to detect information about particular things and events around us, and the intellectual capacity to make generalized conjectures and devise ways to check these conjectures against further evidence; and the particular things and events of which we can be perceptually aware are of kinds, and subject to laws. Otherwise, we couldn't categorize things or discover useful generalizations about them; nor could the natural sciences—deeper and more detailed than everyday empirical inquiry, far more unified, more accurate, yet still thoroughly fallible and imperfect—gradually have managed to identify real kinds of thing or stuff, discern their inner constitution, and discover laws of nature.

This was, by the way, one theme of the talk of mine that prompted Harries's comment: that, as Peirce argued, the very possibility of scientific investigation requires a kind of realism; but that this is a kind of realism we all take for granted when we engage in the most ordinary of empirical inquiry—out of which, as Dewey and Hook observe, the sciences have grown. In this context, I quoted "Some Consequences of Four Incapacities": "Let us not pretend to doubt in philosophy what we do not doubt in our hearts."[37]

To maintain, as I do, that scientific inquiry is continuous with common-sense inquiry of the most ordinary kind is not to deny that for some purposes it is necessary to draw a rough and ready line between science and other things: e.g., as differing from such other activities as clog-dancing or advocacy in being kinds of inquiry, and from other kinds of empirical inquiry such as historical or legal or literary scholarship in its subject matter.[38] But "non-science" is an ample and diverse category, including the many human activities other than inquiry, the various forms of pseudo-inquiry, inquiry of a non-empirical character, and empirical inquiry of other kinds than the scientific; and to make matters even more complicated, there are plenty of mixed and borderline cases. The honorific use of "scientific" and its cognates tempts even scientists themselves, as well as the rest of us, to criticize poorly conducted science as not really science at all; but "not scientific" is no more helpful as a term of generic epistemic criticism than "scientific" is as a term of generic epistemic praise.

The phrase "pseudo-science," which presumably refers to activities that purport to be science but aren't really, derives its pejorative tone in part from its imputation of false pretenses, but also in part from the honorific use of "science." But describing poor work as "pseudo-scientific" is little more than a sneer; it is much better to specify what, exactly, is wrong with it—that it is not serious or honest inquiry; that it rests on assumptions for which there is no good evidence, or which are too vague to be susceptible to evidential check; or that it uses mathematical symbolism, or elaborate-looking apparatus, purely decoratively.

A third synechist theme of mine, and the last I have room to sketch here, focuses proximally on the relation of the social to the natural sciences, and at one remove on the understanding of beliefs, desires, etc.

The phrase "the social sciences," as I understand it, picks out a loose federation of kinds of inquiry, roughly identified by reference to the kinds of question that fall within their scope—as "the natural sciences" picks out a different loose federation of kinds of inquiry, roughly identified by the different kinds of question that fall within their scope. Social-scientific inquiry, like inquiry of every kind, is an effort to discover true answers to the questions within its sphere; although, because the questions they address often concern politically sensitive topics, in the social sciences inquiry has only too often been elided into advocacy (as it sometimes has in the natural sciences, especially in sensitive areas such as environmental science and human biology).

Some areas of social science, such as physical anthropology, are nearly indistinguishable from neighboring areas of natural science; but most social science differs from most natural science in being, so to speak, "intentional"; i.e., including people's beliefs, goals, intentions, etc., in its purview. Psychologists investigate the role of expectation in perceptual error; economists calculate the interactions of consumer confidence and interest rates; sociologists investigate whether political liberals or political conservatives give more generously to charity; anthropologists try to understand why it is taboo to utter these words in the presence of your mother-in-law; and so forth and so on. This extends the picture of the continuum of kinds of inquiry already sketched in my account of the relation of metaphysics to the sciences and of the sciences to everyday empirical inquiry; and in the process accommodates the fact that everyday empirical explanations commonly appeal to people's beliefs and intentions as well as to physical causes.[39]

This larger picture is thoroughly synechistic. It is not, however, reductionist, at least as that term is ordinarily understood. Granted, there are remarkable similarities between human social interactions and those of other social animals; but though human social behavior surely is biologically determined in some respects, it surely is not biologically determined in all. Some of what we do is purely instinctive, some habitual, some due to panic, anger, or confusion; but though it is constrained by biological universals and mediated by cultural specifics, how each person is and behaves depends in part on his beliefs, goals, and intentions. Though a person's beliefs, etc., are certainly physiologically realized, they are not simply reducible to neurophysiological states.

The account I suggested in chapter 6 of *Defending Science* was this: A person who believes that snakes are dangerous will have a very complex multiform disposition—roughly: to shriek at the sight of, and run away from, snakes; to shudder at pictures of snakes; and to assert or assent to sentences in whatever language(s) he speaks to the effect that snakes are dangerous. With such ordinary, garden-variety beliefs, verbal and nonverbal dispositions interlock both causally and referentially: the subject's representing the world to himself this way causally sustains his disposition to act thus and so, and the sentences to which he is disposed to assent are about things in the world with respect to which he is disposed to act thus and so—in the characteristic semiotic triad of person, words, world. These multiform dispositions are realized in enormously complex neurophysiological configurations, meshes of interconnections among receptors (whatever registers input) and activators (whatever initiates behavior, verbal or nonverbal). They must, however, be realizable in more than one way; for while my believing that snakes are dangerous involves among other things a disposition to assert, and assent to, certain sentences of English, Ivan's believing that snakes are dangerous involves among other things a disposition to assert and assent to, certain sentences of Russian.

As the explanation of someone's blushing because of the embarrassing remark he overheard must acknowledge both the connections of his neurophysiological states with these words and with the use of these words in his linguistic community, both the physical realization of a belief and its content are essential. An alarm clock is a physical thing, and its making this noise is brought about by physical goings-on inside the clock; but this doesn't exhaust the explanation of my alarm clock's going off at 7:30 a.m., which also requires reference to human conventions about time. Human beings are also physical things, and their making these noises or marks or movements is brought about by neurophysiological goings-on; but the explanation of my going to the fridge to get a glass of milk isn't exhausted by a neurophysiological account of the firings in my brain, but also requires reference to the content of my belief. And this requires a socio-cultural loop identifying the relevant linguistic, etc., conventions.

After spelling all this out in detail, I summed up the key idea like this: "It's all physical, all right; but it isn't all physics."[40] At the time, G. H. Mead had been a significant influence; but I had never looked more than casually at what Peirce had to say about what is right, and what is wrong, in materialism. Now, however, I am struck by how close I had come, quite unknowingly, to what he had written more than a century before: "No doubt, all nervous physiology shows the dependence of mind upon body. . . . The question is whether mental phenomena are exclusively controlled by blind mechanical law . . ."; but there are "obvious objections" to the idea that they are.[41]

Well. This isn't the first time I have smiled wryly as I recalled that famous observation of George Santayana's, that those who do not study the history of philosophy are destined to repeat it; and I don't suppose it will be the last.

NOTES

1. *The Essential Peirce* (Bloomington: Indiana University Press, 1998), 2:1. Henceforth, *EP*. [References are by volume and page number.]

2. Charles Sanders Peirce, *Collected Papers*, eds. Charles Hartshorne, Paul Weiss, and (vols. 7 and 8) Arthur Burks (Cambridge: Harvard University Press, 1938–51), 6.173 and 6.169 (both 1902; italics mine). Henceforth, *CP*. [References are by volume and paragraph number.]

3. *EP* 2:2 (1893).

4. This page is reproduced in facsimile in Max Fisch and Atwell Turquette, "Peirce's Triadic Logic" (1966), in *Peirce, Semeiotic, and Pragmatism: Essays by Max H. Fisch*, eds. Kenneth Laine Ketner and Christian W. Kloesel (Bloomington, IN: Indiana University Press, 1986), pp. 171–83, p. 175; and transcribed by Robert E. Lane in Susan Haack, ed., *Pragmatism, Old and New: Selected Writings* (Amherst, NY: Prometheus Books, 2006), p. 219.

5. *CP* 6.173, 6.172, and 6.171 (all 1902).

6. "How to Make Our Ideas Clear," *CP* 5.388–410 (1878); "The Fixation of Belief," *CP* 5.358–87 (1877).

7. *CP* 6.163 (1892).

8. *EP* 2:3 (1893).

9. *CP* 6.185–213 (1898).

10. Cimmerii: mythical people described by Homer as dwelling in a remote realm of mist and gloom.

11. *CP* 6.24, 6.25 (both 1891).

12. The quotations come, in order of appearance, from *CP* 1.354 (ca. 1890); 1.386 (ca. 1890); 6.133, (1892); and 6.264 (1892).

13. *CP* 4.551 (1906).

14. *CP* 6.33 (1891).

15. *CP* 6.194 (1898); 6.302 (1893).

16. *CP* 6.202 (1898).

17. *CP* 6.189 (1898).

18. *CP* 6.202 (1898); 6.33 (1891).

19. *CP* 6.5, 6.2 (1898), and 6.6 (ca. 1903).

20. Richard Rorty, *Consequences of Pragmatism* (Hassocks, Sussex: Harvester Press, 1982), p. xxviii.

21. *CP* 5.423 (1905).

22. *CP* 1.129 (ca. 1905).

23. *CP* 1.62 (ca. 1896).

24. *CP* 6.2 (1898).

25. *EP* 2:146 (1903).

26. *EP* 2:375 (1908).

27. *CP*, 6.2 (1898).

28. *EP* 2:146–7 (1903).

29. *CP* 1.129 (ca. 1905).

30. *CP* 6.5 (1898).

31. Richard Rorty, *Consequences of Pragmatism* (n. 19); Susan Haack, "As for That Phrase, 'Studying in a Literary Spirit . . . ,'" (1996), reprinted in Haack, *Manifesto of a Passionate Moderate: Unfashionable Essays* (Chicago: University of Chicago Press, 1998), pp. 48–68.

32. See Haack, "Reflections on Relativism: From Momentous Tautology to Seductive Contradiction" (1996), reprinted in Haack, *Manifesto of a Passionate Moderate* (n. 30), 149–66; and "Realisms and Their Rivals: Recovering Our Innocence," *Facta Philosophica* 4, no. 1 (2002): 67–88.

33. See Haack, "Between the Scylla of Scientism and the Charybdis of Apriorism," in *The Philosophy of P. F. Strawson*, ed. Lewis Hahn (La Salle, IL: Open Court, 1998), pp. 50–73.

34. John Dewey, *Logic: The Theory of Inquiry* (New York: Henry Holt and Company, 1938), p. 88.

35. Sidney Hook, "Naturalism and First Principles" (1956), in Hook, *The Quest for Being* (New York: St. Martin's Press, 1961), 172–95, p. 173; also in Haack, ed. *Pragmatism, Old and New* (Amherst, NY: Prometheus Books, 2006), pp. 529–58, p. 531.

36. Susan Haack, *Defending Science—Within Reason: Between Scientism and Cynicism* (Amherst, NY: Prometheus Books, 2003), chapters 1 through 5.

37. *CP* 5.263 (1868).

38. See also "The Same, Only Different," pp. 37–42 in this volume.

39. Haack, *Defending Science* (n. 35), chapter 6.

40. Ibid., p. 160.

41. *CP* 6.274 (ca. 1893).

6

SCIENCE, ECONOMICS, "VISION"

Why . . . should we not applaud the increasing tendency to envision economics as a science?

          —Robert Heilbroner, *The Worldly Philosophers* (1999)[1]

A s Heilbroner was teaching his seminar on Economic Methodology with Prof. William Milberg at the New School, I was thinking about philosophy of science; so one frequent topic of discussion in our correspondence was whether the social sciences are properly so-called, or whether it is even desirable for these disciplines to aspire to be scientific. In fact, when *Defending Science— Within Reason* was finished, I opened my chapter on the social sciences with a quotation from Adolf Lowe, Heilbroner's own teacher and mentor, to whose work he had introduced me: "[o]nly if a region of inquiry can be opened up in which both the scientific and the humanist approach play their characteristic roles may we ever hope to gain knowledge of man—knowledge rather than figment, and of man rather than of social atoms."[2] In this chapter, guided by the Critical Common-sensist philosophy of science developed elsewhere in the book, I offered my interpretation of Lowe's appealing idea of "social science with a human face" by tracing some main similarities, and some main differences, between the natural and the social sciences.

I didn't, however, specifically tackle the critique of the scientific aspirations

---

of contemporary economics that Heilbroner had developed in "The End of the Worldly Philosophy?", the new final chapter added to *The Worldly Philosophers* in its seventh edition. Given this happy opportunity to remedy the omission, I want to try to sort out what is true in Heilbroner's critique of economics-as-a-science from what is not. It will be helpful to begin, however, with some thoughts about the social sciences generally.

That honorific use of "science" and its cognates as all-purpose terms of epistemic approval has no doubt contributed to psychologists', sociologists', anthropologists', and economists' anxieties about whether what they are doing is really science, and to their preoccupation with methodology. But it is better to ask, not "Are the social sciences *really* sciences?" but "In what ways are the social sciences like the natural sciences, and in what ways unlike?"[3]

A reasonable first response would be that, like "natural science," "social science" refers to a loose federation of kinds of inquiry; in this case, a federation of disciplines that seek to explain social phenomena and events, as the natural sciences seek to explain natural phenomena and events. However, not every field classified by deans or librarians under "social sciences" quite fits this description. At one extreme, such disciplines as physical anthropology or neurophysiological psychology are *less* different from the natural sciences in subject matter and techniques than it suggests—closer to biology than to sociology. At the other extreme, the disciplines sometimes called "social thought" or "political theory," as distinct from social or political science, are *more* different from the natural sciences than it suggests, for the questions of norms and values they investigate are not, at least in the ordinary way, empirical.

In those areas not at either extreme, among the objects and phenomena investigated—e.g., the initiation rituals of New Guinea, gang culture in the inner cities, the trade in blood diamonds—are social phenomena, institutions, roles, and rules. These are real: they are independent of how you, or I, or any individual believes them to be. But they are also socially constructed: they exist, and are as they are, only because of the behavior, beliefs, and intentions of people in the society concerned. While some social institutions are universal, many are culturally specific: everywhere there are differences of status, but only in some cultures are there Sirs and Lords; everywhere people obtain and distribute food, but only in some cultures are there prices and markets, and in even fewer are there hedge funds or pork-belly futures. So the objects of social-scientific investigation are often local to a particular society, and to a time.

Like biologists, legal scholars, investigative journalists, or anyone who inquires into any aspect of the world, social scientists rely on experience, on observation. But while observing people and describing what they do, like observing a cloud chamber or X-ray photograph and describing what you see, requires background knowledge, in this case the background knowledge required is of the peculiar kind needed to conjecture what people's beliefs and motives are, to interpret what they say, and to place their actions in the context of sometimes very culturally specific practices: as with an anthropologist's description of a ceremony as rain dancing, an economist's description of a manager as negotiating next year's contract with the union representatives, or a sociologist's description of academic pecking orders.

Like physicists, historians, detectives, auto mechanics, and the rest of us, social scientists try to explain puzzling phenomena. But the kinds of explanation they seek differ significantly from those sought by natural scientists; they are intentional explanations, couched in terms of human agents and their motivation. An anthropologist might explain that the witch doctor's ritual with bones and feathers is intended to lift the curse from the cattle; a sociologist that this style of suburban house-building caters to the status-striving of middle managers; or an economist that the rising consumption of chicken is due to consumers' fear of mad cow disease.

Though beliefs and goals are presumably neurophysiologically realized, belief-desire explanations are not—at least, not unless the whole history of the world is reducible to physics—reducible to neurophysiological ones; for they require appeal to the content of people's beliefs and desires, their relation to the world, and this can only be understood by reference to language and culture. But such agent explanations are no more mysterious, and no less explanations, than our everyday accounts of missed appointments ("I wrote it on the calendar for *next* Wednesday") or murders ("she was the only person between him and the family fortune"). And these intentional explanations, like all explanations, require a kind of generality; in this case, reference to human commonalities conjectured to lie behind cultural differences.

Social kinds (e.g., money, marriage) are less tightly knit and more historically conditioned than natural ones (e.g., mineral, marsupial); even those social institutions, roles, and rules that are universal or near-universal may be manifested quite differently in different times and places. Nevertheless, there are real but restricted generalities, rooted in human nature but molded by local social institutions, that allow for the possibility of explanation and even prediction—given appropriate limitations of scope and generous ceteris paribus clauses, and ordinarily restricted only to a probability. A newspaper reports a doctor's explanation of the higher rate of HIV infection among migrant workers in South Africa than among other workers: "If you wanted to spread a sexually transmitted disease, you'd take thousands of young men away from their families, isolate them in single-sex hostels, and give them easy access to alcohol and commercial sex. Then to spread the disease around the country, you'd send them home every once in a while to their wives and girlfriends. . . . That is basically the system we have."[4] The patterns of behavior, like the patterns of infection, are local, obtaining here and not there; but to explain them we need to fit them into generalizable categories, to identify kinds of behavior and mechanisms of motivation as well as a kind of virus and mechanisms by which it is passed on.

The underlying modes and procedures of the social sciences, like those of the natural sciences, are continuous with the methods of everyday empirical inquiry; but social scientists need rather different aids to observation and reasoning from those that have proven helpful in various areas of natural-scientific inquiry. Many natural-scientific helps (e.g., microscopes, chromatography, X-ray diffraction photography, etc.) are just not apropos. The controlled experiments that have enabled the medical and other sciences are feasible only in a few areas of social science; and the questionnaire is a more useful instrument of observation than the telescope.

Unfortunately, however, as Robert Merton observes, social scientists often "take the achievements of physics as the standard for self-appraisal. They want to compare biceps with their bigger brothers."[5] And "physics-envy" has sometimes encouraged cargo-cult social science, the form without the substance of real inquiry: much fuss and bother about "methodology," but no real effort to discover the truth; symbolic formulae, but no real precision. The point isn't that quantification or measurement is out of place in social-scientific investigation— on the contrary, it can be enormously useful; but it is worse than useless when it disguises banality, when what is quantified or measured is ill-defined or ambiguous, or when quantification diverts attention from what is important to what can be measured.

Inappropriate borrowing of special techniques from the natural sciences in hopes of looking respectably "scientific" is, of course, only one of the pitfalls of social science. Another is thoughtlessly assuming that what is really a local, parochial social institution—e.g., the division of labor between the sexes in our society now—is universal or inevitable. A third pitfall (to which all investigation is susceptible, but social-scientific investigation probably especially so) is allowing what ought to be inquiry, an effort to discover the truth of some question, to turn into advocacy, an effort to make a case for some proposition determined in advance. Of course, it's perfectly fine for sociologists, economists, etc., as it is for environmental scientists, epidemiologists, and so on, to have views, and to make recommendations, about matters of policy; but it's disastrous if they confuse this with the quite different enterprise of investigating the causes of inflation, of rising mercury levels in fish, or whatever.

In "The End of the Worldly Philosophy?" Heilbroner reaffirms, as he had said in the original text of *The Worldly Philosophers*, that there is no economy, and hence no economics, except in the capitalist context of markets, prices, and so on. Now, however, he adds a regretful critique of recent, "scientific" economics, which he sees as a sadly "desiccated residue" (p. 321): a mathematically sophisticated but deeply unsatisfying enterprise that risks a false assimilation of the behavior of people to the "behavior" of atoms, and of the "laws" of the market to the laws of nature, and pretends to a false objectivity (pp. 316–18); an enterprise, moreover, lacking the capacity or even the aspiration to envision a more socially responsible capitalism. I believe there is both something right and something wrong in Heilbroner's arguments; the challenge is to discriminate the two.

In his second chapter, "The Economic Revolution," Heilbroner had written that, before the eighteenth century, when the "great self-reproducing, self-sufficient world [of capital, markets, prices, etc.] erupted into the bustling, scurrying, free-for-all of the eighteenth century," there could be no economics. There was no need for explanations in terms of supply and demand, cost and value, when reference to the laws of the land, the manor, the Church, the city, and to custom and tradition, sufficed. "[T]here would have been nothing for [Adam Smith] to do." (p. 29). But according not only to my linguistic intuition but also to Merriam-Webster's dictionary, the word "economy" refers to the production and distribution of goods and services, however organized, and "economics" to the discipline that studies these phenomena. To be sure, we could make Heilbroner's thesis true by stipulation, tying the words "economy" and "economics" analytically to markets, prices, and such; but only at the price of turning it into an uninteresting tautology.

Nor would such a stipulation sit easily with Heilbroner's own discussion, in the same chapter, of the rise of pauperism in the aftermath of the English common-land enclosures. Heilbroner quotes the explanation given by one John Hales: ". . . [W]here XL people had their lyvings, now one man and his shepherd hath all. . . . Yes, those shepe is the cause of all these meschieves, for they have driven husbandrie out of the countries, by the which was encreased before all kynde of victuall, and now altogether shepe, shepe." Heilbroner observes that this process of enclosure caused almost unimaginable poverty and misery. For, denied use of formerly common land, peasants could neither sustain themselves as farmers nor hire themselves out as agricultural laborers; and the system of tying paupers to their local parish for poor relief made the only solution—the evolution of a mobile labor force—impossible (pp. 31–32). By my lights (and Webster's), this is an economic explanation. And so, too, are recent accounts of the agricultural disaster in Zimbabwe—formerly the "breadbasket of Africa," now reportedly in desperate decline—as the result of government appropriation of farms; as was the story that remains with me from a long-ago undergraduate course on (yes!) The Soviet Economy: under the first Five Year Plan when production targets were set by weight, a chandelier manufacturer figured out how to beat the system—and several fashionable ceilings in Moscow collapsed.

To be sure, in the absence of markets and so forth, explanations of how goods and services are produced and distributed will appeal in part to the pharaoh's, the king's, or the Party's fiats, and to custom and tradition. In short, economic, political, psychological, and other explanations will be intimately interconnected. Even given markets, prices, etc., understanding the differences between, say, mid-nineteenth-century US capitalism and the late twentieth-century kind, or between capitalism in the United States and in Sweden or India, will require reference to differences in business and labor law, stock exchange regulation, the political power of unions, welfare provisions, and, once again, custom and tradition. But this no more shows that there is no such thing as economics than the fact that biological explanations aren't completely autonomous of physics shows that there is no such thing as biology.

If Heilbroner's insistence on the connection of economics with capitalism seems unduly narrow, his critique of contemporary economics as social science seems somewhat overstated. I don't suppose that even the most scientistic of contemporary economists really supposes that people's beliefs and desires, have no bearing on what they do, or that laws of supply and demand are *just* like the law of gravity. What *is* true, however, is that economists are susceptible to all the usual pitfalls of social-scientific inquiry: and it may well be that the contemporary ethos of economics-as-social-science encourages practitioners to devise elegant mathematical models without asking whether what is measured is what is really important. To overlook the gap between the certainty of mathematical theorems and their much less certain empirical applications; and to forget how local and contingent, particular economic arrangements are—a temptation made even stronger, probably, by the use of "market" as a conveniently expansive concertina concept, applied to people's choice of spouse, for example, as well as to the literal sale of goods or services or stocks, etc. Moreover, rather as the Parsonian functionalist sociology of the family can seem to suggest that "science shows" that a very particular domestic arrangement is a good one, the illusion may be encouraged that "science shows" that this local economic arrangement is not only inevitable, but desirable.

"What does it mean to be 'objective' about such things as inherited wealth or immiserating poverty?" Heilbroner asks (p. 318). He is not encouraging the fudging of inquiry into advocacy; rather, he is stressing that, even if economists were scrupulously aware of their own biases and could somehow discount them, it would still be a mistake for them to think of their recommendations of economic policy as "scientific," or as "stemming unchallengeably from the givens of society." And here, I think, he is exactly right: our knowledge of market forces may yield a means-ends prescription ("if you want to achieve X, raise federal fund interest rates"); but it can't tell us whether or why X is desirable.

This is where the "visionary" economics for which Heilbroner hankers could—should—play an important role. We know, or ought to, that our present, local economic arrangements are not the only ones possible. We know, or ought to, that they are not necessarily optimal from the point of view of human flourishing. It's not that there's anything wrong with economics-as-social-science; the problem is that as it takes center stage it can "crowd out" an important preoccupation of some of the greatest economic thinkers of the past: assessing the benefits and drawbacks of different ways of ordering the production and distribution of goods and services (rather as, taking center stage, contemporary neo-analytic philosophy is in danger of crowding out an important preoccupation of the greatest philosophical thinkers of its past: connecting philosophical analysis with abiding human concerns).

This "visionary" economics would be economics conceived, as I have urged economics should be conceived, broadly; for it would be both comparative and evaluative: comparing the many and various socialized, market, and other economies, and weighing economic efficiencies against other social values (not quite apples vs. oranges, but perhaps grapes vs. potatoes, and certainly guns vs. butter!). Moreover, because it would need to call on political and legal theory and on ethics as well as on the findings of economics-as-social-science this would, as Heilbroner acknowledges, be a task for economics undertaken in the most expansively interdisciplinary spirit. This is hardly something we should expect of every journeyman economist; it's a tough job. But we should be grateful to Heilbroner for reminding us that someone had better do it.

NOTES

1. Robert L. Heilbroner, *The Worldly Philosophers* (1953: seventh edition, New York: Simon and Schuster, 1999), p. 137. All page references in the text are to the 1999 edition.

2. Adolf Lowe, "Comment" (originally published with papers by Hans Joas, Solomon E. Asch, and Erich Hula in *Social Research*, 26 [1959]: 117–66), in Maurice Natanson, ed., *Philosophy of the Social Sciences: A Reader* (New York: Random House, 1959), pp. 152–57. The quotation is from p. 154 in Natanson.

3. In the following section I draw, where appropriate, on my *Defending Science—Within Reason* (Amherst, NY: Prometheus Books, 2003), chapter 6.

4. Mark Schoofs, "Undermined: African Gold Giant Finds History Impedes a Fight Against AIDS," *The Wall Street Journal*, 26 June, 2001, pp. A1 and A10; the quotation is from p. A10.

5. Robert Merton, *Social Theory and Social Structure* (1957; enlarged edition, New York: Free Press, 1968), p. 47.

7

THE INTEGRITY OF SCIENCE

What It Means, Why It Matters

I am not fond of expecting catastrophes, but there are cracks in the universe.

—Sydney Smith[1]

1. "INTEGRITY": ITS MANY MEANINGS

The *Oxford English Dictionary* tells us that the word "integrity" derives from (the negation of) the Latin "*tangere*," suggesting the untouched, what is whole, unadulterated, sound, or pure; and lists among its current meanings the condition of being in an "undivided or unbroken state," of "material wholeness, completeness, entirety"; of "not being marred or violated" but "unimpaired or uncorrupted"; and "soundness of moral principle, esp. in relation to truth and fair dealing," i.e., "uprightness, honesty, sincerity." The *Merriam-Webster Dictionary* tells us that among the current meanings of the word are "completeness," "unity," "incorruptibility," and "firm adherence to values," especially artistic or moral values; and suggests "honesty" as a synonym for the last of these. (According to the *Novo Dicionário da Lingua Portuguesa*, in Portuguese the word "*integridade*" still bears the meaning "chastity, virginity," as the corresponding word also once did in Spanish and, long ago, in English; but this sense, though etymologically as well as sociologically interesting, need not concern us here.)[2]

We may speak of the integrity of a person, such as an artist or politician; of a body of work, such as a writer's or painter's *oeuvre*; or of an institution, such as a voting system, a company, an academic discipline. So thinking about "the integrity of science" leads to a whole snarl of issues: about science *qua* body of work, about individual scientists, and about science *qua* institution; about wholeness, unity, and adherence to values; and about values of different kinds—the ethical, the aesthetic, and the epistemological—and the relations among them.

Questions about wholeness or unity, for example, seem to be best understood as questions about science *qua* body of work (or as we like to say, and as the etymology of "science" suggests, *qua* "body of knowledge"). But the integrity of science in this sense should not be understood as requiring that it be complete, that every possible scientific question have been answered; or that it include no falsehoods, no supposed "knowledge" that will eventually turn out to be mistaken; or even that it be unified, or at least unifi*able*, in the philosophically ambitious sense of the old "Unity of Science" program, reducible in its entirety to the laws of physics. What matters is that, though scientific inquiry is fallible, it is also capable of correcting earlier mistakes and refining earlier ideas as new information comes in, new concepts are devised, and new, synthesizing conjectures are articulated; and that science *qua* body of knowledge is in an important sense integrated, or at least integrat*able*—undivided, as the *Oxford English Dictionary* says.

By no means every component as yet interlocks neatly with the rest; but as we learn more, once-disjoint elements of the scientific body of knowledge come together—as, for example, revised calculations of the age of the earth, modern theories about the mechanisms of genetics (which are very different from the "blending" theory Darwin himself accepted), and recent observations of the emergence of new, drug-resistant strains of bacteria and viruses now harmonize with the (also much-revised) theory of evolution. To be sure, the integration of the social with the natural sciences, even in this quite modest sense, remains a long way off; but it seems reasonable to hope that eventually we will understand how the socio-historical road map of language, beliefs, goals, and actions can be superimposed on the physical contour map of the brain and the nervous system.[3]

Interesting and important as they are, however, in what follows I shall set these issues aside, focusing instead on integrity in the sense of "firm adherence to values," and in particular on how this concept applies to science *qua* institution. I shall begin by identifying and articulating the most relevant values—the epistemological values of evidence-sharing and respect for evidence—and sketching how they are rooted in the character of the scientific enterprise. This will pave the way for an exploration of the circumstances that presently threaten to erode commitment to these core values. Then, looking in some detail at the disturbing saga of the arthritis drugs Vioxx and Celebrex, I will illustrate the threats to the integrity of science that result from the present dependence of much medical research, and especially of the medical journals, on the sponsorship of the pharmaceutical industry. And finally, returning to the broader concerns signaled by my subtitle, I shall try to articulate why the erosion of scientific integrity should concern us.

2. THE INTEGRITY OF SCIENCE: CORE VALUES

If we ask about the integrity of an artist, his adherence to values, our primary concern will probably be the aesthetic or artistic; if we ask about the integrity of a politician, our primary concern will probably be matters of ethical or financial probity. When we ask about the integrity of a scientist, however, the primary concern is likely to be his adherence to *epistemological* values; for inquiry, investigation, is the defining business of a scientist. So when we ask about the integrity of science *qua* institution, the primary concern is likely to be how successfully the institution ensures that everyone involved behaves as nearly as possible in accordance with those epistemological values.

In saying this, I don't mean to deny that there are aesthetic dimensions to scientific work, or even that these may have epistemological significance.[4] Neither do I mean to deny that questions about adherence to ethical values are appropriate to scientists, as to the rest of us—of course, they are; or that adherence to epistemological values is never, also, a matter of ethical concern—of course, it is.[5] But morally acceptable behavior is neither necessary nor sufficient for good scientific work: it is not necessary, because you may do innovative, important, or solid science even though you are unkind to your laboratory animals, arrogant or inattentive in dealing with your students, or ungenerous in giving your collaborators credit; and it is not sufficient either, because you may do poor scientific work even though your behavior is in every respect morally impeccable. To put it another way: sexually harassing a research assistant, putting in a pro forma appearance at a conference as a way of getting your vacation subsidized, bullying your secretary, taking an unauthorized look at a colleague's work-in-progress, failing to get the informed consent of subjects, knowingly helping to make the gas that will efficiently exterminate a despised race, etc., are all objectionable, in varying degrees, on moral grounds; but they don't eat at the scientific core of scientific work, as failures of commitment to the epistemological values inherent in the enterprise do.

The core epistemological values of science are rooted in the central, defining concern of inquiry generally: finding things out. A scientific inquirer starts with a question about what might explain this or that natural or social phenomenon; makes an informed guess; and assesses how well his conjecture stands up to whatever evidence is already available, or can be obtained: i.e., how firmly it is anchored in experimental results and experiential evidence generally; how well it interlocks with the whole explanatory mesh of the body of thus-far well-warranted claims and theories; whether relevant evidence might have been overlooked; and what else could be done to get hold of evidence not presently available. So a scientist needs to take into account not only whatever evidence he can discover for himself, but also whatever evidence others have that may be relevant to the question(s) at issue; and to keep track not only of how well each new conjecture would explain the phenomenon in question, but also of how well it fits in with already well-established claims and theories in the field.

Though nowadays this is quite rare, in the past many scientists have worked more or less alone. But even the greatest scientists of the past have stood on the shoulders of those who went before; and by now a broad and detailed background knowledge of what has already been achieved is essential even to understand what the important open questions in an area are. In short, science as we know it is a deeply and unavoidably social enterprise, the work of many people within and across generations, each with his or her strengths, each with his or her weaknesses, sometimes cooperating, sometimes competing. And it has succeeded as well as it has in part because, thus far, enough of those people have been faithful enough to the key values—the closely interrelated values, as we shall see—of *honesty* and *sharing*, understood specifically as applying to one's relation to evidence. Robert Merton writes of "disinterestedness" and "communism," but these, "communism" especially, carry unwanted connotations; and words like "cooperation" or "trust" would distract attention from the potentially productive aspects of competition and of skeptical mutual scrutiny. So despite the fact that "honesty" and "sharing" have been so debased by their currency in pop psychotherapeutic jargon that one is almost embarrassed to use them, I shall do so without apology.[6]

In this context honesty (or as we might also say, respect for evidence) must be understood as both self- and other-related. Being honest with yourself means avoiding self-deception, both about where the evidence you have leads, and about whether you have the evidence you need to draw any conclusion at all. It doesn't require that you abandon a promising idea in the face of any and every piece of apparently contrary evidence; but it does require that, recognizing how complex and confusing evidence can be, you are ready to follow in good faith wherever it takes you. Being honest with others requires, obviously, that you not present fabricated, fraudulent, or massaged data, but also that when you report your work you include all the relevant evidence. Evidence-sharing doesn't require that you post every passing thought, every casual observation, on the Internet for all the world to read; but it does require that you not withhold significant information from others in the field to advance your, or your sponsor's, interests.[7]

Not every scientist is a paragon of intellectual honesty; not every scientist is cheerfully willing to share his work with others. When things go well, however, the norms of evidence-sharing and respect for evidence will be instilled in young scientists during their long apprenticeship, and reinforced by the acclaim that is the reward of success and the loss of reputation that is the penalty for cheating; and an ethos in which these norms are taken for granted will be transmitted from one generation of scientists to the next. As a result, new information and new ideas will be shared, and each scientist will be able to scrutinize the work of others in his field; making it more likely that flaws will be uncovered, and more likely that potentially promising developments will be spotted and worked out.

Over time the sciences have gradually developed instruments of observation that greatly amplify unaided human senses, and mathematical and statistical methods, computer programs, etc., that greatly refine unaided human powers of reasoning. And over time they have also gradually evolved complicated internal organizational structures and procedures, etc., to protect integrity, i.e., to ensure that results are honestly reported and candidly shared, and to harness grubbier motives, such as the desire for prestige or the hope of besting a rival, to epistemologically desirable ends; including mechanisms—some formalized, some traditional and informal—for assigning resources and positions, disseminating information, training young scientists, and providing incentives to good work as well as penalties for cheating.

But of course all these scientific helps to inquiry, both the technical helps that amplify observation and reasoning and the social helps that enable evidence-sharing and sustain respect for evidence are, like everything human, fallible. Instruments may introduce distortions or artifactual effects; statistical techniques may import false assumptions; computer models may mislead. Most to the present purpose, no internal social organization can by itself guarantee that the scientific ethos will be sustained. When things go badly, the norms of evidence-sharing and respect for evidence can only too easily be undermined or eroded: arrangements that once served as incentives to succeed may come, in changing circumstances, to encourage carelessness or even misconduct; arrangements that once assigned resources in an epistemologically efficient way may, in changing circumstances, be corrupted to serve the interests of a clique or to forward a party line, or may become mired in a self-serving resistance to any exploration of less-familiar ideas; and arrangements for evidence-sharing may become so clogged or fall into such disrepair or corruption that they actually impede communication.

Science interacts in complicated ways with the rest of society—with industry, government, education, law, and so on. Its integrity requires that it be allowed to operate on its own terms; but this doesn't mean that it is either necessary or sufficient that science be wholly autonomous, in the sense of "entirely independent of every other aspect of the society in which it is conducted." It is not necessary, because the mixing of cultures is sometimes harmless, sometimes benign; and it is not sufficient, because threats to evidence-sharing and respect for evidence may come from within as well as from without. Nor is it either necessary or sufficient that science be wholly pure, in the sense of "free of any considerations of utility." It is not necessary, because the hope of finding a cure for the disease that is killing your child, for example, may be a powerful incentive to hard, honest scientific work; and it is not sufficient, because some of the threats to integrity apply no less to pure than to utility-driven science.

However, potentially highly profitable scientific work is in some ways especially vulnerable; and some of the most important threats to the integrity of science do come from the intrusion of the competing values of the larger society in which scientific work takes place. Some social and cultural environments are hospitable to good, honest scientific work; others are in varying degrees inhospitable, or even hostile. And while good, honest scientific work may continue even in a surrounding culture which is less than perfectly hospitable, to the extent that the surrounding culture tends to undermine the norms of evidence-sharing and respect for evidence, or seriously to erode or compromise them, the integrity of science comes under threat. In an emergency—e.g., during the Great Influenza of 1918, as scientists worked desperately to figure out the cause of, and hence a way of dealing with, the worst plague in history—urgency and haste may induce carelessness and jumping to unwarranted conclusions.[8] Again, certain kinds of political regime seem to be inherently hostile environments for scientific work: theocracies are likely to fear scientific discoveries that may threaten their worldview, to deplore scientific methods that offend their moral sensibilities, and to be adamantly opposed to the very idea of investigating certain questions; and, as Merton especially emphasized, totalitarian states, aspiring to control every aspect of citizens' lives, are always ready to distort science to their own ends.[9]

3. THREATS TO SCIENTIFIC INTEGRITY TODAY

Today, some hear echoes of theocratic resistance to scientific advance in President Bush's moral objections to funding human embryonic stem-cell research; others hear echoes of such disturbing concepts as "bourgeois genetics" and "Jewish physics" in some recent radical-feminist talk of "masculinist science" and in radical post-colonialist talk of "Western science."[10] But the most troubling threats to the integrity of science are of another, subtler kind.

In 1946, writing of "Science, Faith and Society"—"faith" referring to the commitment to intellectual honesty and respect for evidence—Michael Polanyi observed that "[i]f each scientist set to work each morning with the intention of doing the best bit of safe charlatanry which would just get him into a good post, there would soon exist no effective standards by which such deception could be detected." After all, he continues: "[a] community of scientists in which each would act only with an eye to please scientific opinion would find no scientific opinion to please."[11] This is wonderfully vivid (and disturbingly close to the uncomfortable truth about too much of the "research and scholarship" that goes on in some areas of the humanities). But it doesn't quite fully capture how insidious the dangers may be; for Polanyi puts categorically what is really a matter of degree.

The more willing the more scientists are to cut corners, to fudge, to obfuscate, to plagiarize, to fake, to conceal unfavorable results, to put their own or their sponsors' interests above discovering the truth, the less effective the internal social mechanisms sustaining the core values of science will be. And today, though the technical helps to inquiry have clearly got better and better, the social helps—always more fragile, more susceptible to failure—are under considerable strain. We don't yet face Polanyi's nightmare scenario in which every scientist sets out each morning to perpetrate whatever charlatanry he can get away with; the danger is, rather, that scientists' commitment to evidence-sharing and respect for evidence will suffer a kind of creeping erosion, that too many will find themselves able to tolerate small dishonesties and small concealments: a little "improvement" of the truth here, a little reticence about inconvenient evidence there, a little corner-cutting to ensure priority, a little compromise about whom to acknowledge, and in what terms, to cultivate a potentially useful contact; and that too many even of those who would not compromise the integrity of their own work will manage to tolerate those who do. Russian mathematician Grigory Perelman comments: "[many] are more or less honest, but they tolerate those who are not honest."[12]

Why so? As science progresses, it tends to get more expensive; in part because many, if not most, of the easily and cheaply obtainable results have been obtained already, and in part because, as the work becomes more complex, it also becomes more costly (especially in fundamental physics, where new knowledge requires observing smaller and smaller particles moving faster and faster).[13] As scientific work becomes more expensive, it must rely more and more on governments and large industrial concerns for support; and these, obviously, are apt to give priority to quite other values than the epistemological norms at the heart of the scientific enterprise. At the very least, it is likely that such sponsors will want answers to some questions more urgently than they want answers to others— even if the latter are of more true scientific importance, or more readily tackled given present knowledge; and it is likely that they will want palatable answers to the questions they want tackled rather than unpalatable ones—sometimes so much so that they find it easy to ignore the risk of coming to believe the palatable answers on the basis of seriously inadequate evidence. So, for example, a government will be reluctant to fund work, however important intellectually, that might prove offensive to some constituency on which it relies; a pharmaceutical company will prefer to fund studies designed to bring out the benefits of its products, and may even try to suppress publication of studies that cast doubt on their effectiveness or safety.

Nor, at this point, are universities unambiguously enough committed to the culture of inquiry to serve as a bulwark against the pressures from elsewhere. As Thorstein Veblen predicted nearly a century ago, universities have become increasingly entangled with the ethos of business, and increasingly bureaucratized;[14] and so even in the academy values of other kinds increasingly pull against evidence-sharing and respect for evidence. Profit is a very different thing from truth; and a bureaucratic culture is deeply inimical to serious intellectual work. The bureaucratized university inevitably stresses money-raising, rankings, numbers of publications, the number and size of grants, volumes added to the library—and bureaucratic administrators strongly prefer conveniently manageable, fungible faculty; while serious intellectual work (whether in the sciences or in history, philosophy, or *any* field) is by its very nature unpredictable and ragged, and requires that those with the talent, originality, patience, penetration, and ingenuity to make real intellectual progress—precisely the least fungible, often the least conformist and manageable—be allowed time, peace of mind, scope for experiment, exploration, mature reflection.[15]

There was a time when a fine scientist like Oswald Avery—who throughout the 1918 epidemic had quietly insisted that the evidence many medical scientists then took to show that influenza was caused by a bacterium was inconclusive— published nothing for almost a decade, and steadfastly refused to put his name on any paper unless he had actually conducted one of the experiments described.

("Disappointment is my daily bread," he averred; "I thrive on it.")[16] We now know, of course, that he was correct in suspecting that influenza is viral, not bacterial; and that in 1944, after his long dry spell, he would publish the pioneering work that led to the identification of DNA, rather than protein, as the genetic material.[17] But sadly, it is hard to imagine how a scientist of such sterling intellectual integrity could survive, let alone thrive, in today's academy.

For academic scientists are now under considerable pressure from their universities to get grants, to publish, to come up with something patentable; and may also find themselves under pressure from their sponsors, or lured by the hope of lucrative patents, large stockholdings, or fat fees as expert witnesses. Nor are scientific journals immune; for as these journals have become serious money-making enterprises, their commitment to scientific values has sometimes come into conflict with their commercial interests. The dangers seem to be greater in the life sciences than in physics, etc.; and especially so in biomedical science. The role of the big pharmaceutical companies in biomedical research in universities, and in medical journals' dissemination of results, is especially disturbing.

4. EROSION OF INTEGRITY IN BIOMEDICAL RESEARCH

According to a recent headline in *The Wall Street Journal*, "Gates Won't Fund AIDS Researchers Unless They Pool Data": Mr. Gates will give $587 million in funding to researchers working on a vaccine for AIDS, but only on condition that they pool their data promptly and without reservation.[18] Shortly thereafter, another headline read, "A Nonscientist Pushes Sharing Bird-Flu Data": with a group of scientists, businessman Peter Bogner has "stitched together a network of the world's top flu scientists . . . to share data that could speed research."[19] Apparently, scientists' commitment to evidence-sharing can no longer be taken for granted. According to another headline, there is a "Worrisome Ailment in Medicine: Misleading Journal Articles":[20] a study finds that in 65 percent of papers surveyed, harmful effects were not completely reported.[21] Apparently, scientists' commitment to honest reporting of their findings cannot be taken for granted either.

Even some editors of major medical journals have expressed concern. The *American Journal of Hypertension* recently split away from the American Society of Hypertension when the editor of the journal concluded that the society had become, in effect, a tool for drug company marketing.[22] An online article by Richard Smith—for twenty-five years an editor of the *British Medical Journal*, and for thirteen of those years editor and chief executive of *BMJ* publishing—is entitled: "Medical Journals Are an Extension of the Marketing Arm of the Pharmaceutical Companies."[23] Richard Horton, editor of *The Lancet*, and Marcia Angell and Jerome Kassirer, both former editors of the *New England Journal of Medicine (NEJM)*, all sound the same theme.[24]

What has gone wrong? Rather than a simple chain of cause-and-effect, many factors contribute to the erosion of integrity. Mechanisms for evidence-sharing that once worked, if not perfectly, well enough, are falling into disrepair as the burdens placed on them have grown. One factor is the increased pressure on scientists to publish. Once, a handful of good papers was enough to secure a scientist's reputation; now, a constant flow of publications is expected. In 1992 a survey showed that over the previous decade the twenty most "productive" scientists in the world published an article at least once every 11.3 days; at the head of the list was Yury Struchov of the Institute for Organoelemental Chemistry in Moscow, who published a paper every 3.9 days.[25] By now the pressure to publish is even more severe: as I can testify from service on university committees, the *curriculum vitae* of a senior medical faculty member will likely list hundreds of papers.

Understandably, some people publish essentially the same material over and over in slightly different forms, and many split their work into shorter papers that can be published separately, a practice so common that scientists themselves talk wryly of "salami publishing" and "minimal publishable units" ("MPUs"). Unfortunately, multiple publications can impede communication. Fragmentation into MPUs may affect the design of a study, e.g., by leading to a focus on intermediate outcomes rather than meaningful endpoints, to controlled trials run over too short a period, to studies that compare a target drug with placebo rather than with proven therapies.[26]

The same pressure to publish has also contributed to the ever-increasing numbers of authors listed on each paper, some of whom may have made only the most minimal contributions to the work reported, or none at all. In 1993 the editor of the *NEJM* accepted the Ig Nobel Prize for Literature on behalf of the 972 scientists listed as coauthors of a ten-page paper—i.e., just two words per author![27] Heads of laboratories or teams may insist on having their name on every paper that the team produces. In 1992, ten geologists at the Russian Institute of Volcanic Geology and Geochemistry went on hunger strike in protest against an "autocratic" director who forced them to put his name on all their work.[28] Sometimes a senior professor will put his name on a study to which he has contributed little or nothing in hopes of helping a junior colleague get it published. Sometimes, after papers have been discovered to be fraudulent, coauthors have denied all knowledge of the perpetrator's fabrications.[29] Even after some major medical journals adopted policies to discourage "honorific" author listings, a study found that many first authors said coauthors had really made little or no contribution;[30] and when all the members of a research team applied for grant money, "their total participation came to 300%."[31]

Along with the ever-swelling flood of submissions, there has been a steady increase in the number, and the size, of journals. A search of PubMed (the NIH's digital archive for biomedical and life sciences journals) turned up a total of 19,355 journals, with 734,858 articles published between January 1, 2005, and January 1, 2006. Many medical journals now carry not only articles but news sections, short summaries, and even summaries of summaries, as well as lots of glossy illustrations; the price of these journals rose, on average, almost 11 percent a year in the period from 1984 to 2001, during which inflation generally was around 3 percent.[32] Now that these journals are serious money-making enterprises, some editors are trying to improve their citation-rate, and thus their journal's library sales, by putting pressure on authors to cite other papers that appeared in their pages.[33]

The peer-review process is severely strained by the enormous number of submissions. Reviewers are estimated to spend an average of only 2.4 hours reading a manuscript and making their recommendations (and more of the reviewers, naturally, are more junior than in the early days, when enough relatively senior scientists could be found to carry the load). Most journals make no independent check of the statistical calculations crucial to the conclusions of many papers. And because there are now so many journals, eventually almost everything submitted gets published—somewhere—perhaps after having been turned down numerous times.[34]

So perhaps it is no wonder that honesty as well as evidence-sharing is under threat. According to a study published in *Nature* in 2005, more than 10% of 3,247 scientists polled admitted that they had withheld details of methodology or results from papers or research proposals, more than 15% that they had dropped inconvenient observations or data points, and more than 27% reported that they had kept inadequate records of research work.[35] According to a study published the same year in the *Journal of the American Medical Association* (*JAMA*), of 45 highly cited studies claiming effective medical interventions, published in the most prestigious journals, 15 were later contradicted in whole or in part by other studies.[36]

Another factor contributing to the erosion both of sharing and of honesty is the role of industrial sponsors, especially the pharmaceutical companies. At a time when government funding is not keeping pace, increasing pressure on faculty to get grants, and increasing collaboration of universities with industry (usually politely described as "technology transfer") has meant that a larger proportion of scientific, and especially medical, research in the universities is funded by industry. This often means that information deemed proprietary must be kept confidential, and that results will be withheld from publication for a time to protect the sponsors' business interests; and it sometimes means that sponsors are allowed to vet, or even control, the publication of results.[37]

The situation is especially severe in the case of medical faculty, who are often obliged, in effect, to secure funding for their own salaries in grant money.[38] At the same time, there are especially attractive financial opportunities for medical scientists who are successful in attracting corporate sponsorship: fees for speaking at company-sponsored conferences, lucrative consultancies, stock holdings, and so on. Other faculty are themselves involved in (sometimes enormously profitable) biotech companies. Universities generally have some kind of conflict-of-interest rules, but there is no uniform standard; in many cases the guidelines are pretty generous or flexible, and often enough policies are not energetically enforced (probably because faculty serving on the relevant committees are reluctant to decline a colleague's grant request).[39]

Though most of the medical societies that run them claim "editorial independence," many journals receive large revenues from drug company advertising. After the *Annals of Internal Medicine* published a study critical of drug company advertisements, the American College of Physicians, which runs the journal, is estimated to have lost between a million and a million-and-a-half dollars of advertising revenue.[40] There is evidence, moreover, that such advertisements are quite often misleading; in particular, the scientific studies cited don't always show what the advertisement claims, usually because "the [advertising] slogan recommended the drug [for] a patient group other than that assessed in the study."[41]

Many medical journals publish symposia organized by pharmaceutical companies, a privilege for which they often charge significant fees; and some suspend the peer-review process for such publications. Many receive large revenues from the sale to such companies of thousands, sometimes hundreds of thousands, of offprints of articles favorable to their products. According to a study published in 1992, between 1975 and 1988 the proportion of pharmaceutical companies' marketing budgets spent on sponsoring symposia rose from $6 million to $86 million. Journal editors reported charges ranging from between $400 and $1,000 per page to a flat fee of $100,000 for publishing the proceedings of such symposia; and journals charged an average of $15 per reprint, of which they sold, on average, 25,000 copies. Eight editors reported that their review procedures were affected by pressure of various kinds from the organizers of the symposia.[42] Once again, it seems likely that by now these problems are not better, but worse.

Most journals require that authors disclose the sources from which they have received support for their work; but disclosure is at best a weak precaution against undue credulity on the part of readers, and few journals impose any real sanctions when disclosure rules are flouted. Jerome Kassirer, former editor of the *NEJM*, writes that in the 1990s it became harder and harder to find people without conflicting drug industry connections to write review articles, as journal policy required. In 2002, the new editor, Jeffrey Drazen, simply gave up the policy as unworkable. The same year, the journal published an article on the anti-depression drug nefazodone, listing 29 authors; the editor noted that "all but 1 . . . of the 12 principal authors have had financial associations with Bristol-Myers Squibb—which also sponsored the study . . . [and] 2 [other authors] are employees of Bristol-Myers Squibb."[43] In 2006, just days after the editor of *JAMA*, Dr. Catherine DeAngelis, had announced more stringent disclosure rules, she ruefully acknowledged—the third such rueful acknowledgment in two months[44]—that the journal had just learned that all six authors of a just-published study linking severe hearts attack to migraines in women had received funding from the manufactures of medicines for migraine or heart-related illnesses.[45] The following week, at the tail end of a press report of a new study of Lipitor, we read not only that all 11 authors of the study, which was funded by Pfizer, but even the doctor recruited by the *NEJM* to write an opinion piece on the study, had financial connections to the company.[46] The week after that, we learned that the editor of the journal *Neuropsychopharmacology* was stepping down after a con-troversy over his having written a favorable review of a new device for the treat-ment of depression without disclosing that he, like all the other eight authors of the article, had financial ties to the manufacturer.[47]

Moreover, there is evidence that company sponsorship has a significant effect on the results reported: reports of work supported by a manufacturer are significantly more likely to be favorable to its products than reports of work not so supported (perhaps the result of a study design more likely to lead to the desired result; perhaps of economy with the truth in reporting; perhaps of simple, optimistic self-deception). As early as 1986, a study found that "in no case was a therapeutic agent manufactured by a sponsoring company found to be inferior to an alternative manufactured by another company";[48] a 1994 study of fifty-six company-sponsored trials of nonsteroidal anti-inflammatory drugs (NSAIDs) found that not one of them presented results unfavorable to the sponsoring com-pany;[49] and a study published in 2004 reported that authors with financial ties to drug companies were between ten and twenty times less likely to report negative findings than authors without such ties.[50]

There is also disturbing evidence of pharmaceutical companies recruiting academic scientists, in return for listing as senior author, to "edit" reports actually produced in-house but submitted to peer-reviewed journals under the supposed senior author's name. Adriane Fugh-Berman describes how it works: on August 24, 2004, she received, from a "medical education company" sponsored by a drug manufacturer, a draft article on warfarin-herb interactions, complete with her name as author and her institutional affiliation. She was asked to review this and suggest any "amends" (*sic*) needed before it was submitted to a peer-reviewed journal—preferably by September 1. (She didn't "make amends," but declined the offer.) As Fugh-Berman observes, this practice is especially hard for readers to detect when, as in this case, the article doesn't specifically mention the company's product, but is designed to increase the perceived need for some drug of theirs.[51]

Moreover, we know that drug companies sometimes put pressure on scientists to withhold findings unfavorable to their products. In 2006, for example, Bausch and Lomb recalled its contact lens solution Renu with MoistureLoc after it was linked to a recent outbreak of fungal eye infections. Shortly thereafter, we learned that the problem (which I was intrigued to see described as a threat to "the integrity of the cornea") had been known since 1999, and that the company had tried to get studies unfavorable to its product suppressed.[52]

It only makes matters worse, of course, that the process of cleaning up the literature after fraud has been discovered, or even after work has been retracted or a journal has published an "expression of concern," is slow and far from thorough. After admitting that they had fabricated data, Friedreich Herrmann and Marion Brach, both with the Max Delbrück Center for Molecular Medicine in Berlin, retracted 11 papers published between 1991 and 1999; but according to Ulf Rapp, who led an investigation of the case for the funding agency, the fabricated data actually appeared in 94 papers, 83 of which were *not* retracted.[53] Even retracted papers often continue to be cited over and over. A year after the US Office of Research Integrity informed ten journals that they had published papers coauthored by Dr. Eric Poehlman based on fraudulent data, only 8 had been retracted; and even after *The Annals of Internal Medicine* had retracted one of these papers, other authors went on innocently referring to it.[54]

5. TRIALS AND TRIBULATIONS: THE TROUBLING TALE OF VIOXX AND CELEBREX

In *Defending Science*, discussing the tensions between the epistemological values of science and the commercial values of pharmaceutical companies that sponsor scientific work, I mentioned in passing the efforts of the Immune

Response Corporation to suppress publication of the unfavorable results of a large clinical trial conducted by a medical scientist at the University of California, San Francisco, and of Merck and Pfizer to suppress evidence that the blockbuster drugs Vioxx and Celebrex might cause heart-related problems.[55] I explore the Remune story in detail in the next essay,[56] but here I want to look more closely at the story of Vioxx and Celebrex, and especially at the role of the journals where this research was published. For this is a story that illustrates just about all the problems that flow from the relation of the medical journals to the pharmaceutical industry: studies designed to produce the desired results, published in prestigious journals whose reviewers didn't notice flaws in their design; large revenues for the sale of offprints of such articles; misleading attribution of drug company papers to academic supposed lead authors; and company efforts to suppress criticism or prevent publication of unfavorable evidence.

For more than forty years, conventional NSAIDs were used for the control of chronic pain; but these drugs carry increased risk of bleeding ulcers in susceptible patients. So it seemed a big advance when new NSAIDs were developed to inhibit the Cox-2 enzyme, which causes inflammation, without affecting the Cox-1 enzyme, which protects against the adverse gastrointestinal effects. These included Vioxx (rofecoxib) and Celebrex (celecoxib), approved for sale by the US Food and Drug Administration (FDA) in 1999.[57]

While Vioxx was on the US market, Merck spent more than $100 million a year on direct-to-consumer advertising; more than 80 million people took the drug; and annual sales exceeded $2.5 billion.[58] But in September 2004, Merck withdrew Vioxx because of concerns over cardiovascular risks; and by mid-December 2006 there were around 27,200 Vioxx lawsuits pending against the company.[59] By November 2007 Merck had made a settlement offer; and by early 2008 press reports suggested that it seemed likely that enough plaintiffs would sign on to seal the deal. (The offer was, however, controversial, because it required lawyers who participate in the settlement to recommend it to all their qualified clients.)[60]

When Merck withdrew Vioxx, Pfizer suspended its huge advertising campaign, but continued to maintain that no studies showed that Celebrex carried cardiovascular risks. Now, however, advertisements for Celebrex warn in bold letters that the drug "may increase the chance of a heart attack or stroke that can cause death." As of January 2008, there were over 2,500 Celebrex cases pending against Pfizer, and a Google search turned up numerous law firms seeking Celebrex clients.[61]

Merck's first large clinical trial, the VIGOR study, showed that Vioxx carried a lower risk of adverse gastrointestinal effects than the rival drug naproxen

(Aleve); as did the company's subsequent, smaller ADVANTAGE study. The FDA approved Vioxx in less than a year, before the VIGOR trial was completed. After FDA approval, a report of the VIGOR study was submitted to the *NEJM*, where it appeared in November 2000.[62] This study indicated the gastrointestinal benefits; but it also suggested a significantly higher rate of myocardial infarction, among patients given one or the other drug for more than eighteen months, in those taking Vioxx than in those taking naproxen.[63] Merck attributed this to a cardio-protective effect of naproxen[64]; but by early 2001 an FDA review concluded that "it is mandatory to conduct a trial specifically assessing the cardiovascular risk of [Cox-2 inhibitors]."[65] No such trial was conducted; but in 2002 Merck was required to add a warning label to the package insert. And in 2004 the drug was taken off the market after Merck's third major clinical trial, the APPROVe study—designed to show that Vioxx lowered the risk of colon polyps—was halted by the data safety-monitoring board when it emerged that patients given 25 mg. of Vioxx for more than eighteen months had a fourfold greater incidence of serious thromboembolic events.[66]

In April 2005, the *New York Times* reported that the published account of the ADVANTAGE trial had omitted three cardiac deaths among the patients given Vioxx. The purported lead author explained that Merck scientists had designed, paid for, and run the study, and written the report; his role was only to give editorial help after the paper was written, and he hadn't known about the additional deaths.[67] In December of that year the *NEJM* published an "Expression of Concern" about "inaccuracies and deletions" in the report of the VIGOR trial: three heart attacks among patients taking Vioxx had been omitted. These adverse events had been included in the data on the FDA website since February of 2001; and two of the three authors had known of them well in advance of the publication of the paper.[68] Their inclusion raised the rate of heart attacks among those taking Vioxx from 0.4% to 0.5% (compared with 0.1% among those taking naproxen); and contradicted the claim in the paper that only those already at risk showed an increase in heart attacks with Vioxx. On behalf of the *NEJM* Dr. Drazen explained to reporters that the study had been "misleading," designed to be more sensitive to gastrointestinal benefits than to cardiovascular risks by continuing to track gastrointestinal effects after it stopped tracking cardiovascular events.

But there is more to the story. We now know that in June 2001 the editors of the *NEJM* had received a letter from pharmacist Jennifer Hrachovec asking that the article be corrected in light of the information on the FDA website, but had declined to publish it on the grounds that "the journal can't be in the business of policing every bit of data we put out." (The same year Merck officials had pressured a leading cardiologist, Dr. Eric Topol, not to publish an article critical of

Merck's claim that the reason for the disparity in the rate of heart attacks wasn't that Vioxx increased the risk, but that naproxen lowered it.)[69] What changed the minds of the editors of the *NEJM* and prompted them to post that "expression of concern"—four and a half years after they were made aware of the problem—was an urgent e-mail from public relations specialist Edward Cafasso that testimony to be presented the next day in a Vioxx case in which executive editor Dr. Gregory Curfman had been deposed made it essential to post something right away, to "drive the media away from the *NEJM* and toward the authors, Merck, and plaintiff attorneys." We also now know that the *NEJM*—which listed $88 million in total publishing revenue for the year ending May 31, 2005—had sold 929,000 offprints of the article (most of them to Merck), for revenue estimated to be between $679,000 and $836,000.[70]

As if this weren't bad enough, in July 2006 the journal posted a correction to the report it had earlier published of the APPROVe study: key results claimed in the article had not in fact been arrived at by the statistical method the authors said they used; and, had they used it, the results would have undermined the claim in the article that cardiovascular risks increased only after eighteen months.[71]

What about Celebrex? The CLASS study, completed and published in *JAMA* in 2000,[72] indicated that Celebrex carried a significantly lower risk of adverse gastrointestinal effects than conventional NSAIDs. Subsequently, however, letters to the journal (including one from Dr. Hrachovec) pointed out that the article reported only data from the first six months of the twelve-month trial, while the more complete information available on the FDA website revealed that "[f]or upper GI safety, and also global safety, there does not appear to be any meaningful advantage for Celebrex"; and that patients with preexisting cardiovascular disease had been excluded from the study.[73] In December 2004, a study published on-line suggested that Celebrex offered some protection against nonfatal myocardial infarction (MI); the same month, however, the National Cancer Institute halted both the Adenoma Protection with Celebrex (APC) trial, and a second trial, the PreSAP study, because of a 2.5-fold increased risk of acute MI and stroke in patients given 400 mg. of Celebrex a day, and a 3.4-fold increase in patients given 800 mg.[74] This led to the warning added to the package insert and advertisements for Celebrex.

Then, a twist in the tale: analysis of the results of the two halted studies, reported at the annual meeting of the American Association for Cancer Research in April 2006, showed a dramatic reduction in risk of colon cancer in patients given Celebrex.[75]

Even after the withdrawal of Vioxx, Merck remains a player in the Cox-2 inhibitor market. In October 2004, after reviewing Merck's application for approval of a new Cox-2 inhibitor, Arcoxia (etoricoxib), the FDA had asked for further data; in August 2006, Merck released preliminary results of the first large-scale trial, the MEDAL study, concluding that Arcoxia has gastrointestinal advantages over the older, widely prescribed NSAID diclofenac (Voltaren, Cataflam), while its heart risks are comparable. But critics noted that the data Merck supplied was very limited; and expressed disappointment at the choice of diclofenac as a comparison treatment, pointing out that this drug "works in the body more like Cox-2 inhibitors than painkillers like naproxen." Only a few weeks later, two analyses of previous clinical trials found that even short-term Vioxx use increased cardiovascular risk—and that the cardiovascular risks of diclofenac (marketed by Novartis) are such as to merit reviewing the regulatory status of the drug.[76] Arcoxia was already on sale in Europe and Latin America,[77] but in April 2007 the FDA rejected Merck's application to market Arcoxia in the United States.[78]

6. WHY THE EROSION OF INTEGRITY MATTERS

In the words of H. L. Mencken, "there is always a well-known solution to every human problem—neat, plausible, and wrong."[79] Even if I had one, a neat, plausible solution to the thicket of problems explored here surely would be wrong. But anyway, having no such solution to offer, I will end instead by trying to articulate briefly why, as my subtitle says, the integrity of science matters, and why the creeping corruption I have described should concern us.

For some people, the commitment to finding out—the "scientific attitude," as C. S. Peirce called it, "the Will to Learn"[80]—is both firm and deep. As Percy Bridgman puts it, some feel the emotional pull of the ideal of intellectual honesty almost as the religious man feels the call to serve Something much more significant than himself.[81] But for many people intellectual honesty flourishes only with the right kind of encouragement and incentives, and with good example; in an inhospitable environment it wilts and withers. So the erosion of integrity feeds on itself: senior scientists whose commitment to the norms of science is weak or ambivalent won't transmit those norms to young colleagues or to students; and the more commitment to those norms becomes professionally disadvantageous, the more ambivalent and the shakier the more scientists' commitment to them will become.[82]

The erosion of commitment to these norms matters, first, because it is apt to impede the progress of science; as a result of which we don't know things we could have known by now, and we lose out on the benefits that knowledge would have provided had we had it. Once again, the saga of Vioxx and Celebrex makes the point vivid. Between 1999 (when Vioxx was approved by the FDA) and 2004 (when it was taken off the market) it is estimated that there were between 88,000 and 140,000 excess cases of serious coronary heart disease in the United States.[83] In late 2004 we learned that Celebrex may protect against colon cancer; and in late 2005 the Cleveland Clinic announced that it would direct a world-wide clinical trial of around 20,000 patients to assess the relative safety of ibuprofen, naproxen, and celecoxib.[81] Think about it: if sponsors' interests hadn't got in the way, mightn't we have known much more, years ago, about which patients which NSAIDs could benefit, and which patients which NSAIDs were likely to harm more than they helped?

Second, and almost as obviously, the erosion of the integrity of science matters because when the public reads, day after day, week after week, one story after another of scientific dishonesty and corruption—e.g., Dr. Hwang Woo Suk's fraudulent work on stem cell cloning; that laughable Columbia "Prayer Study"; the amateurishly fabricated data in Jon Sudbø's oral-cancer study[85]—its confidence in the sciences will inevitably be damaged. Indeed, public trust in science may well be damaged more than the erosion of integrity thus far warrants; especially when, as now, the press takes a particularly keen interest in stories of scientific fraud and misconduct. As a result, the public is likely to become more reluctant to support government funding of an institution it has come to perceive as corrupt and untrustworthy; and again, we lose out on knowledge we might otherwise have had, and on the benefits such knowledge might have brought.

Third, less obviously but perhaps most consequentially, the erosion of the integrity of science matters because it feeds the anti-intellectualism, the cynicism about the very possibility of discovering how things are, even about the very idea of truth, that lies not far beneath the surface of supposedly "civilized" societies. Our capacity to figure things out is one of the best talents human beings have: we aren't especially fast; we aren't especially strong; but if we really want to and are willing to work and think hard, if we have enough patience and enough persistence, if we are ready to fail and try again, perhaps over and over, we can find out something of how the world is. But this is hard work, often painful and frustrating; and there is another, less admirable side of human nature, a side that really doesn't want to go to all the trouble of finding out, that prefers to believe things are as we would like them to be, and that loves the mysterious and the impressively incomprehensible.

Scientific inquiry is not the only kind of inquiry, but it has undeniably been an extraordinarily successful human enterprise. So the erosion of scientific evidence-sharing and respect for evidence matters, also, because allowing the integrity of science to languish—like allowing our talent for music, for dancing, or for storytelling to languish—would be a real tragedy for the human race.

NOTES

1. My source is John R. Gross, *The Oxford Book of Aphorisms* (Oxford: Oxford University Press, 1983), p. 8. (He doesn't give the original source.)

2. The English word "entire," which is etymologically akin to "integrity," still has, I believe, a specialized use in which it refers to an uncastrated animal.

3. See Haack, *Defending Science—Within Reason: Between Scientism and Cynicism* (Amherst, NY: Prometheus Books, 2003), chapter 6.

4. See Haack, *Defending Science* (n. 3), p. 144.

5. See Haack, "'The Ethics of Belief' Reconsidered," in *The Philosophy of R. M. Chisholm*, ed. Lewis Hahn (La Salle, IL: Open Court, 1997), 129–44; reprinted in *Knowledge, Truth, and Duty: Essays on Epistemic Justification, Responsibility, and Virtue*, ed. Matthias Steup (New York: Oxford University Press, 2001), pp. 21–33.

6. See Robert Merton, "Science and Democratic Social Structure," in *Social Theory and Social Structure* (Glencoe, IL: Free Press, 1946), pp. 307–16. A pamphlet entitled *Honor in Science*, published in 1991 by Sigma Xi, the Scientific Research Society, intended for graduate students in the sciences, stresses honesty and "openness."

7. It is worth noting that evidence-sharing can be in tension with the desire for prestige, which is for many an important motive for undertaking the hard and often frustrating work of science; and that plagiarism is epistemologically damaging because it threatens the delicate incentive-structure of science.

8. See John M. Berry, *The Great Influenza: The Epic Story of the Deadliest Plague in History* (New York: Penguin Books, 2004).

9. Robert Merton, "Science and the Social Order," *Philosophy of Science* 5 (July 1938): 321–37; reprinted in *Social Theory and Social Structure* (n. 6), pp. 295–306.

10. See Haack, *Defending Science* (n. 3), chapter 11.

11. Michael Polanyi, *Science, Faith and Society* (London: Geoffrey Cumberledge; Oxford University Press, 1946), p. 40. Polanyi began his career as an X-ray crystallographer, but later in life turned to philosophy of science.

12. Quoted in Sylvia Nasar and David Gruber, "Manifold Destiny: A Legendary Problem and the Battle over Who Solved It," *The New Yorker*, 28 August 2006, pp. 44–57, p. 57.

13. According to Donald Kennedy, this "implacable law of the economics of knowledge" was first stated by Max Planck. See Kennedy, *Academic Duty* (Cambridge: Harvard University Press, 1997), p. 11.

14. Thorstein Veblen, *The Higher Learning in America* (1919; Stanford, CA: Academic Reprints, 1954).

15. See also Haack, "Preposterism and Its Consequences" (1996) in Haack, *Manifesto of a Passionate Moderate: Unfashionable Essays* (Chicago: University of Chicago Press, 1998), pp. 188–208; Pat Duffy Hutcheon, *Building Character and Culture* (Westport, CT: Praeger, 1999), pp. 37 and 139ff.

16. Quoted in Berry, *The Great Influenza* (n. 8), p. 423.

17. Oswald Avery, Colin MacCleod, and Maclyn McCarty, "Studies of the Chemical

Nature of the Substance Inducing Transformation in Pneumococcal Types," *Journal of Experimental Medicine* 79 (1944): 137–58; reprinted in *Conceptual Foundations of Genetics*, ed. Harry A. Corwin and John B. Jenkins (Boston: Houghton-Mifflin, 1976), 13–27. The story is told briefly in Haack, *Defending Science* (n. 3), pp. 102–103.

18. Marilyn Chase, "Gates Won't Fund AIDS Researchers Unless They Pool Data," *The Wall Street Journal*, 20 July 2006, pp. B1, B4.

19. Nicholas Zamiska, "A Nonscientist Pushes Sharing Bird-Flu Data," *The Wall Street Journal*, 21 August 2006, pp. B1, B7 (the quotation is from p. B1).

20. Anna Wilde Matthews, "Worrisome New Ailment in Medicine: Misleading Journal Articles," *The Wall Street Journal*, 10 June 2005, pp. A1. A9.

21. An-Wen Chan et al., "Empirical Evidence for Selective Reporting of Outcomes in Randomized Trials," *Journal of the American Medical Association* 291, no. 20 (May 26, 2004): 2457–65.

22. Robert L. Goodman and Olveen Carrasquillo, "The Corporate Co-author, The Ghost Writer, and the Medical Society," *Journal of General Internal Medicine* 20 (2005): 102.

23. Richard Smith, "Medical Journals Are an Extension of the Marketing Arm of the Pharmaceutical Companies," *Plos Medicine*, 2.5, e138: 03646, available at <www .plosmedicine.org>.

24. Richard Horton, "The Dawn of McScience," *New York Review of Books* 51, no. 4 (2004): 7–9. Marcia Angell, *The Truth About Drug Companies: How They Deceive Us and What to Do About It* (New York: Random House, 2005); Jerome Kassirer, *On the Take: How America's Complicity with Big Business Can Endanger Your Health* (Oxford: Oxford University Press, 2005).

25. Christopher Anderson, "Writer's Cramp," *Nature* 355 (1992): 101.

26. Jerome P. Kassirer, "Reflections on Medical Journals: Has Progress Made Them Better?" *Annals of Internal Medicine* 137, no. 1 (July 2, 2003): 46–48, p. 46.

27. Steve Nadis, "Ig Nobel Prizes Reward Fruits of Unique Labor," *Nature* 365 (1993): 599. The paper in question was "An International Trial Comparing Four Thrombolytic Strategies for Acute Myocardial Infarction," *New England Journal of Medicine* 329, no. 10 (September 2, 1993): 673–82.

28. Anderson, "Writer's Cramp" (n. 25 above).

29. Arnold Relman, "Lessons from the Darsee Affair," *New England Journal of Medicine* 308 (1983): 1417.

30. D. W. Shapiro et al., "The Contributions of Authors to Multiauthor Biomedical Research Papers," *Journal of the American Medical Association*, 271 (1994): 438–42.

31. William J. Broad, "The Publishing Game: Getting More for Less," *Science*, new series, 211, no. 4487 (March 13, 1981): 1137–39, p. 1137.

32. Kassirer, "Reflections on Medical Journals" (n. 26 above), p. 47.

33. Sharon Begley, "Science Journals Artfully Try to Boost Their Rankings," *The Wall Street Journal*, 5 June 2006, pp. B1, B5.

34. See Brief Amici Curiae for Daryl E. Chubin, Edward J. Hackett, David Michael Ozonoff, and Richard Clapp in Support of Petitioners, *Daubert v. Merrell Dow Pharma-*

ceuticals, Inc., 509 U.S. 579 (1993), pp. 11–19; Haack, "Peer Review and Publication: Lessons for Lawyers," *Stetson Law Review* 36, no. 3 (2007): 789–819.

35. Brian C. Martinson et al., "Scientists Behaving Badly," *Nature* 435, no. 9 (June 2005): 737–38.

36. John Ionnadis, "Contradicted and Initially Stronger Effects in Highly Cited Clinical Research," *Journal of the American Medical Association* 294, no. 2 (July 7, 2005): 218–28.

37. See Joshua A. Newberg and Richard L. Dunn, "Keeping Secrets in the Campus Lab: Law, Values and Rules of Engagement for Industry-University R&D Partnerships," *American Business Law Journal* 39 (2002): 187–240.

38. "[E]specially in the health sciences but also in the basic sciences, faculty are often recruited with the understanding that they will have to generate part or all of their salaries through external funding for the duration of their careers at the university": Donald G. Stein (formerly a working scientist, now a senior academic administrator), "A Personal Perspective," in Stein, ed. *Buying In or Selling Out? The Commercialization of the American Research University* (New Brunswick, NJ: Rutgers University Press, 2004), pp. 1–16, p. 3.

39. See e.g., Sheldon Krimsky, *Science in the Private Interest: Has the Lure of Profits Corrupted Biomedical Research?* (Lanham, MD: Rowman and Littlefield, 2003), chapter 3.

40. Goodman and Carrasquillo, "The Corporate Co-author, the Ghost Writer, and the Medical Society" (n. 22).

41. P. Villanueva et al., "Accuracy of Pharmaceutical Advertisements in Medical Journals," *The Lancet* 361 (2003): 27–32. The quotation is from p. 27.

42. Lisa Bero, Alison Galbraith, and Drummond Rennie, "The Publication of Sponsored Symposiums in Medical Journals," *New England Journal of Medicine* 327, no. 16 (October 15, 1992): 1135–40. See also M. K. Cho and Lisa Bero, "The Quality of Drug Studies Published in Symposium Proceedings," *Annals of Internal Medicine* 124 (1996): 485–89.

43. Jerome P. Kassirer, *On the Take* (n. 24), p. 23.

44. "Periscope," *Newsweek*, 7 August 2006, p. 8.

45. Lindsay Tanner, "JAMA Says Docs Misled over Industry Ties," 18 July 2006, available at http://www.chron.com/disp/story.mpl/ap/health/4055561.html.

46. Thomas M. Burton, "Lipitor Shows Limited Benefit for Stroke," *The Wall Street Journal*, 10 August 2006, pp. D1, D4.

47. David Armstrong, "Medical Journal Editor Nemeroff Steps Down Over Undisclosed Ties," *The Wall Street Journal*, 28 August 2006, p. B7.

48. Richard A. Davidson, "Source of Funding and Outcome of Clinical Trials," *Journal of General Internal Medicine* 1, no. 1 (January/February 1986): 155–58, p. 155.

49. Paula Rochon et al., "A Study of Manufacturer-supported Trials of Nonsteroidal Anti-inflammatory Drugs in the Treatment of Arthritis," *Archives of Internal Medicine* 154 (1994): 157–63.

50. Lee S. Friedman and Elihu D. Richter, "Relationship Between Conflict of Interest and Research Results," *Journal of General Internal Medicine* 19 (January 2004): 51–56, p. 54.

51. Adriane Fugh-Berman, "The Corporate Coauthor," *Journal of General Internal Medicine* 20, no. 6 (June 2006): 546–48.

52. Sylvia Pagan Westphal, "Bausch and Lomb Solution Recall Exposes Risks for Eye Infection," *The Wall Street Journal*, 26 July 2006, pp. A1, A12.

53. Laura Bonito, "The Aftermath of Scientific Fraud," *Cell* 124 (March 10, 2006): 873–75.

54. Harold C. Sox and Drummond Rennie, "Research Misconduct, Retraction, and Cleansing the Medical Literature: Lessons from the Poehlman Case," *Annals of Internal Medicine* 144 (March 6, 2006): 609–13; Jennifer Couzin and Katherine Unger, "Cleaning Up the Paper Trail," *Science* 38 (April 7, 2006): 38–43.

55. Haack, *Defending Science* (n. 3), p. 320. The material in the following section is drawn in part from the new (2006) preface to the paperback edition of this book, but updated where necessary.

56. Haack, "Scientific Secrecy and 'Spin': The Sad, Sleazy Saga of the Trials of Remune," pp. 129–45 in this volume.

57. "Cox-2 Nonsteroidal Anti-inflammatory Medication," <www.clevelandclinic .org/arthritis/treat/facts/cox2.htm>, visited March 3, 2006; "Vioxx, Celebrex: Concerns Over Popular Arthritis Drugs," <www.cbc.ca/news/background/drugs/cox-2.html>, visited March 3, 2006.

58. David J. Graham et al., "Risk of Acute Myocardial Infarction and Sudden Cardiac Death in Patients Treated with Cyclo-oxygenase 2 Selective and Non-selective Nonsteroidal Anti-inflammatory Drugs: A Nested Case-control Study," *The Lancet* 365 (February 5, 2005): 475–81, p. 480.

59. "Merck Scores Win in Alabama Court over Vioxx Drug," *The Wall Street Journal*, 16 December 2006, p. A5.

60. Heather Won Tesoriero and Nathan Koppel, "Vioxx Settlement Plan Heads for Key Deadlines," *The Wall Street Journal*, 10 January 2008, pp. B1, B2.

61. In November 2007 a federal judge had ruled the plaintiffs' evidence in a multi-party suit alleging that a 200 mg. daily dose of Celebrex could cause heart attacks and strokes was inadmissible. Paul Sizemore, a plaintiff's attorney with Girard and Keese in Los Angeles, estimated that about 900 Celebrex cases involved such a dose, but added that many patients had taken the drug twice a day. *In Re: Bextra and Celebrex Marketing Sales Practices and Product Liability Litigation*, case no. M:05-CV-01699-CRB, MDI No. 1699, United States District Court for the Northern District of California, 2007 U.S. Dis. Lexis 85382. Nathan Koppel and Heather Won Tesoriero, "Pfizer Legal Win Might Block Some Lawsuits Over Celebrex," *The Wall Street Journal*, 20 November 2007, p. A13.

62. Claire Bombadier et al., "Comparison of Upper Gastrointestinal Toxicity of Rofecoxib and Naproxen in Patients with Rheumatoid Arthritis," *New England Journal of Medicine* 343, no. 21 (November 23, 2000): 1520–28.

63. Some critics suspected that the trial showed no adverse cardiovascular effects in patients taking Vioxx for less than 18 months because it had too little statistical power to detect such effects. Graham et al. (n. 58), p. 479. A Canadian study published in 2006 indicated an increased risk of heart attack within 6 to 13 days after Vioxx therapy began.

Linda E. Levesque, James M. Brophy, and Bin Zhang, "Time Variations in the Risk of Myocardial Infarction among Elderly Users of COX-2 Inhibitors," published electronically at <www.cmaj.ca>, May 2, 2006 (an abridged version is published in *Canadian Medical Association Journal* 174, no. 11 [May 23, 2006]).

64. Susan Okie, "Raising the Safety Bar—The FDA's Coxib Meeting," *New England Journal of Medicine* 352, no. 13 (March 31, 2005): 1283–85, p. 1284.

65. Eric Topol, "Failing the Public Health—Rofecoxib, Merck, and the FDA," *New England Journal of Medicine* 351, no. 17 (October 21, 2004): 1707–1709, p. 1707.

66. "COX-2 Selective Inhibitors—Important Lessons Learned," *The Lancet* 365 (February 5, 2005): 449–51, p. 449.

67. Alex Berenson, "Evidence in Vioxx Suit Shows Intervention by Merck Officials," *New York Times*, 24 April 2005, section 1.

68. David Armstrong, "How the New England Journal Missed Warning Signs on Vioxx: Medical Weekly Waited Years to Report Flaws in Article that Praised Pain Drug," *The Wall Street Journal*, 11 May 2006, pp. A1, A10 (the quotation is from p. A10).

69. Anne Belli and Bill Hensel Jr., "Doctor: Merck Tried to Influence Article: Company Urged Him Not to Publish Warnings against Vioxx Use," *Houston Chronicle*, 4 December 2005, section B.

70. Armstrong, "How the New England Journal Missed Warning Signs on Vioxx: Medical Weekly Waited Years to Report Flaws in Article that Praised Pain Drug" (n. 6), pp. A1, A10.

71. Heather Won Tesoriero, "Vioxx Correction May Add Pressure to Merck's Defense," *The Wall Street Journal*, 27 June 2006, p. A2.

72. Fred E. Silverstein et al., "Gastrointestinal Toxicity with Celecoxib vs. Nonsteroidal Anti-Inflammatory Drugs for Osteoarthritis and Rheumatoid Arthritis: The CLASS Study," *Journal of the American Medical Association* 284, no. 10 (September 13, 2000): 1247–55.

73. Letters, *Journal of the American Medical Association* 286, no. 19 (November 21, 2001): 2398–2400. The quotation from the FDA website appears on p. 2398.

74. Graham et al., "Risk of Acute Myocardial Infarction and Sudden Cardiac Death in Patients Treated with Cyclo-oxygenase 2 Selective and Non-selective Non-steroidal Anti-inflammatory Drugs" (n. 58 above), p. 480, citing M. Kaufman, "Celebrex Trial Halted after Finding of Heart Risk: FDA Chief Urges Patients to Ask about Alternatives," *Washington Post*, 18 December 2004, p. A1.

75. Press Release, American Association for Cancer Research, "Studies Confirm Celecoxib May Help Prevent Colorectal Cancer in High Risk Patients" (April 3, 2006), available at <www.aacr.org?Default.aspx?p=1066&d=608>. Scott Hensley, "Drug Cuts Risks of Colon Cancer in Two Studies," *The Wall Street Journal*, 14 April 2006, p. D6.

76. Peter Loftus, "Merck's Vioxx Tied to New Threat: Heart Risks Early in Study," *The Wall Street Journal*, 13 September 2006, p. A12.

77. Heather Won Tesoriero, "Merck's Possible Vioxx Successor Draws Mixed Results in Study," *The Wall Street Journal*, 14 August 2006, p. D6. See also press release,

<http://www.merck.com/newsroom/press_releases/financial/2006_0420.html> (visited August 24, 2006).

78. Gardiner Harris, "A Decisive Thumbs Down for a New Pain Medication," *The Wall Street Journal*, 13 April 2007, p. A14.

79. H. L. Mencken, "The Divine Afflatus," in *Prejudices: Second Series* (New York: Alfred Knopf, Borzoi Books, 1926), pp. 155–71, p. 158.

80. Charles Sanders Peirce, *Collected Papers*, eds. Charles Hartshorne, Paul Weiss, and (vols. 7 and 8) Arthur Burks (Cambridge: Harvard University Press, 1931–58). [References are by volume and paragraph number.] Peirce describes the "scientific attitude" as "a craving to know how things really are" (1.34), "an intense desire to find things out" (1.14), and the "Will to Learn" (5.583). See also Haack, "As for that phrase 'studying in a literary spirit' . . ." (1996), in Haack, *Manifesto of a Passionate Moderate* (n. 15), pp. 48–68.

81. Percy Bridgman, "Science, Materialism, and the Human Spirit," (1949), in Bridgman, *Reflections of a Physicist* (New York: Philosophical Library, 1955), pp. 452–72, pp. 456–57.

82. The week I wrote this paragraph, a press report on plagiarism problems in the department of mechanical engineering at Ohio University illustrated it: graduate students had copied chunks from earlier dissertations, and faculty, some of whom had supervised more than a hundred theses, hadn't read carefully enough to notice. The report quotes Michael Kalichman, Director of Research Ethics at the University of California, San Diego: "What is going to happen as these [students] become the next generation of faculty members?" Robert Tomsho, "Student Plagiarism Stirs Controversy at Ohio University," *The Wall Street Journal*, 18 August 2006, pp. A1, A10.

83. Graham et al., "Risk of Acute Myocardial Infarction and Sudden Cardiac Death in Patients Treated with Cyclo-oxygenase 2 Selective and Non-selective Non-steroidal Anti-inflammatory Drugs" (n. 58), p. 480.

84. Sarah Treffinger, "Cardiologist at Clinic to Lead Study of Painkillers," *Plain Dealer* (Cleveland), 14 December 2005, p. A1.

85. Nicholas Wade and Choe Sang-Hun, "Human Cloning Was All Faked, Koreans Report," *The New York Times*, 10 January 2006, section A. Bruce Flamm, "The Columbia University 'Miracle' Study," *Skeptical Inquirer* 28, no. 5 (September/October 2004): 25–31. Richard Horton, "Retraction: Non-Steroidal Drugs and the Risk of Oral Cancer: A Nested Case-control Study," *The Lancet* 367 (February 4–10, 2006): 382.

8

SCIENTIFIC SECRECY AND "SPIN"

The Sad, Sleazy Saga of the Trials of Remune

Science is, upon the whole, at present in a very healthy condition. It would not remain so if the motives of scientific men were lowered. The worst feature of the present state of things is that the great majority of the members of many scientific societies, and a large part of others, are men whose chief interest in science is as a means of gaining money. . . .

—C. S. Peirce (1901)[1]

[T]he present concentration of industrial interest in academic science is generating no small measure of concern about whether the academy is selling its soul.

—Barbara J. Culliton (1982)[2]

Entrepreneurialism is rampant in medicine today.

—Arnold Relman (1984)[3]

Entrepreneurial values, economic interests, and the promise of profits are shaping the scientific ethos.

—Dorothy Nelkin (1998)[4]

Today's universities are increasingly encouraging their scientists and doctors to be entrepreneurs and to commercialize their intellectual property. However, the collaboration between industry and academia . . . can easily end in tears.

—editorial in *The Lancet* (2000)[5]

[The industrialization of science] implies the establishment within academic science of a number of practices that are essentially foreign to its culture.

—John Ziman (2000)[6]

T he story is certainly a disturbing one: a drug company funds a large-scale clinical trial of its new AIDS therapy; when the results are unfavorable, the company tries to prevent their publication; when the researchers go ahead with publication anyway, the company seeks millions of dollars in damages; eventually, newspaper headlines tell us the company gets "zilch," but the arbitration proceedings are private, so beyond that we know—well, zilch; the same year, a multi-party suit is filed alleging that the firm had manipulated its stock price by misleading the public about the effectiveness of the drug;[7] four years later, with this suit still pending, the company website affirms that "the results of previous clinical trials demonstrate" that it "has the potential to slow the progression of HIV infection."[8]

Of course, when you look closely things are more complicated than they seem at first. But the complications themselves illustrate some important points about how the ramification of evidence may enable self-deception and obfuscation; about the differences between inquiry and advocacy; and about how secrecy and spin—the very obverse of the core scientific values of evidence-sharing and honest respect for evidence—can impede the progress of science.

1. THE TRIALS OF REMUNE

Since the 1970s the proportion of US "research and development" sponsored by the federal government has been declining, and the proportion sponsored by industry has risen—from 3 percent of all university research in 1970 to 7 percent in 2001—and now amounts to billions of dollars.[9] The dependence of medical research in universities on pharmaceutical-industry sponsorship has become a particular source of concern. "The sad, sleazy saga of the trials of Remune" vividly illustrates the kinds of pressure under which this dependence may put scientists; one such story among many, unusual only in how gross the pressure was, and how admirably stubborn the scientists concerned were in resisting it.

Remune is an AIDS therapy "based on whole HIV particles, stripped of a protein called gp120, and killed by irradiation and chemical treatment."[10] It was conceived by Jonas Salk, the pioneer of polio vaccination, and developed by Immune Response Corporation (IRC), the California biotech company he founded in 1987.[11] Perhaps because of the Salk connection, the drug is sometimes described as a vaccine against AIDS; but it is intended, not to prevent infection, but to boost the immune systems of patients already infected with HIV.[12]

My narrative will begin with approval of the first large-scale clinical trial of the drug by the Food and Drug Administration (FDA), and will follow the story from the early cessation of this clinical trial and Immune Response's efforts to suppress the results, through their publication in the *Journal of the American Medical Association* (*JAMA*) and the ensuing legal dispute between the researchers and their sponsors, to the present state of play with respect to the drug, and the company.

FDA approved the first large-scale study of Remune, funded by IRC, in February 1996. At the time, a diagnosis of AIDS was in effect a death sentence, and AIDS activists were understandably anxious that FDA not delay trials of any therapy that sounded promising; nevertheless, according to an FDA spokesman the advisory committee was "fraught with doubts" about the project, and split on whether to approve it. The chair, Dr. Stanley Lemon of the University of North Carolina, commented that he was "not at all excited about the data" he had seen, but would be "thrilled to be proven wrong."[13] IRC stock soared on news of FDA approval of the trial.[14]

The study began in March 1996, under lead researchers medical scientist Dr. James Kahn, of the University of California San Francisco (UCSF), and statistician Dr. Stephen Lagakos, of Harvard; data were to be collected by a team of researchers at seventy-seven hospitals nationwide. The trial eventually involved 2,527 volunteers, all of whose immune systems were already compromised by HIV, assigned at random to one of two groups. In a double-blind test, patients in one group were given injections of Remune every three months, and those in the other group were given injections of the adjuvant alone.[15] At the time, the FDA required that potential AIDS drugs show a decrease in progression of the disease or in death rates; in line with this, the Remune trial was designed to be sensitive to a 50 percent increase in survival rate attributable to the drug.[16]

Shortly after the trial began, however, the FDA's requirements were changed to allow the use of "surrogate markers," which meant that even if it wasn't shown to lower disease or death rates an AIDS drug could be approved if it was shown to decrease other factors associated with disease or death. Moreover, around the same time a new class of AIDS drugs, the protease inhibitors, was introduced; and as a result of their use the death rate from AIDS slowed from around 6 percent a year to less than 1 percent.[17] The trial design was quickly changed to include AIDS-related illnesses as well as deaths as end points; and participants were allowed also to use any anti-retroviral therapy they chose, including experimental treatments and protease inhibitors, or none at all.[18]

In May 1999, on the recommendation of a five-member Data Safety Monitoring Board (DSMB) selected to help review statistics on patients' responses, Drs. Kahn and Lagakos halted the trial.[19] According to Dr. Kahn, the reason was that preliminary data showed that the drug didn't work: in the first two years of the study fifty-three people in the Remune group had become sicker or died, and so had fifty-three in the control group.[20] According to the then-president and CEO of IRC, Dennis Carlo, the reason was that in view of the now lower expected death-rate from AIDS the sample was no longer large enough to test the effectiveness of the drug. According to Dr. Robert Schooley of the National Institutes of Health (NIH), the reason was that "[t]he study was doomed from the start because the whole method of treating the disease changed during the trial," making it futile to continue.[21]

Shortly after the Kahn-Lagakos study was halted, IRC fired nearly a third of its staff, and many others were forced to take pay cuts.[22] However, with Agouron, a unit of Pfizer to which it had licensed marketing rights for Remune the year before, IRC now initiated two additional Phase III surrogate-marker trials of the drug.[23] A year later, Dr. Kahn notified IRC that he intended to share his negative results with the Clinical Trials Group of the NIH, which had begun enrolling HIV-infected patients in a study of Remune. IRC executives assured Dr. Kahn that this was unnecessary, since the company had already supplied the information. According to Dr. Lagakos, however, NIH didn't have the full data until he gave it to them himself. Eventually, the NIH discontinued one of its Remune trials and substantially modified another.[24]

Dr. Kahn and his colleagues believed that they should publish their analysis of the results of their trial. But in January 2000 Dr. Ronald Moss, medical vice-president of IRC, wrote to Dr. Kahn that the company itself, along with a third-party clinical research outfit, should analyze the study data. Dr. Kahn was "flabbergasted" by this proposal, which he described as "completely unacceptable"; Dr. Lagakos, too, said it was "inappropriate and unacceptable." In July 2000, IRC's lawyer told Dr. Kahn that "data and analysis may be used and published only with IRC's consent. . . . IRC does not consent to your proposed publication";[25] and Dennis Carlo informed Dr. Kahn that "IRC is prepared to enforce its contractual rights," adding that if he were to make any statements suggesting that the company was not acting within its rights in this matter, IRC was prepared to take legal action against him.[26] When Drs. Kahn and Lagakos refused to accept this, the company refused to provide them with the results of participants' final checkups after the trial was halted, and insisted that the results of their own more favorable analysis of a subsample of 10 percent of the subjects whose blood had been tested more frequently should be included in any publication.[27]

In the November 2000 issue of the *JAMA*, Dr. Kahn and his colleagues published a paper based on the 90 to 95 percent of the study data to which they had access. (Had the DSMB not supplied Dr. Kahn with this data, he and his colleagues would presumably have been completely stymied.) This article acknowledged that Remune "elicited significant immunogenicity," but found no significant difference in this effect between the group as a whole and the subgroup on which IRC was placing so much weight—the 200 patients whose blood was tested every twelve weeks instead of every twenty-four. "The results of this trial," the paper concluded, "failed to demonstrate that the addition of HIV-1 Immunogen to ART [anti-retroviral therapy] conferred any effect on progression-free survival relative to that achievable by ART alone."[28]

It is normal practice for such papers to be circulated before publication to all those contributing to the study. But in this case, Dr. Kahn claimed, IRC had refused to provide him with contact information on all the participants; so rather than circulating the paper only to those for whom he had this information, he hadn't circulated it at all.[29] (IRC's Dr. Moss claimed that Dr. Lagakos had all the names and addresses.)[30] Dr. John Turner, the Philadelphia physician who had monitored the group of patients tested more frequently, was reportedly "floored when [he] found out they were coming out with a paper about which [he] knew nothing."[31] In an editorial accompanying Dr. Kahn's paper, the then-editor of *JAMA*, Dr. Catherine DeAngelis, said the journal had decided to publish this study because "the integrity of the research process must be protected and preserved";[32] and the deputy editor, Dr. Drummond Rennie, said the journal had decided to go ahead with publication to "prevent the bias that comes from reporting only those results favorable to sponsors' products."[33]

Some of the letters published in response to the article raised scientific objections (e.g., the trial didn't include true temporal variables, nor explore possible distinguishing characteristics of the subgroup whose response was more promising; there was unpublished data showing that Remune was immunogenic, but suggesting that the response was transient, with no effect on clinical outcomes; it might be the adjuvant, and not Remune, that prompted the response in the immune system). Other letters focused on the relation between the researchers and their sponsors: one, from Peter Lurie and Sidney Wolfe of the Citizens' Health Research Group in Washington, DC, noted that IRC had been accused of improper attempts to influence the presentation of data on Remune before, and in 1995 had even received a Warning Letter from the FDA when two subjects were found to have been excluded from a published article that claimed to include all subjects; another, from Donald M. Poretz of the Georgetown School of Medicine—who had been one of the investigators in the trial and, like Dr. Turner, was upset because he had not been asked to review the manuscript before publication—observed that "[t]he intense pressure on individuals at academic institutions to publish and on sponsoring companies to get their drugs on the market can sometimes produce tensions between the 2 parties, and if results are not favorable, disagreements can develop leading to disputes, innuendos, and even legal action."[34]

That, to put it mildly, is putting it mildly.

By 6:00 p.m. the evening before Dr. Kahn's article came out, IRC stock had fallen more than 19 percent in after-hours trading.[35] The company had spent about $191 million on Remune,[36] and had no other drug in such an advanced stage of development.[37] The vice president of IRC described *JAMA*'s involvement as "tabloid journalism" and Dr. Kahn's article as a "smear campaign." Expressing confidence that "the truth in the long run will come out,"[38] he insisted that the company tried to prevent publication only "because we think there was important information excluded" about the subset of participants whose blood was tested more frequently.[39] Dr. Kahn replied that IRC executives were acting like "bullies in a sandbox," and that their supposedly "important information" was the result of "data-dredging," selectively picking out the information favorable to their product.[40] IRC's analysis stressed that in this subset there was lowered viral load and increased T-cells at weeks 36, 48, 60, 84, 96, and 120; Dr. Kahn replied that "one cannot pick and choose data points to suit one's needs," and that the company was "manipulating data to try to have a positive outcome."[41]

Participants in the study, who now learned for the first time why it had been halted in 1999, expressed concern that they had not been informed of the unfavorable results sooner. IRC spokesperson Laura Hansen declined to comment, instead referring inquirers to the company's website, where numerous news releases about the benefits of Remune were posted. But Dr. Kahn observed that "you should tell [participants] all the information you know," especially since by enrolling in Remune studies they were disqualified from enrolling in many other clinical trials.[42] Indeed: They might have found a more effective treatment had they known Remune didn't work.

Agouron stood by Remune, and biotech stock analyst Alan Auerbach, who was advising clients to buy IRC stock, stood by Agouron: "Agouron/Pfizer is convinced [Remune] works via their analysis, and Pfizer has gotten a lot of drugs approved by the FDA," he commented, asking "[h]ow many drugs has Kahn brought to the FDA?"[43] "If there isn't [any effect on patients], why is Pfizer putting so much money into this? Are you telling me that Jim Kahn is smarter than Pfizer? I have a problem believing that." But Charles Engelberg, who was advising his clients to sell IRC, disagreed: "I've been following this since 1993 and the company has been guilty of massaging data all along. . . ."[44]

The sponsors' contract with Dr. Kahn's university called for binding arbitration in the event of a dispute. In September 2000 IRC had filed an action with the American Arbitration Association to block publication. Shortly after Dr. Kahn's paper appeared, the company filed an action accusing him of omitting favorable data and of violating an agreement to keep certain findings confidential, and demanding $7 to $10 million in damages. The university filed a counterclaim alleging that the company wrongfully withheld data from the researchers.[45]

In March 2000, while the company was disputing with Dr. Kahn over whether his results should be published, IRC stock had risen 43 percent on news that doctors testing Remune in Thailand—where the drug-approval process is "very informal"—would seek authorization from the Thai Minister of Public Health to market the drug.[46] On March 10, 2000, Agouron sold 166,000 shares in IRC for proceeds of $2.5 million.[47] In April 2001, the subset analysis IRC had wanted included in Dr. Kahn's article was published, under the authorship of Dr. Turner (but referring readers to Dr. Moss, at IRC's address, for correspondence) in the European journal *HIV Medicine*. This article concluded that "a beneficial effect of [Remune] was observed on viral load, CD4+ T cells, and HIV-specific immunity."[48] IRC stock rose 115 percent.[49] In May 2001 IRC issued preliminary results of a subset of sixty-six patients in a Spanish Phase II trial, stating that Remune "appeared to enhance allo-immune response along with HIV specific immune responses," and announced positive results from another, fifteen-patient, study.[50]

But in June 2001, IRC acknowledged that the Spanish DSMB had determined that Remune failed to slow the growth of the HIV virus in patients. The company's stock price dropped around 60 percent.[51] In July 2001 a multi-party suit was filed against IRC and Agouron Pharmaceutical for violation of the Securities Exchange Act of 1934, alleging that they withheld and misrepresented the results of clinical trials of Remune, "to artificially inflate the price of Immune stock," so as to enable IRC to complete a public offering of its shares.[52] The same month, Agouron dropped out of the development of Remune. Shares in IRC dropped another 44 percent.[53] On September 11 of that year, the result of the arbitration proceedings against Dr. Kahn and UCSF was reported: IRC had settled "without collecting a cent."[54] A year later, IRC had laid off more than half the workers at its headquarters "under a plan to cut costs and narrow its focus to what it sees as its most promising product," Remune; and Mr. Carlo had resigned as president and CEO.[55] By November 2002, the company was reported to be "close to going out of business."[56]

As of late August 2005, however—with the securities case against IRC (now with a number of new plaintiffs) still pending, and the drug still not approved by the FDA—press releases on the IRC website reported that the company had entered a Standby Equity Distribution Agreement with Cornell Capital Partners,

LP, which had committed to provide up to $15 million of funding for development of its products;[57] that at the July 2005 meeting of the International AIDS Society in Rio de Janeiro the company had presented two posters about the REMIT study, a continuation of the earlier Spanish trial, involving 39 patients; and that Remune is to be included in a new NIH trial, involving 92 patients, of the effects of various therapies in early stages of HIV infection: "[t]he Company believes that results of previous clinical trials demonstrate that REMUNE boosts HIV-specific responses and has the potential to slow the progression of HIV infection when used alone or in conjunction with antiretroviral therapy."[58]

However, acknowledging that its press release about the NIH trial includes "forward-looking statements" signalled by such terms as "could," "will," "might," "plan, "projection," etc., the company concedes that "[a]ctual results could vary from those expected due to a variety of risk factors, including whether the company will continue as a going concern," given, among other things, that it "has not succeeded in commercializing any drug."[59]

In March 2007, the Immune Response Corporation announced that a clinical study of its "investigational T-Cell Receptor peptide vaccine" for the treatment of multiple sclerosis had begun. Remune remained one of its "lead immune-based therapeutic product candidates," but had not been approved by any regulatory agency in any contry.[60] But in July of the same year the company announced that it had discontinued its HIV vaccine development program.[61] In August 2007, the securities fraud case against the company was settled.[62] As of January 8, 2008, the company (now also using the name "Orchestra Therapeutics") was still a going concern.[63]

Does Remune work? In a telephone conversation on December 18, 2004, Dr. Kahn told me that he had no doubt that his study established decisively that it doesn't.[64] Of course, even if I had all the available evidence, I would hardly be competent to judge; still, if I had to bet, I'd bet against it.

2. SOME MORALS OF THE STORY

The clinical trials of Remune illustrate both the potential pitfalls of experimental design, and the confusing complexities of evidence. It should come as no surprise if, in the early stages, the evidence regarding the effectiveness or otherwise of a new drug is ambiguous or unclear; for the design of a large-scale, long-term, multi-center drug study, which inevitably relies on a whole mesh of background assumptions, any of which *may* be mistaken, is a complicated matter in the best of circumstances. And in the present case the inevitable difficulties were compounded, epistemologically, practically, and morally, by the FDA's decision, shortly after the inception of the trial, to allow tests of "surrogate markers," and by the introduction of new therapies that significantly lowered death rates from AIDS. Looked at strictly from an epistemological point of view, one possibility might have been to consider starting again with a new design and a larger sample; but as Dr. Kahn told me, in his opinion the sample was "more than big enough." Another possibility might have been to leave the trial design unchanged, not allowing subjects to use other drugs; but of course moral considerations spoke against forbidding subjects to use the promising new therapies.

Again, the unhappy interaction between the researchers and their sponsors vividly illustrates the difference between genuine inquiry and advocacy research, and about how scientific inquiry can be hampered or perverted by pressure to transform it into boosterism for a product (or a policy). Such pressure damages the fragile social mechanisms that sustain the scientific ethos of honest investigation and encourage free exchange of ideas and information. Getting at the truth about Remune would have been hard enough if everyone involved had been trying their best to do just that; but IRC's efforts to prevent publication and to put their own spin on the results can't have failed to make an already scientifically hard task exponentially harder in other ways. Even though the company didn't succeed in preventing publication, they certainly managed to muddy the waters, and (very likely) wasted resources on new trials.

Of course, it's impossible to know for sure how exceptional, or how typical, the pressure exerted by IRC might be. As Marcia Angell observed, it is "common for companies that sponsor research to assert control over data," but because researchers so seldom stand up to their sponsors as Dr. Kahn did, "there is no way to know how many negative studies have been suppressed—or worse, how many negative studies were converted to positives."[65] But almost every day there is more reason to believe that the iceberg of corruption is sizable: Congress launches an investigation into financial connections between industry and the NIH; Pfizer is fined almost half-a-million dollars for paying physicians to promote its anti-seizure drug Neurontin; Eliot Spitzer, former attorney general of the State of New York, accuses GlaxoSmithKline of hiding evidence that its drug Paxil can trigger suicide; it is revealed that Merck knew the dangers of Vioxx well before it pulled the drug from the market; and so on.[66]

Entanglement with business interests undoubtedly poses a threat to the scientific ethos, and in consequence to the advancement of science. And the advancement of science is undoubtedly of value: because the sciences have revealed so much about the world; because they represent such a remarkable amplification and refinement of the human talent for inquiry; and because of the practical benefits they may bring. This doesn't mean, and I have been careful not to say, that the advancement of science is an overriding value: for example, some ways of procuring evidence, desirable as that evidence might be from a scientific point of view, are unacceptable morally;[67] and regulation of potentially dangerous scientific work is prudentially justified if the benefits outweigh the costs. It *does* mean, however, that the progress of science is not something to be lightly compromised or surrendered.

But how, specifically, is such compromise or surrender to be resisted? Acutely conscious of F. H. Bradley's stern warning that "[i]n the practical sphere the man of mere theory is an useless and dangerous pedant,"[68] it is with more than a little trepidation that I venture my brief concluding thoughts.

The Remune story raises a great tangle of issues: about the FDA, about patent law, about legal sequestering, about journals' financial disclosure policies, and so on. Here I shall comment on just one: university-industry collaborations.

Much attention has been focused on universities' conflict-of-interest policies, their guidelines about collaborative research contracts, etc. Dr. DeAngelis mentions specifically the potential distorting effects of sponsors' gifts and the speaking and consulting fees that sponsors offer researchers;[69] David Korn, senior vice president for biomedical and health sciences at the Association of American Medical Colleges, suggests that medical centers negotiate for control over the data when they accept sponsors' business. Ronald Collins, director of the "Integrity in Science" project at the Center for Science in the Public Interest, focuses on the threat posed by agreements specifying that any disputes go to arbitration.[70]

However, an editorial in *Nature Immunology* comments that while "[c]linical trials sponsored by a product's developer are inherently conflicted, . . . [y]et industry funding is necessary, as public funding for clinical research is inadequate."[71] An editorial in *Nature Biotechnology* asks: "When is it reasonable for academics to expect total freedom over the data they have gathered on a company's behalf, especially if they have signed a confidentiality agreement?"[72] And Dr. DeAngelis observes that "[b]alance must be maintained between the need for research projects to be reasonably funded and performed by the best possible investigators and the relative paucity of public funds for clinical research."[73]

The stress has been on "managing" the problem; and the result has been a patchwork of compromises. Yale will not accept any restriction on publication except for short delays to allow a sponsor to apply for a patent or license;[74] Harvard will not allow a scientist who owns more than $20,000 in publicly traded stock to serve as a principal investigator on research grants funded by the same company, nor to receive more than $10,000 annually in consulting fees or honoraria from companies that sponsor his research. Stanford sets no fixed limits on stock ownership or royalties, but requires that faculty who own more than $100,000 of stock or 0.5 percent of a company notify the university, which then decides cases-by-case whether any restrictions are needed; and MIT regulations focus on whether a faculty member's holdings are large enough to influence stock price, rather than on the dollar amount.[75]

A study of a hundred institutions of higher education from August 1998 to February 2000 found that 55% required disclosure of financial interests from all faculty, 45% only from principal investigators; only 19% set explicit limits on faculty financial interests in corporate-sponsored research; only 12% specified what delay in publication was permissible; and only 4% prohibited student involvement in work sponsored by a company in which a faulty member had a financial interest.[76] Management of conflict and penalties for non-disclosure are invariably discretionary; and it seems that universities rarely ask researchers to forgo financial interests: a study of thousands of disclosure forms at the University of Washington found that the university required researchers to give up financial interests in only 8 of the 321 cases that underwent the university's review process.[77] The authors of a national survey concluded that "academic institutions rarely ensure that their investigators have full participation in the design of the trials, unimpeded access to trial data, and the right to publish their findings."[78]

The University of California, San Francisco's agreement with IRC *did*, in fact, ensure Dr. Kahn's right to publish his findings (subject only to his not disclosing confidential information provided by the company). At Dr. Kahn's suggestion—though only after several, increasingly strongly worded requests to the relevant office at UCSF—I received copies of UCSF's template agreement; the preliminary agreement with IRC; the "Investigational Site Agreement" superseding this earlier agreement; and a document entitled "Protocol 806,"[79] exhibit A of the governing agreement. This provides that IRC should have at least four weeks' advance notice before the submission of any results for publication or presentation "[t]o permit the Immune Response Corporation to delete any proprietary information contained therein"; and that "[p]ublication of the results of this trial is the responsibility of the Steering and Publication Committee," one member of which was to be the Medical Director of IRC. "[I]s the responsibility of" is not amplified in any way; however, the same paragraph continues: "[a]pproval by the Sponsor otherwise [i.e., otherwise than with respect to disclosure of proprietary material supplied by the Sponsor] is not required prior to publication."[80]

All the same, a study of faculty financial relationships with industry at UCSF published in *JAMA* alongside Dr. Kahn's paper concluded that—even though UCSF is subject to relatively stringent state and campus policies—the university committee on relations with industry, which since 1980 has reviewed cases of possible conflict of interest, works "to accommodate all but the most overtly conflicting relationships in the interest of encouraging its faculty and, presumably, encouraging future outside investment in the university."[81]

If they had the will, universities could significantly mitigate the threat to the scientific ethos; but only if—recognizing that the money offered by private sponsors can be a Trojan horse—they are prepared to refuse such money when the terms on which it is offered pose unacceptable restrictions on freedom of inquiry, sharing of evidence, etc.[82] But it isn't clear that they *do* have the will: academic scientists, aware that their professional survival depends on their ability to obtain grants, are likely to be reluctant to hamper colleagues' efforts to secure research funds; more fundamentally, universities are likely to be reluctant to risk putting lucrative opportunities for collaboration with industry in serious jeopardy.

Current UCSF guidelines aver that "[i]n pursuing relationships with industry, the University must keep the public trust and maintain institutional independence and integrity to permit faculty and students to pursue learning and research freely"; and preclude "assigning to extramural sources the right to keep or make final decisions about what may be published," or allowing a sponsor to "exercise any editorial control." Excellent. However, they also describe the university as "exploring innovative . . . approaches to assure support of worthy research and provide significant contributions to . . . scholarship . . . , [and] *that [is] responsive to industry interests.*"[83]

Sheldon Krimsky tells us that Jean Mayer, former president of Tufts, used to joke that "[t]he only thing wrong with tainted money is [that] there t'aint enough of it."[84] It's a nice pun; all the same, it brings Thorstein Veblen's dryly devastating analysis of "the higher learning in America" (1919) nearly irresistibly to mind:

> [T]he intrusion of business principles in the universities goes to weaken and retard the pursuit of learning, and therefore to defeat the ends for which a university is maintained.

and:

> The run of the facts is, in effect, a compromise between the scholar's ideals and those of business, in such a way that the ideals of scholarship are losing ground in an uncertain and varying degree, before the pressure of businesslike exigencies.[85]

I am sorry to say that our universities' disturbing drift to the culture of money shows no signs of abating; and that their present preoccupation with grantsmanship over real achievement, and their eagerness to indulge in boosterism and spin on their own behalf, leave me far from optimistic that they can be relied on to hold the line.

NOTES

1. Charles Sanders Peirce, *Collected Papers*, eds. Charles Hartshorne, Paul Weiss, and (volumes 7 and 8) Arthur Burks (Cambridge: Harvard University Press, 1931–58). References are by volume and paragraph number; this passage is from Peirce's review of Karl Pearson, *The Grammar of Science* (1901).

2. Barbara J. Culliton, "The Academic-Industrial Complex," *Science* 216 (1982): 960–62, p. 960.

3. Arnold Relman, "Dealing With Conflicts of Interest," *New England Journal of Medicine* 310 (May 3, 1984): 1182–83, p. 1182.

4. Dorothy Nelkin, "The Performance of Science," *The Lancet* 352 (September 12, 1998): 893.

5. Editorial, "Medicine's Rude Awakening to the Commercial World," *The Lancet* 355 (March 11, 2000): 857.

6. John Ziman, *Real Science: What It Is, and What It Means* (Cambridge: Cambridge University Press, 2000), p. 79.

7. See *In re Immune Response Secs. Litig.*, 375 F. Supp. 2d 983, 983 (S.D. Cal. 2005). The case originated in ten separate class action suits; the lead plaintiff, Florence Hirschfeld, filed her case on July 10, 2001: *Hirschfeld v. Immune Response Corp.*, No. 01-CV-1237 (S.D. Cal. 2001).

8. Press Release, Immune Response Corporation, 29 March 2005, <http://www.imnr.com/news/2005/2005Mar29.htm>. Site is no longer available. The Immune Response Corporation is now trading under the name "Orchestra Therapeutics"; see n. 63 below.

9. Joshua A. Newberg and Richard L. Dunn, "Keeping Secrets in the Campus Lab: Law, Values, and Rules of Engagement for Industry-University R & D Partnerships," *American Business Law Journal* 39 (2002): 187–240, p. 193; Sheldon Krimksy, *Science in the Private Interest: Has the Lure of Profits Corrupted Biomedical Research?* (Lanham, MD: Rowman and Littlefield, 2003), pp. 27–32.

10. Paul Smaglik, "Reservoirs Dog AIDS Therapy," *Nature* 405 (2000): 270–72, p. 272.

11. "The Immune Response Corporation. Corporate Snapshot," <http://www.imnr.com/corp/corporate.htm>. Site is no longer available. The Immune Response Corporation is now trading under the name "Orchestra Therapeutics"; see n. 63 below.

12. Thomas H. Maugh, "Firm Disputes Handling of Drug Study," *Los Angeles Times*, 1 November 2000, p. A3.

13. Amended Complaint, *Hirschfeld v. Immune Response Corp.* (n. 7), pp. 7–8 (henceforth: "Hirschfeld Complaint").

14. "Stock Comment—New York," *Market Letter*, 26 February 1996.

15. James O. Kahn et al., "Evaluation of HIV-1 Immunogen, an Immunologic Modifier, Administered to Patients Infected with HIV Having 300 to 549 10^6/L CD4 Cell Counts: A Randomized Controlled Trial," *Journal of the American Medical Association* 284, no. 17 (2000): 2193–2202, pp. 2193–94.

16. Maugh, "Firm Disputes Handling of Drug Study" (n. 12); Kahn et al., "Evaluation of HIV-1 Immunogen" (n. 15), p. 2195.

17. Maugh, "Firm Disputes Handling of Drug Study" (n. 12).

18. John S. James, "Bitter Publication Dispute on Remune Study: More Than Meets the Eye?", *AIDS Treatment News*, 3 November 2000, p. 4.

19. Maugh, "Firm Disputes Handling of Drug Study" (n. 12).

20. Hirschfeld Complaint (n. 13), p. 7.

21. Maugh, "Firm Disputes Handling of Drug Study" (n. 12).

22. Maugh, "Firm Disputes Handling of Drug Study" (n. 12).

23. Derhsing Lai and Taff Jones, "Remune Immune Response," *Current Opinion in Investigational Drugs* 3 (2002): 391–98, p. 391.

24. Penni Crabtree, "Scientists Say Firm Tried to Gag Them; Tell of Releasing AIDS Vaccine Data," *San Diego Union-Tribune*, 7 November 2000, p. B1.

25. Thomas M. Burton, "Unfavorable Drug Study Sparks Battle Over Publication of Results," *The Wall Street Journal*, 1 November 2000, p. B1.

26. Crabtree, "Scientists Say Firm Tried to Gag Them" (n. 24).

27. Katherine S. Mangan, "Company Seeks $10 Million from Scientist and University," *Chronicle of Higher Education* (November 17, 2000): A48, A50.

28. Kahn et al., "Evaluation of an HIV-1 Immunogen" (n. 15).

29. Maugh, "Firm Disputes Handling of Drug Study" (n. 12); Kahn et al., "Evaluation of an HIV-1 Immunogen" (n. 15), p. 2202; James O. Kahn and Stephen Lagakos, "In Reply," *Journal of the American Medical Association* 285, no. 17 (May 2, 2001): 2193–95, p. 2194.

30. Maugh, "Firm Disputes Handling of Drug Study" (n. 12).

31. Sabin Russell, "Firm that Paid for UCSF Study Seeks Damages," *San Francisco Chronicle*, 1 November 2000, p. A1.

32. Catherine DeAngelis, "Conflict of Interest and the Public Trust," *Journal of the American Medical Association* 284, no. 17 (2000): 2237–38, p. 2238.

33. Scott Gottlieb, "Firm Tried to Block Report on Failure of AIDS Vaccine," *British Medical Journal* 321 (2000): 1173.

34. Letters, *Journal of the American Medical Association* 285, no. 17 (2001): 2191–98.

35. Penni Crabtree, "Analysts Try to Sort out Flap over Remune," *San Diego Union-Tribune*, 1 November 2000, p. C1.

36. Cheryl Clark and Penni Crabtree, "Carlsbad Firm under Fire on Vaccine Study," *San Diego Union-Tribune*, 1 November 2000, p. A1.

37. Crabtree, "Analysts Try to Sort out Flap over Remune" (n. 35).

38. Clark and Crabtree, "Carlsbad Firm under Fire on Vaccine Study" (n. 36).

39. Gottlieb, "Firm Tried to Block Report on Failure of AIDS Vaccine" (n. 33).

40. Russell, "Firm That Paid for UCSF Study Seeks Damages" (n. 31).

41. Carol Cruzan Morton, "Company, Researchers Battle Over Data Access," *Science* 290, no. 5494 (November 10, 2000): 1063; Russell, "Firm That Paid for UCSF Study Seeks Damages" (n. 31).

42. Cheryl Clark, "A Medical and Ethical Quandary: Fallout Over Vaccine," *San Diego Union-Tribune*, 4 November 2000, p. A1.

43. Crabtree, "Analysts Try to Sort out Flap over Remune" (n. 35).

44. Eric Niler, "Company, Academics Argue over Data," *Nature Biotechnology* 18 (2000): 1235.

45. Clark and Crabtree, "Carlsbad Firm under Fire on Vaccine Study" (n. 36). The American Arbitration Association is a nonprofit group offering settlements without the cost, but also without some of the safeguards, of a court case: proceedings are private, conducted without a jury, and cannot be appealed.

46. Rhonda L. Rundle, "Immune Response Stocks Soar 43% as Thai Doctors Back AIDS Drug," *The Wall Street Journal*, 24 March 2000, p. B6.

47. Hirschfeld Complaint (n. 13), p. 7.

48. John L. Turner et al., "The Effects of an HIV-1 Immunogen (Remune) on Viral Load, CD4 Cell Counts and HIV-specific Immunity in a Double-blind, Randomized, Adjuvant-controlled Subset Study in HIV Infected Subjects Regardless of Concomitant Antiviral Drugs," *HIV Medicine* 2 (2001): 68–77.

49. Penni Crabtree, "Analysis Boosts Carlsbad Biotech: Immune Response Stock Surges with AIDS Drug Results," *San Diego Union-Tribune*, 24 April 2001, p. C1.

50. Hirschfeld Complaint (n. 13), p. 14.

51. Hirschfeld Complaint (n. 13), p. 15.

52. Hirschfeld Complaint (n. 13), p. 2.

53. "Immune Response Stock Falls After Pfizer Ends Deal," *New York Times*, 7 July 2003, p. C3.

54. "Zilch for Maker in AIDS Drug Suit," *San Francisco Chronicle*, 11 September 2001, p. A10.

55. "Immune Response Corp. : Company Lays Off Workers, Shuffles Senior Management," *The Wall Street Journal*, 10 September 2002.

56. Morning Edition: "Company founded by the late Dr. Jonas Salk close to going out of business," NPR radio broadcast, 22 November 2002.

57. Press Release, Immune Response Corporation, "The Immune Response Corporation Signs a $15 Million Financing Agreement" (July 18, 2005), <http://www.imnr.com/news/2005/2005Jul18.htm>. Site is no longer available. The Immune Response Corporation is now trading under the name "Orchestra Therapeutics"; see n. 63 below.

58. Press Release, the Immune Response corporation, "The Immune Response Corporation Presents REMUNE Data at the International AIDS Society Meeting in Rio" (July 27, 2005), <http://www.imnr.com/news/2005/2005Jul27.htm>.

59. Press Release (July 27, 2005) (n. 58).

60. <www.medicalnewstoday.com>, March 8, 2007 (last visited January 8, 2008).

61. "Orchestra Discontinuing HIV Vaccine Programme," ESPICOM Business Intelligence Ltd., July 19, 2007.

62. In re: Immune Response Securities Litigation, Master File No. 01-CV-1237-J (Wme) (August 8, 2007).

63. "Orchestra Therapeutics, Inc.," <http://galenet.galegroup.com.servlet/BCRC

?vrsn=1622locID=miami_richter&3rchtp=glbe...> (last visited January 8, 2008). See also, "The Immune Response Corporation Announces Rebranding to Reflect Expanded Focus on Treatment of Autoimmune Diseases," PR Newswire, <http://www.prnewswire .com/cgi-bin/stories.pl?ACCT=104&STORY=/www/story/04-04-2007/0004559374 &EDATE=>.

64. Telephone conversation with S. H., December 18, 2004.

65. Mangan, "Company Seeks $10 Million from Scientist and University" (n. 27).

66. Shannon Brownlee, "Bitter Medicine," *Mother Jones* (September-October 2004): 83–87, reviewing Marcia Angell, *The Truth About Drug Companies: How They Deceive Us and What to Do About It* (New York: Random House, 2004) and Jerome Kassirer, *On the Take: How Big Business Is Corrupting American Medicine* (New York: Oxford University Press, 2004). Anna Wilde Matthews, "House Panel Grills FDA, Drug Firms," *Wall Street Journal*, 10 September 2004, p. B5. Haack, "The Integrity of Science: What It Means, Why It Matters," pp. 103–27 in this volume.

67. E.g., and quite to the present purpose, testing an unproven AIDS vaccine on healthy patients whom you then deliberately expose to AIDS.

68. F. H. Bradley, *Ethical Studies* (London: Henry S. King & Co., 1876), p. 204.

69. DeAngelis, "Conflict of Interest and the Public Trust" (n. 32), p. 2237.

70. Quoted in Mangan, "Company Seeks $10 Million from Scientist and University" (n. 27).

71. "Collaborative Conflicts," *Nature Immunology* 1, no. 6 (2000): 449.

72. *Nature Biotechnology* 18, no. 2 (December 2000): 1223.

73. DeAngelis, "Conflict of Interest and the Public Trust" (n. 32).

74. Yale University Faculty Handbook, 2002, 102, available at http://www.yale .edu/provost/handbook/faculty_handbook.pdf.

75. Krimsky, *Science in the Private Interest* (n. 9), pp. 130, 48.

76. Mildred K. Cho et al., "Policies on Faulty Conflicts of Interest at U.S. Universities," *Journal of the American Medical Association* 284, no. 17 (2002): 2203–2209, p. 2203.

77. David Wickert, "UW Seldom Cuts Researcher, Corporate Ties," *News Tribune* (Tacoma, WA), 14 October 2002, p. A10.

78. Kevin A. Schulman et al., "A National Survey of Provisions in Clinical-Trial Agreements Between Medical Schools and Industry Sponsors," *New England Journal of Medicine* 374, no. 17 (October 24, 2002): 1335–40, p. 1339.

79. My colleague William Widen helped me sort through the material and identify, from internal clues, the relation between the preliminary and superseding agreements, etc.

80. *Clinical Endpoint Study, Protocol Number 806: A Multi-Center, Double-blind, Phase III, Adjuvant-Controlled Study of the Effect of 10 Units of HIV-Immunogen Compared to IFA Alone Every 12 Weeks on AIDS-Free Survival in Subjects With HIV Infection and CD4 T Lymphocytes Between 300 and 549 Cells/UL Regardless of Concomitant HIV Therapies* (signed February 15, 1996).

81. Elizabeth Boyd and Lisa A. Bero, "Assessing Faculty Financial Relationships with Industry: A Case Study," *Journal of the American Medical Association* 284, no. 17 (November 1, 2000): 2209–15.

82. This is not to suggest that *only* private funding poses such problems. See for example Bernard Wysocki Jr., "As Universities Get Billions in Grants, Some See Abuses," *The Wall Street Journal*, 16 August 2005, pp. A1, A10 (reporting numerous instances of alleged misuse of federal grant money).

83. Guidelines on University-Industry Relations, June 6, 1989, available at <http://www.ucop.edu/raohomecgmemos/89-20.html>; and Frequently Asked Questions, available at <http://www.research.ucsf.edu/iedFAQ.asp>. Last visited December 20, 2004; paper copy on file with the author.

84. Krimsky, *Science in the Private Interest* (n. 9), p. 47.

85. Thorstein Veblen, *The Higher Learning in America* (1919: Stanford, CA: Academic Reprints, 1954), pp. 224, 190.

9

TRUTH AND JUSTICE, INQUIRY AND ADVOCACY, SCIENCE AND LAW

No one will deny that the law should in some way effectively use expert knowledge wherever it will aid in settling disputes. The only question is as to how it can do so best.

—Judge Learned Hand (1901)[1]

Jeremy Bentham writes passionately of "Injustice, and her handmaid falsehood."[2] His splendid metaphor should remind us—if we need reminding—that substantive justice requires factual truth;[3] it really *matters* whether this witness's supposedly "recovered" memory of a crime is genuine, whether the defendant really is the person who committed the crime, whether the plaintiff's injury was caused by his own carelessness or by a defect in this manufacturer's tire or seat belt or lawn chair, whether it was this chemical exposure that promoted the plaintiff's cancer, and so on.[4]

In determining factual truth, in both criminal cases and civil, courts very often need to call on scientists: on toxicologists and tool-mark examiners, epidemiologists and engineers, serologists and psychiatrists, experts on PCBs and experts on paternity, experts on rape trauma syndrome and experts on respiratory disorders, experts on blood, on bullets, on battered women—experts, in fact, on just about every subject imaginable. For, as science has grown, so too has the dependence of the legal system on scientific testimony. Such testimony can be a powerful tool for justice; but it can also be a powerful source of confusion—not to mention of opportunities for opportunism.

Who could have imagined, for example, when DNA was first identified as the genetic material more than half a century ago, that DNA analysis would by now have come to play so large a role in the criminal justice system, and in the public perception of the law? At first, after DNA "fingerprinting" made its way into US legal proceedings in 1987, it was strenuously contested in the courts; but as its solidity, and its power to enable justice, became unmistakable, the "DNA Wars" gradually died down. By now DNA testing has not only helped convict numerous rapists and murderers, but also exonerated many convicted prisoners, including a significant number on death row.[5] In at least one instance, it has both exonerated and convicted the same person: in 1992, after serving nearly 11 years of a 25- to 50-year sentence for rape, Kerry Kotler was released when newly-conducted DNA tests established his innocence; less than three years after his release, he was charged with another rape—and this time convicted on the basis of DNA analysis identifying him as the perpetrator. Even so, many problems remain: police officers and forensic scientists make mistakes, honest or otherwise; juries misunderstand the significance of random-match probabilities, or can't combine them with information about the likelihood that a sample was mishandled; criminals misdirect investigators by planting someone else's DNA; inmates request DNA testing in hopes of creating confusion and raising factitious doubts about their guilt; etc.

And who could have imagined, when Hugo Münsterberg urged in his 1908 *Essays on Psychology and Crime* that US courts follow the European example of looking to the work of experimental psychologists on eyewitnesses, memory, etc.,[6] that such work would by now have proven so useful—or that testimony of supposedly repressed and recovered memories would have become the subject of heated battles in the courtroom, in the press, and in the academy? In the mid-1980s, testimony of recovered memories was crucial in such high-profile trials as the McMartin Preschool case, one of the longest and most expensive US criminal trials ever. The kindergarten teachers at the McMartin School were eventually acquitted of the numerous charges of ritual sexual abuse of the children in their care; and by the mid-1990s it seemed that the skepticism about recovered memories expressed by experimental psychologists like Elizabeth Loftus was vindicated. But recently the "Memory Wars" flared up again, this time in claims against Catholic priests accused of sexual abuse of young people.

Ever since there have been scientific witnesses, lawyers and legal scholars have had their doubts about them. In an 1858 ruling, the US Supreme Court observed that "experience has shown that the opposite opinions of persons professing to be experts may be obtained in any amount";[7] in 1874, John Ordronaux commented in *The American Journal of Insanity* that "[i]f Science, for a consideration, can be induced to prove anything a litigant needs . . . , then Science is fairly open to the charge of venality and perjury, rendered the more base by the disguise of natural truth in which she robes herself."[8] In 1893, Charles Himes wrote that experts "are selected on account of their ability to express a favorable opinion, which, there is great reason to believe is in many instances the result alone of employment and the bias arising out of it."[9] More than a century later, Peter Huber was sounding a similar theme, complaining that "junk science"—"data dredging, wishful thinking, truculent dogmatism, and, now and again, outright fraud"—was flooding the courts.[10]

Some scientists concur. In her study of the silicone breast-implant fiasco, *Science on Trial*, Marcia Angell complained that "[e]xpert witnesses may wear white coats, be called 'doctor,' purport to do research, and talk scientific jargon. But too often they are merely adding a veneer to a foregone, self-interested conclusion";[11] and in her exposé of flimsy psychiatric and clinical testimony, experimental psychologist Margaret Hagen writes of "charlatans and greedy frauds."[12] But others think the problem is, rather, that jurors, attorneys, and judges are too illiterate scientifically to discriminate sound science from charlatanism. Norman Levitt, for example, commenting on the "noisome travesty" of the O. J. Simpson trial, complains that "the basic principles of statistical inference were opaque to all concerned except the witnesses themselves. The lawyers . . . , the judge, the dozens of commentators . . . and certainly the woozy public—all seemed utterly ignorant as to what . . . statistical independence might mean. . . . All the other scientific issues encountered the same combination of neglect and evasion."[13]

There surely are venal and incompetent scientists; and there surely are scientifically ignorant and credulous jurors, attorneys, and judges. But the familiar complaints gloss over many complexities. Flawed scientific testimony may be based on solid science misapplied by a poorly run laboratory, or on serious but highly speculative science, or on sloppily conducted scientific work, or on pseudo-scientific mumbo jumbo; or may be a matter of weak or scanty evidence overemphatically presented. Bias may be due to an expert's greed, his desire to feel important or to help the police or a sympathetic plaintiff, his undiscriminating conservativism about new and radical-sounding ideas, or his undiscriminating attraction to the novel or the radical. Failures of understanding may be due to jurors' or judges' or attorneys' inability to follow complex statistical reasoning, or their ignorance of the controls needed in this or that kind of experiment or study, or their over-deference to science, or their resentment of what they perceive as scientific elitism. Or the problem may simply be their feeling that *someone* should compensate the victim of an awful disease or injury, *someone* should be punished for a horrible crime. Most to the present purpose, the familiar complaints fail to diagnose the deep tensions between science and the law that lie behind the problems in handling scientific testimony.

Peter Schuck describes the interactions of the law with science and with politics as a kind of "multiculturalism," while Steven Goldberg writes of the "culture clash" of law and science in America.[14] But the "two cultures" model is in some respects potentially misleading; "the nature of science and the culture of law" might be a better way to put it. For, though science surely is, among other things, a social institution, scientific inquiry arises from a desire to understand and control natural phenomena, and so is responsible to the character of the world it investigates, as well as constrained by the cognitive powers and limitations of human inquirers; and while details of its practice and etiquette no doubt vary with time and place, science is at its core essentially the same the world over. Legal systems, on the other hand, arise in response to conflict, to disputes, and though no doubt broadly constrained by facts about human nature and society, are largely the product of convention, coming into existence only because of human institutional practices; and they are local, specific to a time and place, in a way that science is not.

The focus here will be on the two kinds of tension between the nature of science and the culture of law signaled by my title: between the adversarialism of the US legal culture, and the quite different procedures of the sciences—as a result of which, I shall argue, the law often gets less from science than science could give; and between the legal concern for prompt and final resolutions, and the open-ended fallibilism of the sciences—as a result of which the law often asks more of science than science could give.

"Science," as I construe it, picks out a loose federation of kinds of inquiry; "law," on the other hand, *Webster's* dictionary tells us, refers to "a body of customs, practices, or rules of conduct recognized as binding or enforced by a controlling authority." It is important not to overstate the contrast. A scientific investigation is an attempt to arrive at the truth of some question; but so, too, it is often said, is a trial. In a 1966 ruling the US Supreme Court averred that "[t]he basic purpose of a trial is the determination of truth";[15] one of the avowed goals of the Federal Rules of Evidence is "that the truth be ascertained"; in her introduction to the 1996 National Institute of Justice Report on DNA evidence, then-Attorney General Janet Reno affirmed that "[o]ur system of criminal justice is best described as a search for truth."[16]

But it is no less important to understate the contrast, to acknowledge, with Justice Blackmun, the "important differences between the quest for truth in the courtroom and the quest for truth in the laboratory."[17] At a trial a jury is asked to decide whether guilt or liability has been established to the desired degree of proof. This is a very special kind of inquiry into a very special kind of proposition, and is constrained not only by the demands of evidence but also by considerations of principle and policy: that it is worse to convict the innocent than to free the guilty; that constitutional rights must be observed;[18] that people should not be discouraged from making repairs which, if made earlier, might have prevented the events for which they are being sued;[19] and so forth. Moreover, the procedures of a trial are quite unlike those of ordinary scientific or historical inquiry, or even of investigative journalism or detective work; as is the very special division of labor inherent in the adversarial system, where competing advocates, held to legally proper conduct by a judge, present the evidence on the basis of which a jury is to arrive at its verdict.

Scientists, like historians or detectives, are by profession inquirers. Inquiry is an attempt to discover the truth of some question or questions; so the obligation of a scientist, *qua* inquirer, is to seek out all the evidence he can, to assess its worth as impartially as possible, to draw conclusions only if and as the evidence warrants doing so—and, when the available evidence is inadequate, to try, acknowledging that at present he simply doesn't know, to get better evidence.[20] Attorneys, by contrast, like lobbyists or clergymen, are by profession not inquirers, but advocates. Advocacy is an attempt to make a case for the truth of some proposition or propositions; and so the obligation of an attorney, *qua* advocate, is to seek out evidence favoring the proposition(s) in question, to present it as persuasively as possible, and to play down, or explain away, unfavorable evidence—or to look for legal grounds for its exclusion.

Once again, it is important neither to overstate nor to understate the contrast. Science is the work of many people, both within and across generations. Often it is cooperative; but sometimes it is competitive, with proponents of rival theories or approaches seeking out the flaws and difficulties in a competing theory that its proponents are motivated to play down or ignore. Such competition can be a real spur to intellectual effort; as with James Watson's (probably exaggerated) perception that Linus Pauling and his team were racing against Francis Crick and himself to solve the structure of DNA. But what Watson wanted wasn't simply to beat out Pauling; it was *to discover the truth about DNA* before Pauling did. Even when science is at its most competitive, its procedures are very far from the adversarial procedures of a trial: there is no real analogue of the legal division of labor between attorneys, judge, and jury;

and scientists' competition for priority is very different from attorneys' competition to win a case.

As C. S. Peirce observed in a lecture of 1898, the idea of science is to keep working at a question, sometimes for generation after generation, until the truth is finally attained.[21] By now, there is a vast body of scientific knowledge, well warranted by evidence, and unlikely to be overturned. But many, many scientific questions are as yet unanswered (not to mention those as yet unaskable), and not all scientific theories are well supported by good evidence: most get discarded as the evidence turns out against them; virtually all are at first only tenuously supported speculations; and even the best warranted are in principle subject to revision should new evidence demand it. For preparedness to revise even the most entrenched claim in the face of unfavorable evidence is essential to scientific inquiry; as is agnosticism, a willingness to admit that you just don't know. In the law, however, a judgment must be reached—a "quick, final, and binding" judgment, in Justice Blackmun's words[22]—however weak or defective the available evidence may be. Peirce comments that this is why the law needs standards of proof; it is also why the law needs statutes of limitations, restrictions on the introduction of new evidence, and final courts of appeal.

Because of the tension of fallibilism with finality, the legal system sometimes asks more of science than science can give, demanding definite answers to scientific questions when no such answers are yet to be had: when courts need an answer to some scientific question (does PCB exposure promote the development of small-cell lung cancer? does this minuscule sample of blood come from the victim? do silicone breast-implants promote systemic connective-tissue disease?), there may still be reasonable disagreement among scientists in the relevant field, or agreement that no warranted answer is yet available; and when a warranted answer *is* available, it may be legally too late—this is new evidence, no longer admissible, the period within which you may prosecute or sue has elapsed, etc. And because of the tension of inquiry with adversarialism, the legal system sometimes gets less from science than science could give, a contrived appearance of scientific controversy instead of the well-warranted scientific answer that is available; for attorneys are motivated by the demands of their profession to seek out experts willing to shade or select the evidence as a case demands, and may encourage maverick, marginal, or less-than-honest scientists into the lucrative business of the professional expert witness—perhaps keeping scientific disputes legally alive long after the scientific community has come to see them as pretty firmly settled.

So it is hardly surprising that it has proven difficult to harness science to the US legal culture, and in particular to domesticate scientific testimony by legal rules of admissibility.

Courts have always needed to determine matters of fact. But in early medieval times "proof was not an attempt to convince the judges; it was an appeal to the supernatural. . . . The common modes of proof [were] oath and ordeal"; for example, in an action for debt a defendant might be required to prove his claim that he owed nothing by swearing to it, and bringing in "oath-helpers"—also known as "con-jurors"—to swear that *his* oath was not perjured.[23] "Proof," here, has its old sense, "test"; and tests by oath and ordeal were based on the assumption that God would punish those who swore falsely, would ensure that an innocent man's arm was not scalded if he plunged it into boiling water, and so forth. After 1215, however, when the fourth Lateran Council prohibited priests from taking part in such tests, courts gradually came to rely on other methods.

In early English jury trials, rather than witnesses being called, jurors could go around and investigate for themselves and, in cases where specialized knowledge was required, jurors might be selected for their expertise—e.g., a jury of hatters when the defendant was accused of selling badly made caps; or the court itself might call an expert—e.g., a master of grammar to help construe doubtful words in a bond. The custom of calling witnesses gradually developed, and then the adversary system, with cross-examination and formal rules governing the admissibility of evidence; until eventually there were expert witnesses in something like the modern sense: experts proffered by one party, subject to cross-examination by the other, and asked, not to testify to what they saw, but to give their informed opinion.[24]

In more recent US law, it was for a long time required only that a scientific witness, like any other expert witness, establish his qualifications as an expert. Then in 1923 the *Frye* ruling imposed new restrictions on the proffered testimony itself. Excluding testimony of a then-new blood-pressure deception test—an early precursor of the polygraph—the D.C. court ruled that novel scientific evidence was admissible only if the principle or discovery on which it is based is sufficiently established to have gained "general acceptance in the field to which it belongs."[25] At first *Frye* attracted little attention; but gradually the "*Frye* rule" came to be widely followed in criminal trials, and by 1975, when the Federal Rules of Evidence (FRE) were enacted, it had been adopted in a majority of states. General acceptance in the relevant field is a better proxy for scientific robustness, obviously, when the field in question is a mature, established scientific specialty than when it is a highly speculative area of research, or, worse, the professional turf of a trade union of mutually supportive charlatans; and it will be more or less demanding according to how broadly or narrowly the relevant field is specified. Nevertheless, the *Frye* rule was commonly criticized as too restrictive.

The Federal Rules set what seemed on its face to be a less restrictive standard: the testimony of a qualified expert is admissible provided only that it is relevant, and not legally excluded on grounds of unfair prejudice, waste of time, or potential to confuse or mislead the jury. In *Barefoot* (1983) the Supreme Court ruled that the constitutional rights of a defendant in a Texas capital-sentencing case had not been violated by the admission of the testimony of two psychiatrists that he would be dangerous in future—even though an amicus brief from the American Psychiatric Association reported that two out of three predictions of future dangerousness are wrong. Writing for the majority, Justice White observed that federal and state rules of evidence "anticipate that relevant, unprivileged evidence should be admitted and its weight left to the fact-finder, who would have the benefit of cross-examination and contrary evidence by the opposing party."[26] In an angry dissent, Justice Blackmun wrote that, in a death-penalty case, this was "too much for [him]," that "a requirement of greater reliability should prevail";[27] and cited Chief Justice Burger: "[t]he very nature of the adversary system . . . complicates the use of scientific opinion evidence, particularly in the field of psychiatry."[28]

By the late 1980s, while legal scholars debated whether the Federal Rules had or hadn't superseded *Frye*, and whether a more or a less restrictive approach to scientific testimony was preferable, there was rising public concern that the tort system was getting out of hand. By 1992, proposals to tighten up the Federal Rules were before Congress; but in 1993 the Supreme Court preempted these proposals when it issued its landmark ruling in *Daubert*[29]—the first case in its 204-year history in which the Court ruled on the standard of admissibility of scientific testimony.

Daubert was a product-liability suit involving the morning-sickness drug Bendectin, alleged to have caused Jason Daubert's severe birth defects; and was a rare instance in which a trial court in a civil case had relied on the *Frye* rule, previously used almost exclusively in criminal cases, in excluding scientific testimony. The Supreme Court agreed to review the case to settle whether the Federal Rules had or hadn't superseded *Frye*; ruling that they had, but that the Rules themselves required judges to screen proffered expert testimony not only for relevance, but also for reliability.

In determining reliability, Justice Blackmun's ruling continues, courts must look not to an expert's conclusions but to his "methodology," to decide whether proffered testimony is really "scientific . . . knowledge," and hence reliable.

Citing Karl Popper and Carl Hempel, the *Daubert* Court suggested four factors for assessing reliability: "falsifiability," i.e., whether the testimony "can be or has been tested"; the known or potential error rate; peer review and publication; and, in a concession to the old *Frye* rule, acceptance in the relevant community. In dissent, however, Justice Rehnquist pointed out that the word "reliable" nowhere occurs in the text of Federal Rule of Evidence 702; expressed doubts about federal judges' ability to assess the reliability of scientific testimony; anticipated that there would be difficulties over whether and if so how *Daubert* should apply to non-scientific experts; and questioned the wisdom of his colleagues' foray into philosophy of science.

Probably Justice Rehnquist was just expressing impatience with Justice Blackmun's philosophical musings; but he was right to be uneasy: the *Daubert* Court's philosophy of science was indeed (if you'll pardon the expression) ill-judged. As I have argued elsewhere,[30] Popper's and Hempel's approaches really can't be reconciled; and neither is likely to be helpful to a court trying to determine whether proffered expert testimony is reliable. Perhaps the Supreme Court has reached the same conclusion—though doubtless by a different route: for since 1993, twice returning to the question of expert and scientific testimony, it seems quietly to have disassociated itself from Justice Blackmun's philosophical efforts.

In *Joiner* (a 1997 toxic tort case involving PCB exposure),[31] Justice Rehnquist, now writing for the majority, cast doubt on the legitimacy of the distinction between methodology and conclusions on which the Court had insisted in *Daubert*. And two years after that—trying to sort out the problems with non-scientific experts which, as Justice Rehnquist anticipated, soon arose in the wake of *Daubert*—the Court ruled in *Kumho* (a 1999 product-liability case involving a tire blowout),[32] that the key word in Rule 702 is "knowledge," not "scientific"; what matters is whether proffered testimony is reliable, *not* whether it is science.

However, in these later decisions the Supreme Court has continued to affirm judges' gatekeeping responsibilities: the *Joiner* Court held that a judge's decision to allow or exclude scientific testimony, even though it may very well determine the outcome of a case, is subject only to review for abuse of discretion, not to any more stringent standard; and the *Kumho* court, stressing that the *Daubert* factors are "flexible," ruled that a judge may use any, all, or none of them. The "*Daubert* trilogy," as legal scholars call this line of cases, gives federal judges substantial responsibility and broad discretion in screening expert testimony, but offers them little really substantive guidance about how to do this.

No wonder then, that, besides these efforts to domesticate scientific testimony by legal rules, there have also been some notable modifications both of the concern for finality and of adversarialism, as the legal culture has adapted to accommodate scientific evidence.

Among the ripple effects of the dramatic DNA exonerations—besides reinforcing reservations about the death penalty and prompting renewed scrutiny of the other kinds of evidence on which those exonerated by DNA (and doubtless many others) were originally convicted—have been significant modifications of the legal restrictions on new evidence, on statutes of limitations, etc. Many jurisdictions have enacted statutes allowing convicted prisoners access to DNA testing;[33] some states have increased the statute of limitations on crimes for which DNA evidence may be available; and some prosecutors have begun to issue "John Doe" warrants, identifying suspects only by their DNA, on the eve of the expiration of the statute of limitations, effectively suspending the statute should the suspect's DNA turn up in one of the data-banks.[34] It is salutary to remember that the brouhaha over recovered memories also prompted some modifications of statutes of limitations, to enable prosecution of (supposed) long-ago crimes. Still, when new scientific work makes it possible to establish that an innocent person has been convicted, it seems more than reasonable to make some compromise of finality in the service of truth.

And the new responsibilities for scrutinizing proffered expert testimony imposed on federal judges by *Daubert*, *Joiner*, and *Kumho* have given rise to small but significant modifications of adversarialism. Since 1975, under FRE 706 and many state equivalents, a court has had the power to "appoint witnesses of its own selection," a power used in a number of asbestos cases between 1987 and 1990, in response to a wave of lawsuits against the manufacturers of silicone breast-implants in the late 1990s, and occasionally since then.[35]

Most to the present purpose, this new reliance on court-appointed experts, though quite modest in scale, represents a significant modification of the adversarial culture of the US legal system, more radical than *Frye*'s oblique deference to the relevant scientific community, or even than *Daubert*'s (and *Joiner*'s and *Kumho*'s) extension of judges' gatekeeping powers—as proponents of the practice, including Learned Hand,[36] have recognized from the beginning. Some critics complain that the practice is "elitist" and "undemocratic," even "totalitarian," a move in the direction of an "inquisitorial" system.[37] Less melodramatically, others uneasy about this compromise of the adversary system fear that jurors will be unduly influenced by the testimony of an expert they know to be court-appointed.[38]

Even if I were qualified to do so, it obviously isn't feasible for me to undertake a comprehensive comparison of adversarial and inquisitorial legal systems here; but allow me to conclude with some brief reflections on these kinds of criticism.[39] There is no question that trial by jury is a better way of getting at the truth than trial by oath or ordeal; nor that citizens' service on juries is an expression of the democratic ethos. But it seems something of an exaggeration to deny that countries like Germany or the Netherlands are democracies simply because court-appointed experts are the rule rather than the exception. Perhaps we might better conceive of democracy as having many facets: some, like universal suffrage and a free press, most central, and others, like referenda or civil jury trials, less so.

Moreover, the rhetoric of "adversarial" versus "inquisitorial" legal systems disguises the fact that the "inquisitorial" legal cultures of civil-law countries include "adversarial" aspects; and the slightly sinister term "inquisitorial" conveys the impression—I trust, the false impression—that German, Dutch, etc. civil law judges may be in the habit of racking defendants or pulling out their fingernails. It also encourages us to forget that in recent decades—even as the overall volume of legal activity has been steadily rising—the proportion of US cases decided by juries has fallen significantly, and is now quite tiny. Between 1962 and 2002 the proportion of federal civil cases resolved by means of a trial fell from 11.5% to 1.8%; there had been a 60% decline in the absolute number of trials since the mid-1960s; and a similar decline in the number of trials was seen in state courts, both criminal and civil. Legal scholars write of "the vanishing trial."[40]

Some might argue that it is hardly surprising if cases where the scientific evidence concerned is uncontroversial end in settlement or summary judgment; and that where the scientific evidence *is* controversial, the fairest way to proceed is an adversarial trial at which each party has the opportunity to present its own experts and cross-examine the other party's. But one might wonder exactly what the content of "fair" could be; for in practice the ability of many plaintiffs and of indigent criminal defendants to call their own experts is severely limited. Think of Mr. Joiner, going up against the vast resources of General Electric Company; or of Mr. Barefoot, at the time of whose sentencing the defense in a Texas death-penalty case was allotted just $500 for "investigation and experts."

All this said, and with the essential caveats in place about the dangers of imagining that arrangements that work in one cultural niche can simply and easily be adopted or adapted in another, I will venture to say that, while trial by jury *is* one expression of the democratic ethos, I don't believe civics education for jurors could justify avoidable, consequential factual errors; that it seems reasonable to be willing to adapt the adversarial culture of the US legal system a little if this would better serve the fundamental purpose of protecting citizens from arbitrary and irrational determinations of fact; and that it would make sense, as we explore the benefits and drawbacks of such an adaptation,[41] to look to the experience of other legal systems. For, as Learned Hand observed more than a century ago, in its search for factual truth the law must rely on expert knowledge, and the only question really *is* "how it can do so best."

NOTES

1. Learned Hand, "Historical and Practical Considerations Regarding Expert Testimony," *Harvard Law Review* 15 (1901): 40–58, p. 40.

2. Jeremy Bentham, *Rationale of Judicial Evidence* (1827; New York: Garland, 1978), vol. 1, p. 22.

3. With which, however, considerations of procedural justice sometimes compete; e.g., when the person who committed a crime goes unpunished, or a person who suffers an injury goes uncompensated, for lack of admissible evidence making the case to the required degree of proof.

4. Though sometimes courts deliberately sidestep this principle: famously, in *Summers v. Tice*, 199 P.2d 1 (Cal. 1948), where two hunters were both found liable for injury to a third person in whose direction both had negligently fired, though only one could actually have hit him.

5. For a list, see <http://www.innocenceproject.org>.

6. Hugo Münsterberg, *On the Witness Stand: Essays on Psychology and Crime* (New York: McClave, 1908). Shortly after the publication of his book, Münsterberg was mercilessly satirized by the celebrated evidence scholar John Wigmore, who put Münsterberg himself "on the witness stand" in his "Professor Münsterberg and the Psychology of Testimony," *Illinois Law Review* 3, no. 9 (1909): 399–445.

7. *Winans v. New York and E. R. Co.*, 62 U.S. 88, 101 (1858).

8. John Ordronaux, "On Expert Testimony in Judicial Proceedings," *The American Journal of Insanity* 30 (1874): 312–22, p. 312.

9. Charles F. Himes, "The Scientific Expert in Forensic Procedure," *Journal of the Franklin Institute* 85 (1874): 407–36, p. 409.

10. Peter Huber, *Galileo's Revenge* (New York: Basic Books, 1991), p. 3.

11. Marcia Angell, *Science on Trial* (New York: W. W. Norton, 1996), p. 132.

12. Margaret Hagen, *Whores of the Court* (New York: HarperCollins, Regan Books, 1997), p. 73.

13. Norman Levitt, *Prometheus Bedeviled* (New Brunswick, NJ: Rutgers University Press, 1999), p. 213.

14. Peter Schuck, "Multiculturalism Redux: Science, Law, and Politics," *Yale Law and Policy Review* 11 (1993): 1–46; Steven Goldberg, *Culture Clash: Law and Science in America* (New York: New York University Press, 1994).

15. *Tehan v. United States*, 382 U.S. 406, 416 (1966).

16. Janet Reno, "Introduction" to *Convicted by Juries, Exonerated by Science: Case Studies in the Use of DNA Evidence to Establish Innocence After Trial* (National Institute of Justice, 1996), p. 1.

17. *Daubert v. Merrell Dow Pharm., Inc.*, 509 U.S. 579, 596–97 (1993).

18. The ruling from *Tehan* (n. 15) continues: "by contrast, the Fifth Amendment Privilege against self-incrimination is not an adjunct to the ascertainment of truth . . . but stands as a protection of quite different constitutional values. . . ."

19. Federal Rule of Evidence 407 provides *inter alia* that evidence of "subsequent repair" is inadmissible.

20. Of course, in applied science—in medicine or engineering, for example—practical decisions may have to be made in the absence of good evidence.

21. Charles Sanders Peirce, *Collected Papers*, eds. Charles Hartshorne, Paul Weiss, and (vols. 7 and 8) Arthur Burks (Cambridge: Harvard University Press, 1931–58), 6.3. [References are by volume and paragraph number.]

22. *Daubert* (n. 17), 597.

23. F. W. Maitland, *The Forms of Action at Common Law* (Cambridge: Cambridge University Press, 1909), lecture II.

24. According to Learned Hand, the first case of an expert witness as an exception to the rule that the conclusions of a witness are inadmissible was *Alsop v. Bowtrell*, Cro. Jac. 541 (1620). Learned Hand, "Historical and Practical Considerations Regarding Expert Testimony" (n. 1), p. 45. According to Stephan Landesman, one of the earliest cases of expert witnesses called by the parties and subject to cross-examination was *Folkes v. Chadd*, 3. Doug. 157 (1782). Stephan Landsman, "Of Witches, Madmen and Product liability: An Historical Survey of the Use of Expert Testimony," *Behavioral Science and Law* 13 (1995): 130–57, p. 141.

25. *Frye v. United States*, 54 App. D.C. 46, 293 F.1013 (D.C. Cir. 1923).

26. *Barefoot v. Estelle*, 483 U.S. 880, 898 (1983). Mr. Barefoot was executed in 1984.

27. *Barefoot* (n. 26), p. 916.

28. *Barefoot* (n. 26), p. 933. Warren E. Burger, "Psychiatrists, Lawyers, and the Courts," *Federal Probation* 28 (June 1964): 3–10, p. 6.

29. *Daubert* (n. 17).

30. "Trial and Error: The Supreme Court's Philosophy of Science," pp. 161–77 in this volume.

31. *General Electric Co. v. Joiner*, 522 U.S. 136 (1997).

32. *Kumho Tire Co. v. Carmichael*, 526 U.S. 137 (1999).

33. Kathy Swedlow, "Don't Believe Everything You Read: A Review of Modern 'Post-Conviction' DNA Testing Statutes," *California Western Law Review* 38 (2002): 355–87, gives a list and notes some significant restrictions.

34. Mark Hansen, "The Great Detective," *American Bar Association Journal* 87 (2001): 36–44, 77.

35. See "Trial and Error: The Supreme Court's Philosophy of Science" (n. 30) for more details.

36. Hand, "Historical and Practical Considerations Regarding Expert Testimony" (n. 1).

37. See e.g., M. N. Howard, "The Neutral Expert: A Plausible Threat to Justice," *Criminal Law Review* 1991 (1991): 98–114, p. 101.

38. See Michael H. Graham, *Evidence: An Introductory Problem Approach* (St. Paul. MN: West Group, 2002), p. 339.

39. I have relied in what follows on Herbert J. Liebesny, *Foreign Legal Systems: A Comparative Analysis* (Washington, DC: George Washington University Press, 1981), pp. 327–45; John Langbein, "The German Advantage in Civil Procedure," *University of Chicago Law Review* 52 (1985): 823–66; and Petra van Kampen, *Expert Evidence Compared: Rules and Practices in the Dutch and American Criminal Justice System* (Antwerp: Intersentia, 1998).

40. See William Glaberson, "Juries Find Their Central Role in Courts Fading," *New York Times*, March 2, 2001. Marc Galanter, "The Vanishing Trial: An Examination of Trials and Related Matters in Federal and State Courts," *Journal of Empirical Legal Studies* 1, no. 3 (November 2004): 459–570, pp. 459–60; and "The Hundred Year Decline of Trials and the Thirty Years War," *Stanford Law Review* 57 (2005): 1255–74. Kimberlee K. Kovach, "The Vanishing Trial: Land Mine on the Mediation Landscape or Opportunity for Evolution: Ruminations on the Future of Mediation Practice," *Cardozo Journal of Conflict Resolution* 7 (Fall 2005): 27–75.

41. On the US experience, see for example Joe S. Cecil and Thomas E. Willging, "Assessing Causation in Breast Implant Litigation: The Role of Science Panels," *Law and Contemporary Problems* 64 (2001): 139–90; John Monahan and Laurens Walker, "Scientific Authority: The Breast Implant Litigation and Beyond," *Virginia Law Review* 86 (2000): 801–33. Interestingly enough, at a workshop at Albany Law School in December 2006 I learned from Dr. Mark Frankel (of the American Academy for the Advancement of Science CASE project) that the commonest upshot, when a judge announces that he intends to call on the association to find experts to advise him, is that a settlement is promptly reached.

10

TRIAL AND ERROR

The Supreme Court's Philosophy of Science

It seems to me that there is a good deal of ballyhoo about scientific method. I venture to think that the people who talk most about it are the people who do least about it. . . . No working scientist, when he plans an experiment in the laboratory, asks himself whether he is being properly scientific. . . . When the scientist ventures to criticize the work of his fellow scientist, he does not base his criticism on such glittering generalities as failure to follow the "scientific method," but his criticism is specific. . . . The working scientist is always too much concerned with getting down to brass tacks to be willing to spend his time on generalities.

—Percy Bridgman[1]

W hile pregnant with her son Jason, Mrs. Daubert had taken Bendectin for morning sickness (which, though often just a nuisance, is sometimes serious enough to warrant hospitalization—and occasionally fatal). Believing that Bendectin had caused Jason's severe birth defects, in 1989 the Dauberts brought suit against Merrell Dow Pharmaceuticals, the manufacturers of the drug. At trial, however, the experts they proffered to testify on the question of causation were excluded under the *Frye* Rule: the consensus in the relevant scientific community was that Bendectin is not teratogenic, does not cause birth defects. With the Dauberts' causation experts excluded, there was no case to answer, and the trial court granted summary judgment in favor of Merrell Dow; the appeals court affirmed.

This was a very rare instance in which the *Frye* Rule—which arose in a criminal case, and had until then been cited in criminal cases almost exclusively—had been used in a civil trial. Moreover, the status of the *Frye* Rule was in question, since the relevant provision of the Federal Rules of Evidence (FRE) enacted in 1975 made no reference to *Frye* or to "general acceptance." And so *Daubert v. Merrell Dow Pharmaceuticals* ended up at the Supreme Court.[2] The court agreed to hear the case to determine whether the Federal Rules had or hadn't superseded *Frye*. But Justice Blackmun's ruling in this landmark 1993 case did more than settle whether *Frye* had survived the Federal Rules; it was also a remarkable judicial foray into philosophy of science.

Yes, Justice Blackmun wrote for the majority, the FRE *had* superseded *Frye*; but the rules themselves require judges to screen proffered expert testimony not only for relevance, but also for reliability. The legal or "evidentiary" reliability of scientific testimony, he continued, is a matter of its scientific "validity"; and in assessing whether proffered scientific testimony is legally reliable, courts must look, not at the conclusions an expert draws, but at the "methodology" by which he reached them, to determine whether the proffered evidence is really "scientific . . . knowledge," and hence reliable. As to what that methodology is, citing law professor Michael Green citing philosopher of science Karl Popper, quoting an observation of Carl Hempel's for good measure, Justice Blackmun's ruling suggests a flexible list of four factors that courts might use in assessing reliability: "falsifiability," i.e., whether proffered evidence "can be and has been tested"; the known or potential error rate; peer review and publication; and (in a nod to *Frye*), acceptance in the relevant community.[3]

In partial dissent, however, noting that the word "reliable" nowhere occurs in the text of Rule 702, Chief Justice Rehnquist anticipated that there would be difficulties down the road about whether, and if so how, *Daubert* should be applied when courts determine whether a non-scientific expert's testimony is admissible; worried aloud that federal judges, few of whom have any scientific training, were in effect now required to decide substantive scientific issues on which even experts in the field disagree; and argued that it would have been better for the Court simply to have settled the narrow question of the standing of *Frye*, rather than engaging in an ambitious argument about the nature of "scientific . . . knowledge."

Justice Rehnquist was right to suspect that something was seriously amiss; indeed, this paper might be read as an exploration, amplification, and partial defense of his reservations about his colleagues' philosophical excursus.

1. *DAUBERT*'S CONFUSIONS: POPPER AND HEMPEL

Apparently equating the question of whether expert testimony is reliable with the question of whether it is genuinely scientific, taking for granted that there is some scientific "methodology" which, faithfully followed, guarantees reliable results, and casting about for a philosophy of science to fit this demanding bill, the *Daubert* Court settled on an unstable amalgam of Popper's and Hempel's very different approaches—neither of which, however, is suitable to the task at hand.

Popper describes his philosophy of science as "Falsificationist" (by contrast with the "Verificationism" of the Logical Positivists),[4] because he holds that scientific statements can *never* be shown to be true, or even probable. Hence his criterion of demarcation: to be genuinely scientific, a statement must be "testable"—meaning, in Popper's mouth, "refutable" or "falsifiable," i.e., susceptible to evidence that could potentially show it to be false (if it *is* false). Curiously, Popper acknowledged from the beginning that his criterion of demarcation is a "convention"; and in 1959, in his Introduction to the English edition of *The Logic of Scientific Discovery*, even affirmed that scientific knowledge is continuous with common-sense knowledge.[5] Nevertheless, his criterion of demarcation is a very important element of his philosophy of science. Falsifiability is to discriminate real empirical science (such as Einstein's theory of relativity) from pre-scientific myths, from non-empirical disciplines like pure mathematics or metaphysics, from non-scientific disciplines like history, and from such pseudo-sciences as Freud's and Adler's psychoanalytic theories and Marx's "scientific socialism."[6] It is also vital to Popper's account of the scientific method as "conjecture and refutation": making a bold, highly falsifiable guess, testing it as severely as possible, and, if it is found to be false, giving it up and starting over rather than protecting it by *ad hoc* or "conventionalist" modifications. (Readiness to accept falsification, and repudiation of *ad hoc* stratagems to protect a theory from contrary evidence, is Popper's "methodological criterion" of the genuinely scientific.)

Popper also describes his philosophy of science as "Deductivist," by contrast with "Inductivism," whether in the strong, Baconian form that posits an inductive logic for arriving at hypotheses or in the weaker, Logical Positivist form that posits an inductive logic of confirmation. According to Popper, David Hume showed long ago that induction is unjustifiable. But science doesn't need induction; the method of conjecture and refutation requires only deductive logic—specifically, *modus tollens*, the rule invoked when an observational result predicted by a theory fails.

Theories that have been tested but not yet falsified are "corroborated": degree of corroboration at a time depending on the number and severity of the tests passed. But that a theory is corroborated, to however high a degree, doesn't show that it is true, or even probable; indeed, the degree of testability of a hypothesis is *inversely* related to its degree of logical probability—the more testable the theory, the lower its probability.[7] Corroboration is not a measure of verisimilitude, but at best an indicator of how the verisimilitude of a theory *appears*, relative to other theories, at a time;[8] and that the fact that a theory is corroborated doesn't mean that it is rational to believe it. (It *does* mean, Popper writes, that it is rational to prefer the theory as the basis for practical action; not, however, that there are good reasons for thinking the theory will be successful in future—there *can be no* good reasons for believing this.[9] So it seems that all this "concession" amounts to is that in deciding how to act we can do no better than go with theories we don't yet know to be false.)

The first problem with the *Daubert* Court's reliance on Popper is that applying his criterion of demarcation is no trivial matter; as Justice Rehnquist pointed out, observing wryly that, since *he* didn't really know what is meant by saying that a theory is "falsifiable," he doubted federal judges would, either.[10] Indeed, Popper himself doesn't seem quite sure how to apply his criterion. Sometimes, for example, he says that the theory of evolution is not falsifiable, and so is not science; at one point he suggests that "survival of the fittest" is a tautology, or "near-tautology," and elsewhere that evolution is really a historical theory, or perhaps metaphysics. Then he changes his mind: evolution *is* science, after all.[11] It's ironic; for Popper's criterion of demarcation had already found its way into the US legal system, a decade before *Daubert*, in a 1982 first amendment case: *McLean v. Arkansas Board of Education*, where Michael Ruse's testimony that creation science is not science, by Popper's criterion, but the theory of evolution is, apparently persuaded Judge Overton.[12]

But there is an even more serious problem with the *Daubert* Court's reliance on Popper, of which Justice Rehnquist doesn't seem aware: Popper's philosophy of science is signally inappropriate to the Court's concern with reliability. When Popper describes his approach as "Critical Rationalism," it is to emphasize that the rationality of the scientific enterprise lies in the susceptibility of scientific theories to criticism, i.e., to testing, and potentially to falsification, *not* in their verifiability or confirmability. True, early on Rudolf Carnap translated Popper's word "*Bewährung*" as "confirmation"; and for a while, thinking the issue merely verbal, Popper let it go—even, occasionally, using "confirm" himself. But in a footnote to the English edition of *The Logic of Scientific Discovery* he comments that this had been a bad mistake on his part, conveying the false impression that a theory's having been corroborated means that it is probably true.[13] Except for the weak moments when he condoned Carnap's (mis)translation,[14] Popper insisted that corroboration must not be confused with confirmation.

The degree of corroboration of a theory represents its past performance only, and "*says nothing whatever about future performance, or about the 'reliability' of a theory*"; even the best-tested theory "is not 'reliable'"[15]—so scornful is Popper of the concept of reliability that he refuses even to use the word without putting it in precautionary scare quotes! Reiterating that he puts the emphasis "on *negative arguments*, such as negative instances or counter-examples, refutations, and attempted refutations—in short, criticism—while the inductivist lays stress on '*positive instances*,' from which he draws 'non-demonstrative *inferences*,' and which he hopes will guarantee the '*reliability*' of the conclusions of these inferences," Popper specifically identifies Carl Hempel as representative of those inductivists with whom he disagrees.[16]

Hempel is not, perhaps, the prototypical inductivist: he describes the method of science as "hypothetico-deductive"; he affirms that scientific claims should be subject to empirical check or testing; and he doesn't follow Reichenbach and Carnap in explaining confirmation by appeal to the calculus of probabilities. Nevertheless, Popper is surely right to see Hempel's approach as very significantly at odds with his own: Hempel is not centrally concerned with demarcating science; he questions the supposed asymmetry between verification and falsification, and argues that Popper's criterion "involves a very severe restriction of the possible forms of scientific hypotheses," e.g., in ruling out purely existential statements;[17] when he speaks of "testing" he envisages both disconfirmation *and confirmation* of a hypothesis; and one of his chief projects was to articulate the "logic of confirmation," i.e., of the support of general hypotheses by positive instances.

Apparently the Supreme Court hoped, by combining Hempel's account of confirmation with Popper's criterion of demarcation, to craft a crisp test to identify genuine, and hence reliable, science. But, though Hempel's philosophy of science *is* more positive than Popper's, it isn't much more help with the question of reliability. For one thing, the confirmation of generalizations by positive instances that preoccupies Hempel is just too simplified to apply to the enormously complex congeries of epidemiological, toxicological, and other evidence at stake in a case like *Daubert*. For another, what Hempel offered was an account of the supportiveness of evidence, or as he said, of "relative confirmation," the *relation between* observational evidence and a hypothesis, expressible as "E confirms H [to degree n]," or "H is confirmed [to degree n] by evidence E." This, as Hempel acknowledged, falls short of an account of "absolute confirmation," the warrant of a scientific claim, which would be expressed in non-relative terms, as

"H is confirmed [to degree n], period." To discriminate reliable testimony from unreliable, however, seems to require an account of the absolute concept—which Hempel doesn't supply. Moreover, Hempel himself seems eventually to have concluded that the "grue" paradox shows that confirmation isn't a purely syntactic or logical notion after all,[18] and late in life began to think that maybe Thomas Kuhn had been on the right track in focusing on the historico-politico-sociological, rather than logical, aspects of science.[19]

2. *DAUBERT*'S CONFUSIONS: "SCIENTIFIC" AND "RELIABLE"

So, the *Daubert* Court mixes up its Hoppers and its Pempels; but isn't this just a slip, of merely scholarly interest? No. It is symptomatic of the serious misunderstanding of the place of the sciences within inquiry generally revealed by the Court's equation of "scientific" and "reliable."

The honorific use of "science" and its cognates is unmistakably at work in the *Daubert* ruling; indeed, it seems to be implicit even in the way Justice Blackmun writes of "scientific . . . knowledge," strategically excising three not insignificant words from the reference in FRE 702 to "scientific or other technical knowledge," and apparently signalling an expectation that a criterion of the genuinely scientific will also discriminate reliable from unreliable testimony.

If "scientific" is used honorifically, it is a tautology that "scientific" = "reliable"; but this tautology, obviously, is of no help to a judge trying to screen proffered scientific testimony. If "scientific" is used descriptively, however, "scientific" and "reliable" come apart: for, obviously, physicists, chemists, biologists, medical scientists, etc., are sometimes incompetent, confused, self-deceived, dishonest, or simply mistaken, while historians, detectives, investigative journalists, legal and literary scholars, auto mechanics, etc., are sometimes good investigators. In short, not all, and not only, scientists are reliable inquirers; and not all, and not only, scientific evidence is reliable. Nor is there a "scientific method" in the sense the Court assumed: no uniquely rational mode of inference or procedure of inquiry used by all scientists and only by scientists. Rather, scientific inquiry builds on the inferences, desiderata, and constraints common to all serious investigation by means of its vast array of constantly evolving local ways and means of stretching the imagination, amplifying reasoning power, extending evidential reach, and stiffening respect for evidence.

Every kind of empirical inquiry, from the simplest everyday puzzling over the causes of delayed buses or spoiled food to the most complex investigations of detectives, of historians, of legal and literary scholars, and of scientists, involves making an informed guess about the explanation of some event or phenomenon, figuring out the consequences of its being true, and checking how well those consequences stand up to evidence. This is the procedure of all scientists; but it is not the procedure *only* of scientists. Something like the "hypothetico-deductive method," really *is* the core of all inquiry, scientific inquiry included. But it is not distinctive of scientific inquiry; and the fact that scientists, like inquirers of every kind, proceed in this way tells us nothing substantive about whether or when their testimony is reliable.

The sciences have extended the senses with specialized instruments; stretched the imagination with metaphors, analogies, and models; amplified reasoning power with numerals, the calculus, computers; and evolved a social organization that enables cooperation, competition, and evidence-sharing, allowing each scientist to take up his investigation where others left off. Astronomers devise ever more sophisticated telescopes, chemists ever more sophisticated techniques of analysis, medical scientists ever more sophisticated methods of imaging bodily states and processes, and so on; scientists work out what controls are needed to block a potential source of experimental error, what statistical techniques to rule out a merely coincidental correlation, and so forth. But these scientific "helps" to inquiry are local and evolving, not used by *all* scientists.

You may object that, since I have acknowledged that scientific inquiry is continuous with everyday empirical inquiry, I have in effect agreed with Popper that science is an extension of common sense. Indeed, I think science *is* well described, in Gustav Bergmann's wonderfully evocative phrase, as the Long Arm of Common Sense.[20] But the continuity is not between the content of scientific and of common-sense knowledge, but between the basic ways and means of everyday and of scientific inquiry; and it is precisely because of this continuity that the Popperian preoccupation with the demarcation of science from non-science is a distraction.

Or you may object that the *Daubert* Court's Popperian advice that courts ask whether proffered scientific testimony "can be and has been tested" surely is potentially helpful. This is true; but it is no real objection. "Check whether proffered testimony has been tested" *is* very good advice when a purported expert hasn't made even the most elementary effort to check how well his claims stand up to evidence: such as the knife-mark examiner in *Ramirez*,[21] who testified that he could infallibly identify this knife, to the exclusion of all other knives in the world, as having made the wound—though no study had established the assumed uniqueness of individual knives, and his purported ability to make such infallible identifications had never been tested. This is not, however, because falsifiability is the criterion of the scientific, but because *any* serious inquirer is required to seek out all the potentially available evidence and to go where it leads, even if he would prefer to avoid, ignore, or play down information that pulls against what he hopes is true.

Yes, this is a requirement on scientists; as Darwin recognized when he wrote in his autobiography that he always made a point of recording recalcitrant examples and contrary arguments in a special notebook, to safeguard against his tendency conveniently to forget negative evidence.[22] But it is no less a requirement on other inquirers, too; as we all realized a few years ago when a historian who announced that he had evidence that Marilyn Monroe had blackmailed President Kennedy turned out to have ignored the fact that the supposedly incriminating letters were typed with correction ribbon, and that the address included a zip code—when neither existed at the time the letters were purportedly written![23]

The honorific use of "science" and its cognates tempts us—like the *Daubert* Court—to criticize poorly conducted science as not really science at all. But rather than sneering unhelpfully that this or that work is "pseudo-scientific," it is always better to get down to those "brass tacks" Bridgman talks about, and specify what, exactly, is wrong with it: that it is not honestly or seriously conducted; that it rests on flimsy or vague assumptions—assumptions for which there is no good evidence, or assumptions that aren't even susceptible to evidential check; that it seeks to impress with decorative or distracting mathematical symbolism or elaborate-looking apparatus; that it fails to take essential precautions against experimental error; or whatever.

3. *DAUBERT*'S LEGAL PROGENY

So, the *Daubert* Court's philosophy of science was muddled; but haven't subsequent Supreme Court rulings cleared things up? Not exactly: it would be more accurate to say that in *Joiner* (1997) and *Kumho* (1999) the Supreme Court quietly backed away from *Daubert*'s confused philosophy of science.[24] At any rate, those references to Hepper, Pompel, falsifiability, etc., so prominent in *Daubert*, are conspicuous by their absence from *Joiner* and *Kumho*. But there are points of epistemological interest.

In *Joiner* there is a kerfuffle over "methodology" worthy of our attention: Mr. Joiner's attorneys had argued that the lower court erred in excluding their proffered expert testimony because, instead of focusing exclusively on their experts' methodology—which, they maintain, was the very same "weight of evidence" methodology used by the other party's (i.e., G.E.'s) experts—improperly concerned itself with the experts' conclusions. Apparently anxious to sidestep this argument, the *Joiner* Court (with the exception of Justice Stevens) denies the legitimacy of the distinction between methodology and conclusions. Opining that this is No Real Distinction, the Court sounds like nothing so much as a conclave of medieval logicians; but given their citation to *Turpin*[25] it seems likely that they didn't really intend to make a profound metaphysical pronouncement, only to acknowledge that if an expert's conclusions are problematic enough, this alerts us to the possibility of some methodological defect—as Judge Becker had suggested in *Paoli*,[26] the case on which the court of appeals had relied in reversing the trial court's exclusion of Joiner's experts.[27]

This focus on "methodology"—an accordion concept expanded and contracted as the argument demands[28]—obscured a much deeper epistemological question. Mr. Joiner's attorneys proffered a collage of bits of information, none sufficient by itself to warrant the conclusion that exposure to PCBs promoted Mr. Joiner's cancer, but which, they argued, *taken together* gave strong support to that conclusion. G.E.'s attorneys replied, in effect, that piling up weak evidence can't magically transform it into strong evidence. In response, Mr. Joiner's attorneys refer to the EPA guidelines for assessing the combined weight of epidemiological, toxicological, and other evidence. But no one addresses the key question: is there a difference between a congeries of evidence so interrelated that the whole really is greater than the sum of its parts, and a collection of unrelated and insignificant bits of information, between true consilience and the "faggot fallacy"[29]—and if so, what is it?

There *is* a difference. Evidence of means, motive, and opportunity may interlock to give much stronger support to the claim that the defendant did it than any of these pieces of evidence alone could do. Similarly, evidence of increased incidence of a disease among people exposed to a suspected substance may interlock with evidence that animals biologically similar to humans are harmed by exposure to that substance and with evidence indicating what chemical mechanism may be responsible to give much stronger support to the claim that this substance causes, promotes, or contributes to the disease than any of these pieces of evidence alone could do. However, the interlocking will be less robust if, e.g., the animals are unlike humans in some relevant way, or if the mechanism postulated to cause damage is also present in other chemicals not found to be associated with an increased risk of disease, or, etc.[30]

"Interlocking" is exactly the right word, given the ramifying, crossword-like structure of evidence. And because of the ramification of reasons, the desirable kind of interlocking of evidence gestured at in *Joiner* is subtle and complex, not easily captured by any mechanical weighting of epidemiological data relative to animal studies or toxicological evidence. Nor, moreover—as Justice Rehnquist already saw in the context of *Daubert*—can its quality readily be judged by someone who lacks the necessary background knowledge.

In *Kumho* the Supreme Court made a real epistemological step forward. In this product liability case focused on the proffered testimony of an expert on tire failure, the Court tried to sort out the problems with non-scientific experts which, as Justice Rehnquist had anticipated, soon arose in the wake of *Daubert*; and ruled that judges can't evade their gatekeeping duty on the grounds that proffered expert testimony is not science: the key word in FRE 702, after all, is "knowledge," not "scientific." No longer fussing over demarcation, recognizing the gap between "scientific" and "reliable," in *Kumho* the Supreme Court acknowledges that *what matters is whether proffered testimony is reliable, not whether it is scientific.* Quite so.

Far from backing away from federal courts' gatekeeping responsibilities, however, the *Joiner* Court had affirmed that a judge's decision to allow or exclude scientific testimony, even though it may be outcome-determinative, is subject only to review for abuse of discretion, not to any more stringent standard; and the *Kumho* Court, pointing out that (depending on the nature of the expertise in question) the *Daubert* factors may or may not be appropriate, held that it is within judges' discretion to use any, all, or none of them. A year later, revised Federal Rules made explicit what according to *Daubert* had been implicit in Rule 702 all along: admissible expert testimony must be based on "sufficient" data, the product of "reliable" testimony "reliably" applied to the facts of the case. As a result, federal judges now have large responsibilities and broad discretion in screening not only scientific testimony but expert testimony generally; but they have very little specific guidance about how to perform this difficult task.

Post-*Daubert* courts seem to have been significantly tougher than before on expert testimony proffered by plaintiffs in civil cases. This isn't the place for a full-scale discussion of the frequently heard criticism that *Daubert* and its progeny tend to favor defendant corporations over plaintiffs; but I will say that I think things are a lot more complicated than this criticism suggests. No doubt there are heartless and unscrupulous companies more concerned with profit than with the dangers their products may present to the public; and it is certainly easier to sympathize with poor Jason Daubert or with poor Mr. Joiner than with a vast, impersonal outfit like Merrell Dow or G.E. But no doubt there are also greedy and opportunistic plaintiffs and plaintiffs' attorneys—and the people thrown out of work when meritless litigation forces a company to downsize or close also deserve our sympathy. Moreover, while we certainly hope the tort system will discourage the manufacture of dangerous substances and products, we also want it *not* to discourage the manufacture of safe and useful ones. And I will add that, while it seems that since *Daubert* courts have not, at least not yet, been as tough on expert testimony proffered by prosecutors in criminal cases as they have on plaintiffs' experts in civil cases, we surely also want to avoid convicting innocent criminal defendants on flimsy forensic testimony—and leaving the real offenders at liberty. That said, I will leave it to others to pursue *Daubert*'s policy ramifications,[31] and pick up the epistemological thread once more.

4. WHERE DO WE GO FROM HERE?

So, since *Kumho*'s epistemological step forward, the other problem Justice Rehnquist worried about—that judges generally lack the background knowledge that may be essential to a serious appraisal of the worth of scientific (or other technical) testimony—looms larger than ever. But hasn't the legal system by now found ways to help judges handle their quite burdensome responsibilities for keeping the gate against unreliable expert testimony? Up to a point; but only up to a point. Ways have been explored to give judges some of the background knowledge they may need, and to enable them to call on the scientific community for help; but these have been relatively small steps, and sometimes (understandably) fumbling.

Daubert prompted various efforts to educate judges scientifically. In May 1999, for example, about two dozen Massachusetts Superior Court judges attended a two-day seminar on DNA at the Whitehead Institute for Biomedical Research. A report in the *New York Times* quoted the director of the institute assuring readers that, while in the O. J. Simpson case lawyers had "befuddled everyone" over the DNA evidence, after a program such as this judges will "understand what is black and white . . . what to allow in the courtroom."[32] To be candid, this report leaves me a little worried about the danger of giving judges the false impression that they *are* qualified to make subtle scientific determinations; when it is hardly realistic to expect that a few hours in a science seminar will transform judges into scientists competent to make subtle and sophisticated scientific judgments, any more than a few hours in a legal seminar could transform scientists into judges competent to make subtle and sophisticated legal determinations.

It really isn't feasible to bring—let alone keep—judges up to speed with cutting-edge genetics, epidemiology, toxicology, or whatever. (I mean, not to denigrate judges' abilities, but to draw the analogy with expecting a few lessons to turn a professional football player into a ballet dancer, or me into a concert pianist.) It should be feasible, however, to educate judges in the elements of probability theory, to give them a sense of how samples may be mishandled or this or that kind of mistake made at the laboratory, and to explain how information about the probability that the lab made a mistake is such-and-such affects the significance of a random-match probability. More generally, it seems both feasible and useful to try to ensure that judges understand the more commonly employed scientific ideas they are likely to encounter most frequently: the role of suggestion, for example, and its significance for how DNA samples or suspect knives, etc., should be presented, or how photo arrays or lineups should be conducted. Of course, when the issues are subtle, the subtleties need to be conveyed: one would hope, for example, that judges understand the concept of statistical significance—but also that they grasp the element of arbitrariness it involves.

Since 1975, under Federal Rule 706 and many state equivalents, courts have had the power to appoint experts of their own selection. Used in a number of asbestos cases in 1987 and 1990,[33] the practice came to public attention in the late 1990s in the context of a wave of lawsuits against the manufacturers of silicone breast implants, when it was adopted by Judge Jones in *Hall*,[34] and most notably by Judge Samuel Pointer, who in 1996 appointed a National Science Panel to help him sift through the scientific evidence in the several thousand federal silicone breast-implant cases that had been consolidated to his court. And it seems that, as their gatekeeping responsibilities have grown, more judges have been willing, as Justice Breyer urged in *Joiner*, to call directly on the scientific community for help:[35] court-appointed experts have advised judges on the potential dangers of seat-belt buckles, the diet drug fen-phen, and the anti-lactation drug Parlodel; and, in the Court of Appeals in Michigan, on Bendectin.[36] At the American Academy for the Advancement of Science (AAAS) the CASE (Court-Appointed Scientific Experts) Project makes available "independent scientists . . . [to] educate the court, testify at trial, assess the litigants' cases, and otherwise aid in the process of determining the truth." Duke University's Registry of Independent Scientific and Technical Advisors also provides the names of independent experts.

Sometimes it is thought that there *are no* neutral experts. If neutrality is taken to mean freedom from all preconceptions, it is true that there are few if any neutral experts: anyone competent to the task of a court-appointed scientist is virtually certain to have some view at the outset. And if neutrality is taken to mean freedom from all contact, direct or indirect, with either party, again there probably won't be many neutral scientists: for, given the dependence of much medical research on drug company funding,[37] most scientists competent to the task will probably know people involved with one party or the other. But it doesn't follow, and it isn't true, that some experts aren't, in the essential sense, more neutral, or less biased, than others: i.e., more willing to go where the evidence leads, even if it pulls against what they were initially inclined to believe.

Bias, in the sense at issue here, is not the same as conflict of interest; nevertheless, we certainly want to avoid conflicts of interest, both because they may lead to bias in the relevant sense, and because, even if they don't, we want to avoid the appearance of such bias. But we should be conscious that there is a broad continuum from a court-appointed scientist being financially supported in some way by a defendant company or plaintiffs' attorneys, to his discussing his court-appointed work with an acquaintance who is supported in some way by a defendant company or plaintiffs' attorneys, to his simply having such acquaintances, . . . , to his being completely out of any professional loop in the field in question.

Yes, it is disturbing that, while serving on Judge Pointer's panel, one scientist signed a letter asking for financial support for another project from one of the defendant companies; and worrying that just four scientists were, in effect, responsible for the disposition of thousands of cases. Moreover, given that even competent and honest scientists will sometimes legitimately disagree, we need to think about what will happen when court-appointed scientists are not of one mind. Both legal issues and practical questions need to be addressed, among them:[38] Should court-appointed experts help judges with their *Daubert* screening duties, or should they testify before juries, along with the parties' experts? How could court-appointed experts best be selected? Who should pay for their services? How should they be instructed about conflicts of interest? We could learn a lot from Judge Pointer's experience, and (if we are careful to avoid the pitfalls of facile cross-cultural comparisons) from the experience of other legal systems, about how and when court-appointed experts might be most helpful.

Such experts are potentially very useful in some kinds of case; but of course they are no panacea—in fact, I don't suppose for a moment that there *is* a panacea. Rather, there is a range of possibilities worth pursuing: thinking about the unhappy interaction of the FDA and the tort system in the silicone breast-implants affair, for example, you might wonder how the FDA could have acted to prevent the panic in the first place;[39] thinking about the AAAS's willingness to help, you might wonder about other ways of making the scientific community more responsive when legal disputes turn on scientific issues irresoluble by the presently available evidence; thinking of the weaknesses of other techniques of forensic identification, and the mistakes made by crime labs, etc., revealed in the wake of those dramatic DNA exonerations, you might wonder how we could make the forensic-science business more rigorous (the temptation to say "more scientific" is strong; but I shall resist it!).

Shortly before *Daubert*, writing of expert testimony in pharmaceutical product liability actions—and echoing Judge Learned Hand's diagnosis of the problem, that we "set[] the jury to decide, where experts disagree," when "it is just because they are incompetent for such a task that the expert is necessary at all"[40]—Marc

Klein had written that:

> Expert testimony is an absurd enterprise. We require expert testimony in pharmaceutical product liability actions because the medical and scientific details are well beyond the comprehension of laymen. Yet, we then ask those same laymen to choose between the competing sets of experts and resolve the very issues that are, by definition, beyond their comprehension.[41]

Daubert shifted more of the burden to the judge; but the fundamental problem remains. Almost a century after Hand posed the essential question—how can the legal system make the best use of expert testimony?—we are still fumbling toward an answer.

NOTES

1. Percy Bridgman, "On 'Scientific Method'" (1949), in Bridgman, *Reflections of a Physicist* (New York: Philosophical Library, 1955), pp. 81–83, p. 81.

2. *Daubert v. Merrell Dow Pharmaceuticals, Inc.*, 509 U.S. 579 (1993).

3. The *Daubert* Court did not itself scrutinize the disputed testimony; on remand, Judge Kozinski argued that the plaintiffs' proffered experts would have to be excluded under *Daubert* as they were under *Frye*. (Merrell Dow had taken Bendectin off the market in 1984, more than a decade before Judge Kozinski's ruling on remand; litigation costs had made the product uneconomic.)

4. Verificationism, however, was proposed as a criterion of the empirically meaningful; it is not, like Popper's Falsificationism, a criterion of the scientific. (I write about this difference in *Defending Science—Within Reason: Between Scientism and Cynicism* [Amherst, NY: Prometheus Books, 2003], p. 34, but won't pursue it here.)

5. Karl R. Popper, "Preface, 1959" to *The Logic of Scientific Discovery* (1934: English edition, London: Hutchinson, 1959), p. 18.

6. Karl R. Popper, "Philosophy of Science: A Personal Report," in *British Philosophy in Mid-Century*, ed. C. A. Mace (London: Allen and Unwin, 1957), reprinted in Karl R. Popper, *Conjectures and Refutations: The Growth of Scientific Knowledge* (New York: Basic Books, 1962), p. 33.

7. Popper, *The Logic of Scientific Discovery* (n. 5), section 83.

8. Karl R. Popper, *Objective Knowledge: An Evolutionary Approach* (Oxford: Oxford University Press, 1972), p. 102.

9. Popper, *Objective Knowledge* (n. 8), p. 22.

10. *Daubert* (n. 2), p. 600. Some federal judges evidently understand falsifiability better than others. In *U.S. v. Havvard*, 117 F.Supp. 2d 848, 854 (2000), admitting finger-

print identification testimony, Judge Hamilton observes that "the methods of latent print identification . . . have been tested. .. for roughly 100 years . . . in adversarial proceedings." But in *Llera-Plaza I*, 2002 WL 27305 (E.D.Pa, Jan. 2, 2002), Judge Pollak points out that "'adversarial' testing in court is not . . . what the Supreme Court meant when it discussed testing as an admissibility factor." (Shortly thereafter, Judge Pollak reconsidered and revised his ruling, but on grounds unrelated to the point at issue here.)

11. Karl. R. Popper, "Natural Selection and Its Scientific Status," excerpted from a lecture of 1977, in *The Pocket Popper*, ed. David Miller (London: Fontana, 1983), pp. 239–46.

12. *McLean v. Arkansas Board of Education*, 529 F.Supp. 1255 (1982). Judge Overton's ruling and Ruse's testimony, along with Larry Laudan's properly scathing critique, can be found in *But Is It Science? The Philosophical Question in the Creation/Evolution Controversy*, ed. Michael Ruse (Amherst, NY: Prometheus Books, 1996).

13. Popper, *The Logic of Scientific Discovery* (n. 5), pp. 251–52, n. *1, added in the English edition. When Popper uses "confirm" for "corroborate"—as he does in his 1957 "Philosophy of Science: A Personal Report" (n. 5)—the effect is powerfully confusing.

14. I am being deliberately noncommittal about whether this really is a mistranslation. *Pons' Globalwörterbuch Deutsch-Englisch* (1983) explains *"Bewärhung"* as "proving one's/its worth"; and gives as a secondary meaning, "probation."

15. Popper, *Objective Knowledge* (n. 8), pp. 18, 22.

16. Popper, *Objective Knowledge* (n. 8), p. 20; the reference to Hempel is in Popper's footnote 29.

17. Carl G. Hempel, "Studies in the Logic of Confirmation," *Mind* 54 (1945): 1–26 and 97–121; reprinted in Carl G. Hempel, *Aspects of Scientific Explanation and Other Essays in the Philosophy of Science* (New York: Free Press, 1965), pp. 3–46. See also his "Empiricist Criteria of Cognitive Significance: Problems and Changes" (adapted from two papers previously published in 1950 and 1951), and "Postscript (1964) on Confirmation," in *Aspects of Scientific Explanation*, pp. 99–122.

18. Hempel, "Postscript (1964) on Confirmation" (n. 17), p. 51. Goodman defines "*x* is grue" as: "either *x* is first examined before time *t*, and *x* is green, or *x* is not examined before *t*, and *x* is blue." The paradox is that (setting *t* as some future time, say 2050) it apparently follows that the evidence we have confirms, e.g., "All emeralds are grue" as well as it confirms "All emeralds are green." Nelson Goodman, "The New Riddle of Induction," in *Fact, Fiction, and Forecast* (1954; 2nd ed., Indianapolis, IN: Bobbs-Merrill, 1965), pp. 59–83. See also Haack, *Defending Science—Within Reason* (n. 4), pp. 84–86.

19. Carl G. Hempel, "The Irrelevance of Truth for the Critical Appraisal of Scientific Theories" (1990), reprinted in *Selected Philosophical Essays*, ed. Richard Jeffrey (Cambridge: Cambridge University Press , 2000), pp. 75–84, p. 75. Thomas Kuhn, *The Structure of Scientific Revolutions* (Chicago: University of Chicago Press, 1962).

20. Gustav Bergmann, *Philosophy of Science* (Madison: University of Wisconsin Press, 1957), p. 20; it is from Bergmann, of course, that I adopted "The Long Arm of Common Sense" as the title of chapter 4 of *Defending Science—Within Reason* (n. 4).

21. *Ramirez v. State*, 542 So. 2d 352 (Fla. 1989); *Ramirez v. State*, 651 So. 2d 1164 (Fla. 1995); *Ramirez v. State*, 8120 So. 2d 836 (Fla. 2001). Florida remains officially a *Frye* state, but seems to be rapidly evolving in the direction of (as Michael Saks puts it) *Fryebert*.

22. Charles Darwin, *Autobiography and Letters*, edited by Francis Darwin (New York: D. Appleton and Company, 1893; reprinted New York: Dover, 1952) p. 45.

23. Evan Thomas, Mark Hosenball, and Michael Isikoff, "The JFK-Marilyn Hoax," *Newsweek*, 6 June 1997, pp. 36–37.

24. *General Electric Co. v. Joiner*, 522 U.S. 136 (1997); *Kumho Tire Co. v. Carmichael*, 526 U.S. 137 (1999).

25. *Turpin v. Merrell Dow Pharm. Inc.*, 959 F.2d 1349 (6th Cir. 1992), *cert. denied*, 506 U.S. 137 (1999).

26. *In re Paoli R.R. Yard PCB Litig.*, 35 F.3d 717 (3rd. Cir. 1994).

27. *Joiner v. General Electric Co.*, 78 F.3d 524 (11th Cir. 1996).

28. The term "accordion concept" was introduced in Wilfrid Sellars's "Scientific Realism or Irenic Instrumentalism," *Boston Studies in Philosophy of Science*, vol. 2, eds. Robert Cohen and Marx Wartofsky (New York: Humanities Press, 1965), pp. 171–204, p. 172.

29. The word "consilience," meaning etymologically "jumping together," was coined by the nineteenth-century philosopher of science William Whewell, and recently made famous as the title of E. O. Wilson's best-selling book, *Consilience* (New York: Knopf, 1998), on the unity of science. The phrase "faggot fallacy" was introduced in Petr Skrabanek and J. McCormick's *Follies and Fallacies in Medicine* (1989; reprinted, Amherst, NY: Prometheus Books, 1997), and adopted by G.E. attorneys' in *Joiner*.

30. See "An Epistemologist Among the Epidemiologists," pp. 179–82 in this volume.

31. As one character says to another in a cartoon for which I have a particular fondness, "Politically, I suppose you could say I'm a member of the lunatic middle."

32. Cary Goldberg, "Judges' Unanimous Verdict on DNA Lessons: Wow!" *New York Times*, 24 April 1999, p. A10.

33. See Carl R. Rubin and Laura Ringenbach, "The Use of Court Experts in Asbestos Litigation," *Federal Rules Decisions* 137 (1991): 35–52.

34. *Hall v. Baxter Healthcare Corp.*, 947 F.Supp. 1387 (D. Or. 1996).

35. See Howard M. Erichson, "Mass Tort Litigation and Inquisitorial Justice," *Georgetown Law Journal* 87 (1999): 1983–2024.

36. *DePyper et al. v. Paul V. Navarro*, No. 19149, 1998 WL 1988927 (Mich. App. Nov. 6, 1998); "Denial of Expert Witness Testimony Violates *Daubert*, Appeal States," *DES Litigation Report* (December 1998).

37. See "The Integrity of Science: What It Means, Why It Matters," pp. 103–27 in this volume.

38. See for example Joe S. Cecil, Laurel J. Hooper, and Thomas E. Willging, "Assessing Causation in Breast Implant Litigation: The Role of Science Panels," *Law and Contemporary Problems* 64 (2001): 139–90; John Monahan and Laurens Walker, "Scientific Authority: The Breast Implant Litigation and Beyond," *Virginia Law Review* 86 (2002): 801–33.

39. The wave of litigation began after the FDA banned silicone breast implants, formerly "grandfathered in"; they were not known to be unsafe, but the manufacturers had failed to submit evidence of their safety, as they had been required to do.

40. Learned Hand, "Historical and Practical Considerations Regarding Expert Testimony," *Harvard Law Review* 15 (1901): 40–58, p. 54.

41. Marc S. Klein, "Expert Testimony in Pharmaceutical Product Liability Actions," *Food, Drug, and Cosmetics Law Journal* 45 (1990): 393–42, pp. 341–42.

11

AN EPISTEMOLOGIST AMONG THE EPIDEMIOLOGISTS

A ll that ballyhoo about "scientific method," Percy Bridgman observes, seems pointless to a working scientist, who will use "any method or device whatever which in the particular situation before him seems likely to yield the correct result."[1] Somewhat in this spirit, Sander Greenland defends "risk-factor epidemiology";[2] i.e., epidemiological studies where data is collected without any test-hypothesis being stipulated in advance, or where data collected for other purposes is analyzed to look for correlations between this or that exposure and these or those diseases. But critics like Alvan Feinstein or Petr Skrabanek, who write pejoratively of "black-box epidemiology," or "data-dredging," think such studies substandard: Feinstein argues that they are especially susceptible to unreliability,[3] and Skrabanek complains that often they are just "scaremongering made respectable by the use of sophisticated statistical methods."[4] This is quite a tangle; but I will try, in what remains of my 1,000 words, to *disentangle* it.

As Feinstein points out, when a hypothesis is specified before data are collected, it is possible to take precautions against relying on poor information about exposure, dosage, or diagnosis, against mistaking higher diagnosis rates for higher disease rates, etc.—something that may be impossible when masses of data collected for other purposes are searched for unanticipated correlations. This

---

seems right. Moreover, when very large numbers of statistically significant correlations are discovered in a search of multiple data sets, some of them will likely be due to chance. But all this is quite compatible with Greenland's argument, which is that the correlations such studies turn up may prompt us to speculate fruitfully about what causal mechanism might tie the apparently unrelated factors together; and, with evidence from toxicology, animal studies, and the like, these studies can help confirm a causal hypothesis. And this also seems right; as Greenland's example of the role of lipid peroxidation in causing renal cancer, and the epidemiological and other evidence that supports it, illustrates very nicely.

Feinstein's observation that no amount of toxicological, in vivo, etc., evidence can turn a poor statistical study into a good one, though of course correct, doesn't undermine Greenland's argument either. How warranted a hypothesis is depends on how supportive the evidence is with respect to the claim at issue, how secure the evidence is, independent of that claim, and how comprehensive it is.[5] Now we see that Feinstein is concerned with the potential *insecurity* of the results of the controversial kinds of study, but Greenland, by contrast, with their potential *supportiveness* with respect to a claim about the cause of a disease or condition.

Like security, supportiveness comes in degrees. How strongly evidence supports a claim depends on how well the evidence and the claim fit together in an explanatory story: as evidence from genetics, phage studies, stereochemistry, X-ray crystallography, etc., interlock to support the conclusion that DNA is a double-helical, backbone-out macromolecule with like-with-unlike base pairs more strongly than any one of these pieces of evidence does. Similarly, statistical evidence of a correlation between risk-factor F and disease D, toxicological evidence of the physiological ill-effects of F, studies showing an increased occurrence of D in animals exposed to F, etc., may interlock to support the conclusion that exposure to F causes elevated risk of D more strongly than any component piece of evidence alone could do. Granted, supportiveness and security interact: if the epidemiological evidence is weak on independent security, the degree of warrant of the conclusion will be lessened. On the other hand, independent evidence of a causal mechanism may justifiably boost confidence in the reliability of the epidemiological evidence.

Skrabanek's concerns are in part, like Feinstein's, about security; but mainly he complains that in this era of epidemiology without epidemics much of what goes on in the discipline is trivial or alarmist. Doubtless—aided and abetted by journalists eager for a saleable story and attorneys eager for a new cause of action—unreliable epidemiological studies often *do* raise unnecessary public alarm; and doubtless there *is* plenty of banal work being done. But *everywhere* in the academy the "publish or perish" mentality has encouraged a flood of academic busywork;[7] *everywhere* in the sciences pressure to obtain grants has encouraged special pleading for "further research" into this or that, and created incentives for scientists to go prematurely to press; and *everywhere* research has a potential relevance to policy, the line between inquiry and advocacy tends to get blurred.[8]

In any case, this too is irrelevant to Greenland's argument; for these are matters, not of "methodology," but of the health of our academic culture—indeed, of our intellectual culture generally. Skrabanek's complaints about "poor data . . . manipulated to reach a foregone conclusion"[9] bring to mind the lapidary reply that French sociologist Georges Sorel gave when asked to identify the most important method in his field: "Honesty."[10]

This prompts the following concluding thought: methodological protocols, procedures, and rules, etc., have their place; but they are no substitute for well-informed imagination, shrewd judgment of the weight of evidence, and good faith in inquiry—as, I suspect, in his era of epidemiology without methodological ballyhoo, John Snow[11] understood well enough.

NOTES

1. Percy Bridgman, "On 'Scientific Method'" (1949), in Bridgman, *Reflections of a Physicist* (New York: Philosophical Library, 1955), pp. 81–83, p. 83.

2. Sander Greenland, Manuela Gago-Dominguez, and José Esteban Castelao, "In Defense of Risk-Factor Epidemiology," *Epidemiology* 15, no. 5 (September 2004): 529–35.

3. Alvan R. Feinstein, "Scientific Standards in Epidemiologic Studies of the Menace of Everyday Life," *Science* 242, no. 4883 (1988): 1257–63.

4. Petr Skrabanek, "The Poverty of Epidemiology," *Perspectives on Biology and Medicine* 35, no. 2 (1992): 182–85, p. 182. See also Skrabanek, "The Epidemiology of Errors," *The Lancet* 342 (1993): 1502; "The Emptiness of the Black Box," *Epidemiology* 5 (1994): 553–55; Petr Skrabanek and James McCormick, *Follies and Fallacies in Medicine* (1989; Amherst, NY: Prometheus Books, 1990).

5. See Robert C. Olby, *The Path to the Double Helix* (Seattle: University of Washington Press, 1974); Franklin H. Portugal and Jack S. Cohen, *A Century of DNA: A History of the Discovery of the Structure and Function of the Genetic Substance* (Cambridge: MIT Press, 1977); or, for a brief summary, Susan Haack, *Defending Science—Within Reason: Between Scientism and Cynicism* (Amherst, NY: Prometheus Books, 2003), pp. 77–82.

6. See Haack, *Evidence and Inquiry: Towards Reconstruction in Epistemology*

(Oxford: Blackwell, 1993; 2nd ed. Amherst, NY: Prometheus Books, forthcoming 2009), chapter 4; Haack, *Defending Science—Within Reason* (n. 5), chapter 3.

7. See Haack, "Preposterism and Its Consequences" (1996), in Haack, *Manifesto of a Passionate Moderate: Unfashionable Essays* (Chicago: University of Chicago Press, 1998), 188–208.

8. See Haack "Science, Economics, 'Vision,'" pp. 95–102 in this volume, and "The Integrity of Science: What It Means, Why It Matters," pp. 103–27 in this volume.

9. Skrabanek, "The Epidemiology of Errors" (n. 4), p. 1502.

10. Georges Sorel's response is reported in Stanislav Andreski, *Social Science as Sorcery* (New York: St. Martin's Press, 1972), p. 232.

11. John Snow (1813–58), the founder of epidemiology, was responsible for the discovery that cholera is water-borne. John Snow, *On the Mode of Communication of Cholera* (London: Churchill, 1849). See also Stephanie J. Snow, "Commentary: Sutherland, Snow and Water: The Transmission of Cholera in the Nineteenth Century," *International Journal of Epidemiology* 51 (2002): 908–11.

12

FALLIBILISM AND FAITH, NATURALISM AND THE SUPERNATURAL, SCIENCE AND RELIGION

In the face of the fact, the scientist has a humility almost religious. . . . [He has] a feeling of spiritual attainment in that he has made a step forward in his adjustment to things as they are.

—Percy Bridgman[1]

As I wrote in *Defending Science—Within Reason*, science is best thought of, not as a body of belief, but as a federation of kinds of inquiry into natural and social phenomena, differentiated from other kinds of inquiry such as history or literary scholarship primarily by the questions within its scope.[2] Science is continuous with everyday empirical inquiry, and relies, as all empirical inquiry does, on experience and reasoning.

Thomas Huxley put it this way: "[t]he man of science . . . uses with scrupulous exactness the methods which we all, habitually and at every minute, use carelessly."[3] Like everyone who tries to find something out, scientists make an informed guess at what might explain a puzzling event or phenomenon, figure out what else would have to be the case if their guess were right, and check out how well those consequences stand up to whatever evidence they have, or can get. But controlled experiments help scientists isolate the evidence they need; instruments of observation help them look more closely; statistical techniques and computer programs help them to keep closer track of consequences; and the knowledge that their work may be scrutinized by others in the field encourages them to persist in seeking out evidence, and to take care in assessing its worth.

The evidence with respect to a scientific claim or theory, like the evidence for the most ordinary empirical claims, is a mesh of observational evidence and background beliefs; and its strength depends on how firmly it is anchored in sensory interactions with the world, how broad it is in explanatory scope, how specific in explanatory details, and how tight in explanatory integration. The natural sciences seek explanations of natural, and the social sciences of social, phenomena and events. In the natural sciences (as in cookery or auto mechanics) the explanations sought are in terms of physical events, forces, and laws; in the social sciences (as in history or detective work) they are in terms of human beings' beliefs, goals, etc., and the actions they prompt. Both the social and the natural sciences are in an important sense "naturalistic": they traffic neither in purported explanations appealing to the purposes and actions of supernatural beings, nor in the supposed evidence of religious experience or of sacred texts.

The goal of scientific inquiry, as of any inquiry, is to find true answers to the questions within its scope. In their professional capacity scientists accept many propositions as true, some of them very confidently and firmly, and not a few pretty dogmatically; but at any time there are many new speculations as yet untried, many contested issues, and many competing theories and theory fragments. Most scientific conjectures are discarded, sooner or later, when the evidence turns out against them; and no scientific claim is in principle beyond the possibility of revision should new evidence demand it.

According to the best-warranted scientific world-picture we have, the earth is just one small corner of a vast universe, a small corner hospitable to life; and in this corner of the universe, human beings evolved from earlier life-forms. Inevitably, parts of this presently accepted scientific account of the origin of the universe and our place in it are better warranted than others, but much of it is well supported by strong evidence.

Unlike science, religion is best conceived, not as a kind of inquiry, but as a body of belief, a creed; by my lights anyway, vague spirituality doesn't count. At the core of a religious creed is the belief that a purposeful spiritual being (or beings) brought the universe into existence, and gave human beings a very special place; and that this spiritual being is concerned about how we behave and what we believe, and can be influenced by our prayers and rituals. Moreover, religious belief is supposed to be, not tentative or hedged, but a profound commitment. This is why we sometimes describe religious people as "believers," and people with a passion for some political or other idea as holding it "with religious fervor." (Among the religious, unbelief is sometimes regarded as sinful, and faith as a virtue.) Unlike the various branches of science, the different religions are not complementary and interlocking parts of a common enterprise; they are rivals, sometimes embroiled in bitter conflict.

Theology, unlike religion, sets out to be a form of inquiry. But unlike scientific inquiry, theological inquiry welcomes, indeed seeks, supernatural explanations, in terms of God's making things so. And when it is not purely a priori, theology calls on evidential resources beyond reasoning and the senses: religious experience and revelation. So, by contrast with the continuities between scientific inquiry and everyday empirical inquiry, there are significant *dis*continuities between theological inquiry and such everyday inquiry: in the kinds of explanation they offer, and in the kinds of evidential resource to which they appeal.

Much attention has been focused on the relations between the content of current scientific theorizing and the content of religious doctrine. *Incompatibilists* believe there are real inconsistencies between now-accepted cosmological and biological explanations of the origin of the universe, the place of the earth, and the evolution of human life, and theistic explanations in terms of the actions and intentions of a powerful supernatural agent. *Religious incompatibilists*, as one might call them, believe that the relevant religious doctrines are true and the competing scientific ideas false; while *scientific incompatibilists* believe that it is the scientific ideas that are true, or at any rate better warranted. *Compatibilists* believe that any appearance of inconsistency between science and religious doctrine is *mere* appearance. Some compatibilists maintain that scientific theorizing concerns only the material, or only the realm of the factual, while religious belief concerns only the spiritual, or only the realm of values; others hold that scientific results actually support religious doctrine; and others again claim that supernatural explanations can fill the gaps in the scientific picture, or explain how scientific explanations are possible.

In *Defending Science*, and in the first version of this paper, I wrote that there is real incompatibility between the scientific and the religious world-pictures; now, however, I think it better to say, more cautiously, that there are deep tensions between the scientific and the religious world-pictures.[4] This acknowledges that scientific theories say nothing one way or another about God; and so do not strictly logically preclude, for example, the possibility that God brought about the Big Bang, or initiated the evolutionary process, or etc. (Though the silence of scientific theorizing about such matters seems to me very different from its silence about, say, the law regarding death-penalty sentencing in Texas,[5] or the publication history of Samuel Butler's *The Way of All Flesh*.)[6] Nevertheless, it seems to me, as to both religious and scientific incompatibilists, that the scientific world-picture of a vast universe in one small corner of which human beings have evolved is profoundly inhospitable to the idea that we are the chosen creatures, with a special relation to a divine creator.

The Psalmist is eloquent:

> When I consider thy heavens, the work of thy fingers, the moone and the starres which thou hast ordained:
> What is man, that thou art mindfull of him? and the sonne of man that thou visiteth him?
> For thou has made him a little lower than the Angels; and hast crowned him with glory and honour.[7]

But eloquent as this is, it sounds to me like whistling in the dark; for, like the scientific incompatibilists, I believe the scientific world-picture—incomplete and fallible as it is—is far better warranted than the religious.

But science and religion differ from each other not only in their conception of the essential character of the universe and our place in it, but also in what they regard as genuinely explanatory; and not only in *what* they believe, but in *why* and *how* they believe it. I want to focus in what follows on these other dimensions of difference: on the deep tensions between the reliance of the sciences on the evidence of the senses, and theological appeals to a distinctive, scientifically inaccessible religious experience; between the natural explanations sought by scientists, and the supernatural explanations sought by theologians; and between the fallibilism of the sciences, and religious dogma and appeals to faith. In the process I will suggest what is wrong with the commonly heard objection that science itself requires a leap of faith; but also what is right in the less-familiar idea that the demands and satisfactions of science itself, the self-transcendence required of any serious inquirer, can be, if not "spiritual" in a religious sense, genuinely uplifting to the human spirit.

Is religious experience an evidential resource on a par with the evidence of the senses? I don't believe so.

All of us rely, in the most mundane of empirical inquiries, and, for that matter, simply in getting around without bumping into things, on the competence of our senses to detect information about objects and events around us. We know, of course, that even the sharpest human eyes, ears, noses, etc., have their limitations, that many people have defective eyesight or hearing, and some are blind or deaf; that even for those whose senses are in good working order, things can go wrong if conditions of observation are poor or misleading, and that background expectations can prompt perceptual misjudgments; that puzzle-pictures deliberately confuse and mislead; and that drugs or mental disorders cause hallucinations. If we suspect our senses are deceiving us, we routinely get someone else to check, to make sure we're not "seeing things."

But fallible and imperfect as it is, our sensory experience plays an essential evidential role in anchoring our beliefs to the world and contributing to their warrant. It plays this evidential role in virtue of connections set up as language is learned: in the way, for example, a child first encounters the word "dog" by hearing it used in the presence of visible, audible, etc., dogs; even though subsequently, encountering dimly perceived distant bushes, stuffed or robotic toy dogs, miniature horses, holograms, and the like, he will soon learn "I thought I saw . . . ," ". . . looked just like a dog," and such.

Like our everyday empirical beliefs, scientific claims and theories are ultimately supported by our sensory interactions with the world; though scientific observations are often mediated by sophisticated instruments—which, the possibility of instrumental failure notwithstanding, have vastly extended human beings' unaided sensory reach. Moreover, scientific observations can be controlled, blinded, and when necessary repeated by several people to minimize the danger of observer bias; and by now the sciences of psychology, optics, and related fields have discovered a good deal about perception and misperception, the effects of suggestion, and the workings and weaknesses of instruments. Of course, like the rest of us, scientists rely on their senses even as they figure out whether or why this or that sensory evidence, this or that observational result, is misleading.

The case of putative interactions with God could hardly be more different. Such interactions involve no special sensory organ, nor any above-average sensory powers. Only a minority of people claim to have experienced them; and of these only a privileged elite—most of them long dead—are taken at all seriously. And such interactions do not, and cannot, play anything like the evidential role of our sensory interactions with the world around us.

Virtually everyone who learns the word "dog" does so in the first instance by hearing it used in the presence of a dog visible or audible both to the teacher and to the learner; but no one is introduced to the word "God" in this way. Granted, some children first encounter the word "zebra" in the presence not of zebras but of pictures of zebras; and perhaps some first encounter the word "God" in the presence of a picture of an old man with a long white beard speaking to Moses. But the picturing relation is utterly different in the two cases; after all, a child might first encounter "zebra" by being shown *photographs* of zebras, but no one learns "God" by being shown a photograph of God. (It is possible to imagine a child picking up "God" by being shown a photo of "God's house"; but impossible to miss how different this would be from picking up the word "president" by being shown a photo of the White House.) Moreover, virtually everyone who is told what a zebra is, and is subsequently in the visible or audible presence of a zebra, sees or hears it; but by no means all of those told about God subsequently report seeing or hearing him.

Most of us have to rely on others' assurances that they have seen black swans; but if need be we could go to Australia ourselves to check. Again, we may rely on the assurances of those with more sensitive color vision than our own that they see subtle differences we can't; but if need be we can devise tests to determine whether they are discriminating consistently. Some people claim to have spotted Elvis Presley at their local supermarket, some to have seen the Loch Ness monster, and some, even, to have extrasensory awareness of distant objects and events; but even here there is no in-principle difficulty about checking whether their claims are true. But with claims to have seen or heard God we are dealing with the testimony of a relatively few others who claim to have had experiences of a kind radically different from any that we have ever had.

To be sure, terms like "religious experience" or "sensing the presence of God" cover not only actual voices and visions—the focus of my discussion thus far—but also (as "sense" shifts from a literal to a figurative use) religious interpretations of mundane events, and even vague feelings of being taken out of oneself. "Religious experience" covers Moses' hearing the voice from the burning bush, and Martin Luther's waking suddenly to find Satan disputing with him; but also the supposedly miraculous appearance of an image of the Virgin Mary on the window of the Ugly Duckling car rental firm in Clearwater, Florida,[8] and the emotional stirrings prompted by the Hallelujah Chorus or a glorious sunset. But religious experience in the weaker sense is a matter of distinctively religious interpretations of ordinary things and events, and is not even a candidate for analogue of the evidence of the senses.

Brain scientists conjecture that religious experience, broadly conceived, may be associated with electrical disturbances in the temporal lobes, disturbances that can be triggered by anxiety, lack of oxygen, low blood sugar, or fatigue. That may be; but this doesn't tell us *either* that any supposed religious experience is authentic, *or* that none is. Religious people will aver that their experience is *self*-authenticating; and may urge unbelievers to overcome their spiritual blindness by opening their hearts to God (a very different matter from going to Australia to check on reports of sightings of black swans). But skeptics may find David Hume's shrewd advice, not to trust a witness who is too vehement, coming unbidden to mind: Some purported religious experience is probably outright hallucination, and some wishful or fearful over-interpretation of responses to natural phenomena or to religious music or ritual; and whether any, in the end, provides any evidence at all of the truth of religious claims is doubtful.

Are supernatural explanations on a par with natural explanations? Again, I don't believe so.

Some claim that the Bible story better explains the origin of the universe and of human life than current cosmological and evolutionary theorizing; some that the workings of cilia, flagella, blood-clotting mechanisms, and so forth, can only be explained by divine design; others that God must have caused the Big Bang, or fine-tuned the world to make it hospitable to human life; and others again that only divine purposeful action can explain why there is a universe at all, and why there are natural kinds and laws for science to discover. Each of these claims faces particular difficulties of its own: e.g., in the case of explanations in terms of divine design, the sub-optimality of the biological mechanisms at issue. More to the present point, all take for granted that supernatural explanations are genuinely explanatory.

Some have suggested that (metaphysical or, more often, methodological) naturalism is a convention of science.[9] The sciences do indeed eschew supernatural explanations; but this is much more than a "convention." A good explanation combines specificity and scope, providing a specific account of the causal mechanism responsible for a particular phenomenon (e.g., the role of lipid peroxidation in causing renal cancer), interlocking with a larger explanatory picture (of epidemiological patterns, chemical and physiological theory, etc.).[10] Supernatural explanations are of the broadest possible scope. However, they cannot be made specific—for reasons of principle: they appeal to the intentions of an agent, which, being non-physical, cannot put Its intentions into action by any conceivable physical means. In short, supernatural "explanations" *don't really explain at all.*

This is why, beyond (flawed) arguments that the mechanisms in question could not have evolved, Intelligent Design "Theory" seems to amount to nothing more than a flat assertion that a divine designer must have devised those "irreducibly complex systems"; and why supernatural explanations of the Big Bang, supposed cosmic fine-tuning, etc., all stop short of saying *how* God puts his intentions into effect. Jesuit theologian Michael Buckley simply concedes that "we really do not know how God 'pulls it off'";[11] but this is to highlight the problem, not to solve it. "He spake, and it was done"; "He commanded, and it stood fast"—these are no explanations at all; and neither is "It's a mystery."

Richard Swinburne thinks it sufficient to point out that many natural-scientific explanations appeal to unobservable entities or forces, and that most social-scientific explanations appeal to the intentions and actions of human agents.[12] This is true; but it doesn't speak to the fundamental difficulty, which is *not* that God is unobservable, and *not* that he is an intentional agent, but that he is not physical. Perhaps Swinburne thinks our beliefs and intentions aren't physical, either; but if they weren't, it would be just as mysterious how they could explain our physical actions as it is how God's beliefs and intentions could explain worldly events—this is, indeed, the central mystery of Cartesian dualism. (Perhaps I need to add that although, in my view, mind is physical, the explanation of intentional action is not reducible to physics. But that's a whole other story.)[13]

Older, more anthropomorphic conceptions took God to be, as Andrew Dickson White puts it, a kind of giant toy-maker.[14] And as older conceptions of the physical, as simply material stuff, have given way to an understanding of the equivalence of mass and energy, some have been tempted to try to avoid the difficulty about supernatural explanations by identifying God with whatever force brought the universe into being. This avoids the problem of a supposed non-physical cause of physical events; but it brings a new and no less formidable problem of its own: it makes no sense to imagine such a force listening to our prayers, performing the occasional miracle, or taking any interest in what humans do or believe.

"Can science explain everything?" theists ask pointedly. No, science *can't* explain everything; but it doesn't follow that supernatural explanations can fill the gaps. Science can't explain why my cow was struck by lightning, but not yours, or why their church was destroyed by the hurricane, while ours was left untouched; but this is because no such explanation is either necessary or possible. Events like these are explicable in natural terms; but its being *my* cow rather than yours, *their* church rather than ours, is coincidental. And there are many legitimate questions within the competence of science that it can't yet answer, and many legitimate questions—legal and literary, commercial and culinary, and so on—outside its competence altogether; but no one supposes that such questions can be resolved by supernatural explanations.

The contrast between the fallibilism of the sciences and the faith demanded by religion is complicated by an ambiguity in the phrases "faith in God," and "belief in God," which may mean: *unshakable belief, indifferent to ordinary evidence, that God exists;* but also: *trust in God*. It's worth noting for the record that trust in God presupposes the existence of a God in whom to place one's trust; but it is the first sense, firm belief that God exists, that is relevant here.

If what is meant when it is said that belief has no place in science is that scientists don't, or shouldn't, give any degree of credence to their theories, it is false; scientists surely *do* place credence in well-warranted theories, and reasonably so. Sometimes, moreover, a scientist may have a strong hunch in advance of or even contrary to the then-available evidence that this or that theory is right; and such hunches sometimes prove to be correct. All this said, however, an important sense remains in which faith is alien to science: for, inherent in the scientific enterprise, is a kind of fallibilism that demands willingness to revise even the most firmly accepted claims should the evidence require it.

To say this is by no means to subscribe to the popular stereotype of science as essentially skeptical, and of scientists as accepting nothing on authority. On the contrary: there is a vast body of presumed scientific knowledge, which—even though it may yet have to be revised—must be taken for granted as the work proceeds. If it weren't, each scientist would have to start on that vast crossword alone and from scratch. To say that fallibilism is "inherent in the scientific enterprise" means simply that science is a kind of inquiry, and that willingness to take negative evidence seriously is an important aspect of the intellectual honesty demanded of any genuine inquirer; and to say that intellectual honesty requires willingness to take negative evidence seriously simply means that negative evidence shouldn't be ignored or suppressed and, if it can't plausibly be explained away or accommodated, must be acknowledged as undermining previously accepted claims or theories. Bridgman puts the essential point less carefully perhaps, but more pithily: "for the scientist faith can be no virtue, because it is inconsistent with the resolution to accept the fact as supreme."[15]

Accusing "Darwinists" of a dogmatic denial that a supernatural being could influence natural events or communicate with natural creatures like ourselves, and a dogmatic insistence that science is the only reliable source of knowledge, Phillip Johnson voices the common objection that science *does* depend on faith—faith in naturalism, faith that nature is governed by laws, faith that those laws are discoverable by creatures like us, faith in the senses.[16] Scientists themselves sometimes suggest something of the kind. Michael Polanyi, for example, writes that "no one can become a scientist unless he presumes that the scientific doctrine and method are fundamentally sound and that their ultimate premises can be unquestioningly accepted," and goes on to describe this as "*fides quaerens intellectum*, faith in search of understanding."[17] And Einstein, likening science to working on "a well-designed word puzzle," remarks that "[i]t is a matter of faith that nature—as she is perceptible to our five senses—takes the character of such a well-formulated puzzle."[18]

But scientific inquiry requires no peculiar "leap of faith" beyond what we all take for granted all the time. No, the sciences are not the only source of knowledge. And yes, they eschew supernatural explanations. Moreover, the very possibility of scientific inquiry does presuppose that we have sensory organs capable of detecting particular things and events around us, and that there are some lawful patterns into which those things and events fall—though (as Bridgman points out) it does not require that all natural events are governed by laws. But these are presuppositions not only of the possibility of scientific inquiry, but also of the possibility of everyday inquiry of the most ordinary kind; otherwise, we could never successfully predict, as in fact we do every day, how people, animals, or stuff will behave.

We humans are capable—gradually, stumblingly, and sometimes painfully—of figuring things out, and of taking pleasure in understanding; but we also have a talent for elaborate obfuscation, and a weakness for the mysterious and the impressively incomprehensible. So, as older, religious entries in the crossword puzzle have gradually been displaced by newer, scientific entries, there have always been those who felt this as a loss: John Keats, for example, with his famous toast "to Newton's health, and confusion to mathematics"—Newton had destroyed the poetry of the rainbow, Keats believed, when he reduced it to a prism. But there have also always been those who have felt this demystification as a gain, a liberation: H. L. Mencken, for example, with his cheerful acknowledgment that "everything we are, we owe to Satan and those bootleg apples."[19]

I agree with Mencken; and, again, with Bridgman, when he writes that "the refusal of the scientist to follow the mystic, and his resolution to submit to the discipline of the actual . . . touch[es] the human spirit." The true scientist, Bridgman continues, feels that there is something "abhorrent and unclean" in the mystic's willingness to live in a world of his own construction; and, responding to the challenge of difficult questions, the freedom to devise whatever approach seems likeliest to resolve them, and the satisfaction of knowing that he is doing his honest best to arrive at true answers, finds the discipline of following the evidence where it leads both liberating and rewarding. As Bridgman notes, the twin ideals of the exercise of intelligence in tackling challenging problems and intellectual integrity in facing the evidence squarely touch the spirit not only of scientists but of all serious inquirers.[20] Indeed.

NOTES

1. Percy W. Bridgman, "Science, Materialism, and the Human Spirit" (1949), in Bridgman, *Reflections of a Physicist* (New York: Philosophical Library, 1955), pp. 452–72, pp. 456 and 457.

2. In what follows, I have, where appropriate, drawn quite freely on my *Defending Science—Within Reason: Between Scientism and Cynicism* (Amherst, NY: Prometheus Books, 2003), chapter 10.

3. See J. W. Grove, *In Defense of Science: Science, Technology and Politics in Modern Society* (Toronto: University of Toronto Press, 1989), p. 13. (He doesn't give the original reference.)

4. See "Coherence, Consistency, Cogency, Congruity, Cohesiveness, &c.," pp. 61–77 in this volume.

5. See "Trial and Error: The Supreme Court's Philosophy of Science," pp. 161–77 in this volume.

6. See "The Ideal of Intellectual Integrity, in Life and Literature," pp. 195–208 in this volume.

7. Psalm 8, from the King James version in its original spelling (which I learned from Adam Nicholson, "God's Work Via Committee," *The Wall Street Journal*, 30 September 2006, p. P14.)

8. See Michael Shermer, *How We Believe: The Search for God in an Age of Science* (New York: W. W. Freeman, 2000), pp. 34–35 and 65–69.

9. This idea left its mark on Judge Jones's ruling in *Kitzmiller v. Dover Area School District*, 400 F.Supp. 2d 707 (2005), of which there is more detailed discussion in the new preface to the paperback edition of my *Defending Science* (2007).

10. See Sander Greenland, Manuela Gago-Dominguez, and José Estaban, "In Defense of Risk-Factor Epidemiology," *Epidemiology* 15, no. 5 (September 2004): 529–35; and "An Epistemologist Among the Epidemiologists," pp. 179–82 in this volume.

11. Michael Buckley, "Religion and Science: Paul Davies and John Paul II," *Theological Studies* 52 (1990): 310–24.

12. Richard Swinburne, *Is There a God?* (New York: Oxford University Press, 1996), p. 37.

13. See Haack, *Defending Science* (n. 2), pp. 154–61, and "Not Cynicism, but Synechism," 79–94 in the present volume.

14. Andrew Dickson White, *A History of the Warfare Between Science and Theology in Christendom* (1896; New York: Dover, 1960), vol. 1, p. 2.

15. Bridgman, "Science, Materialism, and the Human Spirit" (n. 1), p. 456.

16. Phillip E. Johnson, *Darwin on Trial* (Washington, DC: Regnery Gateway, 1991), pp. 114–16.

17. Michael Polanyi, *Science, Faith and Society* (London: Geoffrey Cumberledge, Oxford University Press, 1946), p. 31.

18. Albert Einstein, "Physics and Reality," in *Ideas and Opinions of Albert Einstein*, translated from the German by Sonja Bargmann (New York: Crown Publishers, 1954), pp.

290–322, p. 295. (This is not intended, obviously, as a full account of Einstein's ideas about science and religion, which would require a whole other paper.)

19. H. L. Mencken, *Treatise on the Gods* (New York: Knopf, 1930), p. 292.

20. Percy Bridgman, "The Struggle for Intellectual Integrity" (1931), in *Reflections of a Physicist*, pp. 361–79, pp. 365–66.

13

THE IDEAL OF INTELLECTUAL INTEGRITY, IN LIFE AND LITERATURE

Certainly there be that delight in giddiness, and count it a bondage to fix a belief; affecting free-will in thinking, as well as in acting. . . . But it is not only the difficulty and labour which men take in finding out of truth, nor again that when it is found it imposeth upon men's thoughts, that doth bring lies in favour; but a natural though corrupt love of the lie itself. . . . Doth any man doubt, that if there were taken out of men's minds vain opinions, flattering hopes, false valuations, imaginations as one would, and the like, but it would leave the minds of a number of men poor shrunken things, full of melancholy and indisposition, and unpleasing to themselves?

. . . But howsoever these things are thus in men's depraved judgements and affections, yet . . . the inquiry of truth, which is the love-making or wooing of it, the knowledge of truth, which is the presence of it, and the belief of truth, which is the enjoying of it, is the sovereign good of human nature.

—Francis Bacon[1]

I n just a few short lines, Bacon presents the ideal of intellectual integrity with almost poetic precision and compactness; sketches some of the characteristic intellectual vices to which human beings are susceptible; suggests how these vices arise from the interference of the will with the intellect; and describes the "vain opinions, flattering hopes, and false valuations" to which they in turn give rise.

The remarkable brief essay, "Of Truth," from which these lines are taken is a rhetorical, a psychological, and a philosophical *tour de force*, illuminating questions about the traits of character that make some people strong, honest, thorough inquirers, and others weak, dishonest, or perfunctory: questions profoundly consequential for our understanding, and our conduct, of the life of the mind.

Of course, many others have also shed light on these questions; scientists and social thinkers as well as philosophers—I think of John Locke, C. S. Peirce, Friedrich Nietzsche, W. K. Clifford, Thorstein Veblen, and Percy Bridgman—have wrestled hard and helpfully with them. Many novelists, too—I think of George Eliot, Samuel Butler, Sinclair Lewis, William Cooper[2]—have explored the tangled roots and described the bitter fruits of ignorance, self-deception, hypocrisy, carelessness, and of those vain opinions, flattering hopes, and all their horrid kin, in the magnificently messy detail that imaginative literature makes possible, but from which dry philosophical analysis must abstract.

Inevitably, I, too, will abstract, as philosophers do. But in the spirit of Stanislav Lec's shrewd advice—"think before you think!"[3]—I will first remind myself, and you, of the vast variety and rich diversity of our vocabulary for describing and appraising a person's character or temperament *qua* believer, *qua* inquirer, or *qua* thinker. Here is an off-the-top-of-my-head list: sloppy, meticulous, thorough, patient, hasty, slapdash, credulous, skeptical, flighty, obstinate, willful, dogmatic, conventional, unconventional, iconoclastic, sober, light-minded, playful, serious, imaginative, fanciful, stodgy, original, derivative, reliable, unreliable, responsible, irresponsible, casual, prejudiced, partisan, honest, dishonest, slippery, simple-minded, crude, subtle, flexible, rigid, self-deceiving, independent, formulaic, crass, emotional, logical, illogical, confused, clear, ambivalent, penetrating, superficial, trenchant, sharp, dull, deep, shallow, critical, uncritical, quick, slow, thoughtful, curious, diligent, circumspect, cursory, accurate, picky, negligent, slack, loose, constipated, vague, foggy, vacillating, parochial, gullible, intuitive, dilettantish, hackneyed, sophisticated, blundering, perspicacious, judicious, inept, doctrinaire, timid, bold, conscientious, interested, disinterested, uninterested, engaged, perfunctory, pedestrian, plodding, persistent, painstaking. . . .

A detailed categorization of these terms, as in a thesaurus, might classify them according as they relate to honesty, to thoroughness and care, to effort, to intellectual styles and strengths, and so forth. I shall focus here on honesty, carefulness, and diligence, and of course also on dishonesty, carelessness, and sloth; questions about intellectual styles, gifts, knacks, and kinks will have to wait for another occasion.

A work of literature can convey, in prose that engages and delights us, some of the very truths that a work of philosophy, sometimes very ponderously and laboriously, states and elaborates; moreover, the way the narrative structure of a novel tracks its protagonists' thoughts and actions over time is especially well suited to explorations of character, epistemic character included. So, not to lose sight of how subtle and complex epistemic character can be, I am going to begin, not with philosophers' analyses, but with a novelist's exploration of willfulness and self-deception in belief and inquiry.

V. S. Pritchett wrote of *The Way of All Flesh*, published the year after Butler's death, that it is "one of the time-bombs of literature. . . . One thinks of it lying in [his] desk for thirty years, waiting to blow up the Victorian family and with it the whole great pillared and ballustraded edifice of the Victorian novel." William Maxwell observed in the *New Yorker* that while the novel is often read by "the young, bent on making out a case against their elders," Butler was fifty when he finished working on it, and "no reader much under that age is likely to appreciate the full beauty of its horrors. . . ."[4] True, all true; but from our perspective the important thing is that this is also one of the finest epistemological novels ever written: a semi-autobiographical *Bildungsroman* that traces not only the moral but also the intellectual growth of its central character, Ernest Pontifex, as he fumbles his way from a fog of self-deceptive pseudo-belief and sham inquiry to an appreciation of what it means really to believe something, and what is involved in really trying to find something out.

Brought up in an "atmosphere of lying and self-laudatory hallucination" (291) by his cruel, domineering clergyman father, Theobald, and his socially self-aggrandizing and spiritually self-deluded mother, Christina, further trained in humbug by Dr. Skinner at Roughborough School and then as a student in Cambridge, Ernest is none-too-subtly maneuvered by his parents (as, a generation before, the reluctant Theobald had been by his), into becoming a minister. As his ordination approaches, he briefly gets religion in—well, in earnest; at which—as Mr. Overton, Ernest's godfather and Butler's dryly deadpan narrator,[5] observes—"[e]ven Christina refrained from ecstasy over her son's having discovered the power of Christ's word, while Theobald was frightened out of his wits" (241).

Ernest's ambivalence soon returns, in spades. Still, as a troubled young curate he chooses to live among his poorest parishioners; and, feeling he ought to try to convert someone, resolves to begin with the other tenants in the seedy rooming house in Ashpit Place where he takes up residence. Too timid to tackle the loud, wife-beating tailor in the room above, he approaches the Methodist couple on the top floor, only to discover that he doesn't actually know what it is

he's trying to convert them *from*. He ends up in the front kitchen, trying to convert the free-thinking tinker, Mr. Shaw; but faced with the tinker's challenge to
give the story of the Resurrection of Christ as told in St. John's gospel, he is
embarrassed to find himself running the four gospel accounts hopelessly
together. If Ernest will go away and get the different accounts straight, Mr. Shaw
tells him, he may pay him another visit, "for I shall know you have made a good
beginning and mean business" (277). Ernest does as he is asked: he really tries
"to find out, not that [the four gospels] were all accurate, but whether they were
accurate or no. He did not care which result he should arrive at, but he was
resolved that he would reach one or the other" (280). He gets his first glimpse of
the difference between really trying to figure something out, and merely trying to
make a case for a predetermined conclusion.

But then, disaster: Ernest's unhealthily over-excited effort to convert another
neighbor, a young woman of easy virtue, is interrupted by one of her gentleman
callers, Mr. Towneley—an affluent, affable, and self-assured fellow, "big and very
handsome" (229), whom Ernest knows slightly from Cambridge. Ernest is
crushed; and blushing scarlet with humiliation at the contrast between himself and
the worldly Towneley, slinks away. "He knew well enough what he wanted now"
(282); kicking his Bible into a corner, he blunders into making a crass, clumsy
pass at another young woman in the house—rashly assuming that she and Miss
Snow are birds of a feather. Scared, agitated, and insulted, the naive and innocent
Miss Maitland hurries from the house; and returns with the police, who cart our
hero off to the magistrates' court, where he is sentenced to six months' hard labor.

This double humiliation is the making of him. In prison, slowly recovering
from the illness brought on by shock and shame, too weak for the treadmill but
allowed to have a Bible, Ernest returns to Mr. Shaw's challenge. Reading his New
Testament "as one who wished neither to believe nor disbelieve, but cared only
about finding out whether he ought to believe or no" (297), one day he experiences
a kind of revelation: that "very few care two straws about truth, or have any confidence that it is righter and better to believe what is true than what is untrue, even
though belief in the untruth may seem at first sight most expedient. Yet it is only
these few who can be said to believe anything at all; the rest are simply unbelievers
in disguise" (299). He has begun to appreciate the ideal of intellectual integrity.

And so, Ernest finds his way—though hardly all at once or directly, for "like
a snipe" he zigs and zags before settling to a steady flight (213). He cuts off communication with his ghastly parents; he makes his living as a secondhand clothes
dealer during a sad "marriage" to the pretty, good-natured—but hopelessly alco-
holic, and, it turns out, bigamous—Ellen. (Dry as ever, Overton muses: "Is it not
Tennyson who has said: 'T'is better to have loved and lost, than never to have

lost at all'?" [361]).[6] But eventually Ernest comes to see his time in Ashpit Place and in prison as far more valuable than his misspent years at Roughborough and Cambridge; he is even able to appreciate the irony of Theobald's pleonastic plea at family prayers, that Christina and himself, their children and servants, be made "*truly* honest and conscientious" (107, 230, 400).

Gradually realizing the potential that his godfather and his independent-minded, affectionate aunt Alethea (yes!) had seen in him, by the end of the book Ernest is, like Butler himself, a modestly successful if not very popular writer. When Overton wishes he would write more like other people, he replies that he "must write as he does or not at all" (429). When his publisher points out that his reputation is suffering because of his reluctance to form alliances in the literary world, he replies in one word: "Wait" (430).

"Those who know [Ernest] intimately," the book concludes, "do not know that they wish him greatly different from what he actually is" (431). I for one certainly wouldn't wish Ernest greatly different; and not least because his story has so much to teach us about intellectual character. For one thing, it illustrates very vividly how various and how individual intellectual character is, and how inextricably intertwined in each person's ever-evolving personality. For another, and most to the present purpose, Ernest's story brings home to us that to understand what intellectual integrity involves means thinking about the role of the will and the mechanisms of self-deception; about the nature of belief and pseudo-belief; and about the differences between inquiry and advocacy, and what happens when the two are blurred. And it nudges us to ask why intellectual integrity is not only an achievement, but a rare and difficult one—and why there are so many who, rather than recognizing it as an ideal, scorn or denigrate it as a kind of superstition.

◆ ◆

The phrase "intellectual integrity," with its etymological connotation of wholeness or unity, suggests that what is involved is a kind of harmony. The harmony involved is not, however, simply consistency or coherence at the intellectual level; rather, as expressions like "willful ignorance" and "wishful thinking" suggest, it is a kind of concordance of the will with the intellect. The phrase "intellectual honesty"—which Merriam-Webster's dictionary, as well as my linguistic intuition, tells me is a synonym for "intellectual integrity"—suggests that self-deception is the special kind of willfulness that intellectual integrity requires us to avoid. As Peirce writes, a man "must be single-minded and sincere with himself. Otherwise, his love of truth will melt away, at once" (1.49).[7] Articulating what is involved, however, calls for caution if we are to avoid suggesting *either* that belief is voluntary, that one can simply decide what to believe, *or* (at the opposite and equally faulty extreme) that a person's hopes, desires, and fears can have no legitimate bearing on his intellectual life.

To believe that *p* is to hold *p* true; to inquire into whether *p* is to try to find out whether *p* is true; and evidence that *p* is an indication that *p* is true. As this suggests, intellectual integrity is, at its heart, a matter of conducting your intellectual life from the motive of truth-seeking. Peirce is eloquent on the subject: the year after James's *The Will to Believe* was published, dedicated to "my old friend, Charles Sanders Peirce," we find him referring to the "Will to Learn" (5.583). Elsewhere he writes: "[t]he *spirit* . . . is the most essential thing—the *motive*" (1.34); for genuine inquiry requires "actually drawing the bow upon truth with intentness in the eye, with energy in the arm" (1.235), looking into things "without any sort of axe to grind" (1.44), seeking the truth "regardless of what the color of that truth may be" (7.605). I might put it, more prosaically, like this: really inquiring into a question requires that you want to find the true answer. But when what you want is not the truth, but a palatable conclusion, or a theologically or politically correct conclusion, or the conclusion you have already committed yourself to in print, or, . . . etc., your desires are pulling against your intellect.

However, since belief isn't simply voluntary, much as you might want to reach that theologically or politically correct conclusion, you can't just *make* yourself believe it; you can't just *decide* to believe that things are as you would like. You have to go about things less directly: to deceive yourself about where the evidence really points. As this reveals, "intellectually honest," like many of our terms for appraising intellectual character ("thorough," "meticulous," "responsible," "diligent," "negligent," and so on) has to do with a person's relation to evidence; for intellectual integrity requires a willingness to seek out evidence, and assess it, honestly.

Some philosophers have found the phenomenon of self-deception puzzling, since the idea of a person's lying to himself seems far more problematic than the idea of his lying to someone else. The better analogy is not with the flat-out lie, but with selective presentation, misdirection, being "economical with the truth." You *can't* simply tell yourself that not-*p*, and believe it, while being well aware that *p*.[8] You *can*, however, willfully pay attention selectively, concentrating your attention on this, favorable evidence, and not dwelling on that other, less favorable information; for this is, up to a point, a voluntary matter: hence our talk of "willful" ignorance, and "wishful" (and "fearful") thinking.

Those who "delight in giddiness, affecting free-will in thinking, as well as in acting," as Bacon so charmingly puts it, want to believe that things are as they would like them to be: a goal best achieved by not looking into things too closely, and actively ignoring or strenuously trying to explain away any inconvenient evidence you can't avoid altogether. And not only the irresponsibly light-minded, who want to change their opinions whenever they feel like it, but also the obstinately dogmatic, who don't want to change their opinions at all, do this in one way or another. But, as Ernest gradually comes to understand, when the will habitually pulls against the intellect, the price is steep; inevitably, you are drawn into pseudo-belief and pseudo-inquiry.

Someone who really believes that p will have a disposition, when circumstances demand it, to agree, or to aver, that p; and, when circumstances demand it, to act as if p.[9] Since it is true that p just in case p,[10] this is as much as to say that he holds p true. (Depending on the degree of intensity of his belief, the strength of his conviction that p, these dispositions may be strong or weak; depending on the degree of entrenchment of his belief, they may be more or less easily budged as new evidence comes in.)

Someone who really believes that not-p, but is pretending to believe that p—to avoid flak from his boss, say, or to escape the perils of the Inquisition—will say that p, when he must, and act as if p, when he can't avoid it; but his dispositions to assert and to behave as if not-p will remain untouched.

But someone who would very much like it to be the case that p (or very much fears that it is the case that p), and who willfully concentrates on evidence that p while willfully ignoring evidence that not-p, all the while telling himself that of course, p, is in a state of pseudo-belief. Like the person who really believes that not-p but is pretending to believe that p, he will aver that p, when this is expedient or is expected of him, and act as if p, when there will be no serious consequences; e.g., he may, like Ernest, affirm the creed unquestioningly, and even hope to convert unbelievers from a supposed heterodoxy he doesn't understand to a supposed orthodoxy he doesn't understand either. But he doesn't really believe either way; he isn't even straightforwardly pretending to others that he believes. Instead, he is *pretending to himself* that he believes that p. So he must deceive himself about deceiving himself, studiously ignoring the evidence that he is studiously ignoring the evidence that not-p—and so on. No wonder he is in a mental fog!

Someone who is really inquiring into a question wants to discover the truth of that question, no matter what that truth may be. Whether he wants the true answer out of pure scientific curiosity, "an impulse to penetrate into the reason of things,"[11] or he wants it for some ulterior reason, such as to find the cure for his child's illness, or to make money, or to become rich or famous; whether he is a deeply engaged inquirer who wants the true answer very badly, obsesses over the question, and works all the hours God sends to answer it, or he is a merely dutiful inquirer who goes home at five and gives his question no more thought until the next day, the truth of the matter is what he wants. (However, someone may want to know the truth with respect to some question, or want that truth to be known, without inquiring into it himself: think of a person who devotes himself to raising money so that others more competent than he can look into, say, a cure for macular degeneration.)

A person who knows full well that he isn't actually trying to work out the answer to the question he is supposedly investigating, but is goofing off—telling his boss or the dean that he is making progress, that he has written a draft of the eventual article, etc., when actually he has done nothing—is pretending to inquire; as, in a different way, is a person who knows full well that he has no idea, really, whether p or not-p, and doesn't really *care* whether p or not-p, but is busily seeking out evidence that p, and finding ways to hide or explain away any indication that not-p, because he wants the boss, the dean, the external evaluators, the voting public, or whomever, to believe that p.

But someone who is seeking out evidence that p, and finding ways to avoid, ignore, or explain away any indication that not-p, while telling himself that he is trying to find out whether p, is engaged in pseudo-inquiry. Perhaps he is already unbudgeably convinced that p, and couldn't be persuaded by any evidence to the contrary; or perhaps he doesn't give a damn about whether p, only about the fact that being known as a proponent of p will make his name in the profession or ensure his boss's approval. In any case, such a person isn't really inquiring; he isn't even straightforwardly pretending to others that he is inquiring; he is *pretending to himself* that he is inquiring. Like the pseudo-believer, the pseudo-inquirer is obliged to conduct his intellectual life in a self-induced mental fog; in this case, a fog in which inquiry becomes indistinguishable from advocacy—the art of the attorney, the lobbyist, the politician, and (as Butler doesn't fail to remind us) of the clergyman. Advocacy is all very well in its place;[12] but pseudo-inquiry *has* no legitimate place in the life of the mind.

Allow me to add—recalling the wonderfully funny hypothesis that bullshit is so called "because it is very loose and copiously produced"[13]—that pseudo-belief and pseudo-inquiry stand to real belief and real inquiry rather as a bull session stands to a genuinely truth-directed discussion.

Our capacity to inquire is a remarkable human talent; but of course we don't always inquire successfully. Sometimes, even when we really want to know, we just can't figure something out: our imaginations fail us, and we can't think of a plausible hypothesis; or we can't see, or reason, well enough. But sometimes we don't really want to know: we are ambivalent about inquiring, or about what we might discover if we look into things too carefully. Sometimes we don't care enough to bother finding out; and sometimes we really want *not* to discover what we fear will be unpalatable truths, and go to some lengths to avoid finding out. And so we not only often make mistakes and often fail to come up with answers; we not only often inquire reluctantly, half-heartedly, dragging our heels about it; we also often fudge, fake, and obfuscate so as to disguise, even from ourselves, that we aren't really inquiring at all. This is the sad fact that dawns on Ernest in his prison cell: pseudo-belief and pseudo-inquiry are ubiquitous.

"Real [intellectual] power," Peirce observes, "is not *born* in a man; it has to be worked out."[14] The same is true of intellectual integrity; it is an achievement, and a difficult one at that. For that tendency to self-serving mental fogginess is just as much part of human nature as the capacity to inquire. A whole sleazy crew of motives, desires, hopes, and fears conspires to impede the intellect: among them sloth (we don't care to do the work involved in looking into a question thoroughly), impatience (we cut corners because we want quick and easy answers), and timidity (we sense the dangers involved should we have the misfortune to discover that the conventional "wisdom" is no such thing). And then there's hubris: as Peirce observes, the desire to learn requires that you acknowledge that "you do not satisfactorily know already" (1.13); but it hurts our pride to admit that we don't know, or that we were mistaken.

"Your discovery of the contradiction [the paradox of the class of all classes that are not members of themselves] . . . has shaken the basis on which I intended to build arithmetic," Gottlob Frege writes in response to Bertrand Russell's letter pointing out the inconsistency in his logic; and sets to work to try again in an appendix to be added to the second volume of his *Grundgezetze der Arithmetik*, then in press.[15] When Rosalind Franklin points out that DNA contains ten times as much water as his model has room for, "Honest Jim" Watson candidly admits his embarrassing mistake and goes back to the drawing board—as he will do again, many times, before the problem is finally solved.[16] Such expressions of intellectual honesty are striking and inspiring precisely because we all know how hard it can be to admit that you screwed up, and to take up a difficult task again after failing once (or twice, or . . .). As my title indicates, intellectual integrity is an ideal—something to strive for, but something achieved only imperfectly at best.[17]

Writing in 1933 of "The Struggle for Intellectual Integrity,"[18] Percy Bridgman observes that "animals and morons are incapable of intellectual honesty." Moreover, he continues, appreciation of this ideal requires not only a certain intellectual power, but also "example and practice" (364–65). It isn't always easy to recognize when rationalizing has crept into your thinking; and the opportunity for the practice of intellectual integrity is possible only in a society far enough from bare subsistence that an appreciable fraction of people can engage in intellectual pursuits. Intellectual integrity can and should be an ideal for intellectual workers in every field, Bridgman adds; but "in scientific activity the necessity for continual checking against the inexorable facts of experience is so insistent, and the penalties for allowing the slightest element of rationalizing to creep in are so immediate" that even the dullest understand that "intellectual honesty is the price of even a mediocre degree of success" (365–66).

More than that: the ideal of intellectual integrity can come to make a strong emotional appeal; one "finds something fine in . . . rigorously carrying through a train of thought careless of the personal implications; he feels a traitor to something deep within him if he refuses to follow out logical implications because he sees they are going to be unpleasant. . . ." Though only a small fraction of people have yet caught the vision, Bridgman believes, "enough have caught it . . . that a new leaven is working in society" (366–67). But the consequences for someone who does grasp the ideal are likely to be uncomfortable. His first reaction will be "a complete repudiation in his own mind of the bunk that he is asked to accept. So much he must do, though it slay him." But, Bridgman continues, "he must also continue to live in society as he finds it" (368)—and this won't be easy. Moreover, at least in the short term, the effects of this new leaven in society may be far from benign; alluding to the Germany of his day, Bridgman predicts that a period of disruption and instability is inevitable, for there is bound to be resistance to the ideal, and hostility to those who feel its power.

When Bridgman likens the discovery that we are capable of responding to the ideal of intellectual integrity to "that other great discovery of the human race about itself, that it responds emotionally to music" (366), I am reminded yet again of *The Way of All Flesh*. Noticing that the callow fourteen-year-old Ernest can hum and whistle all kinds of classy stuff, Alethea sets him to building an organ: a project which, she hopes, will develop both his puny muscles and his puny character. "'He likes the best music,' she thought, 'and he hates Dr. Skinner. This is a very fair beginning'" (148). And when she dies, Ernest proposes to his godfather that they inscribe on her tombstone a bar of music from the last of Handel's six grand fugues—music that "might have done for Leonardo da Vinci himself," Overton comments, as he chuckles over the last line of Ernest's letter: "if you do not like it for Aunt Alethea I shall keep it for myself" (166–67).

When Bridgman stresses the importance of intellectual integrity to "the scientific worker," I am reminded of Peirce's use of "the scientific attitude" as a synonym for "genuine, good-faith inquiry" (1.43ff.). But neither Bridgman's nor Peirce's point is really about the sciences as such. For as Bridgman acknowledges, not only scientists but serious inquirers of every kind (and, I would add, in every age) have some grasp of the ideal of intellectual honesty. Moreover, the whole sad panoply of intellectual dishonesties from wishful thinking to outright fraud is to be found both in the history of science and in its current practice. In fact, of the vast array of helps to inquiry that scientists have gradually devised over the centuries, it is precisely the social mechanisms that, by and large and in the long run have, thus far, kept most scientists, most of the time, reasonably honest, that are the most fragile. They are, moreover, ever more susceptible to failure as science gets bigger, more expensive, and more potentially profitable to its practitioners.[19]

Elsewhere, suggesting how the natural sciences have achieved their remarkable successes, I have addressed issues about scientific dishonesty and fraud in detail.[20] Here, however, I want to develop some thoughts prompted by Bridgman's observation that there will inevitably be many who regard the ideal of intellectual integrity with indifference, and some who attack it as an illusion, a kind of superstition. Since Bridgman alludes to the rise of fascism, I will begin by reminding you of these words of Hitler's: "I don't want there to be any intellectual education. . . . [W]e stand at the end of the Age of Reason. . . . A new era of the magical explanation of the world is rising, an explanation based on will rather than knowledge. There is no truth, in either the moral or the scientific sense. Science is a social phenomenon, . . . limited by the usefulness or harm it causes."[21]

The rhetoric of "a new era of magical explanation" sounds dated; but the remarkable thing about "there is no truth," and "[s]cience is a social phenomenon, . . . limited by the usefulness or harm it causes," and so on, surely, is how *un*remarkable these ideas sound today. For in our times disillusion with the idea of truth and the ideal of honest inquiry has become almost an orthodoxy; and we face a veritable barrage of arguments purporting to show that the concept of truth is irredeemable and the supposed ideal of intellectual honesty is just another sham. Elsewhere, spelling out why we should value intellectual integrity, I have tried to show that these arguments are, one and all, unsound.[22] Here, however—noting for the record that if the cynics really believed, as they profess to, that the concept of truth is irredeemable, there would be no point in their offering arguments at all—I will try to suggest why so many apparently find the cynics' arguments appealing, their (often manifest) unsoundness notwithstanding.

Ours, it is said, is the Age of Information; but of course it is also the age of misinformation, of boosterism, advocacy "research," creative accounting, official cover-ups, propaganda, and PR. *Pravda* (and *Veritas*) is full of propaganda, spin, and outright lies; the scientific breakthrough or miracle drug trumpeted in the press often turns out to be no such thing; in their zealous pursuit of clients' interests advocates commonly employ, in Judge Frankel's words, "time-honored tricks and stratagems to block or distort the truth";[23] much of the boasted wealth of electronic "information" out there is dross; and so on and on.

You might think that universities would be the exception. Indeed, in principle a university should be in the business of inquiry; and from time to time real inquiry actually does take place. Too often, however, it is crowded out by preoccupations of quite other kinds, such as football or politics, but also by intellectual busywork, political axe-grinding, and pseudo-inquiry of every variety imaginable, masquerading as the real thing. Worse, only too often a decline of good-faith inquiry is accompanied by an escalation of boosterism and hype, creating an ethos eerily reminiscent of the "atmosphere of lying and self-laudatory hallucination" in which young Ernest Pontifex grew up. ("Survival of the slickest" is the phrase that comes to mind.)[24]

Here is Bridgman once more: "A dog is content to turn around three times before lying down; but a man would have to invent an explanation of it. . . . There is not a single human social institution which has not originated in hit or miss fashion, but, nevertheless, every one of these institutions is justified by some rationalizing argument as the best possible, and, what is worse, the community demands the acceptance of these arguments . . ." (368).[25] Is it any wonder, then, if in today's academy some set to work to cook up arguments purporting to show that the concept of truth is humbug, and the supposed ideal of intellectual integrity an illusion, or that others eagerly embrace the conclusion? After all, if that conclusion were—pardon the expression!—true, there would be no shame in failing to engage in what old-fashioned prigs like Peirce and I confusedly describe as "genuine inquiry";[26] for there could be no such thing.

This suggests the role of the cynics' arguments in the psychic economy of those to whom they appeal: to generate a thick-enough mental fog to enable the pseudo-inquirer, who must somehow disguise his dishonesty from himself, to ease the strain of studiously ignoring the fact that he is studiously ignoring unfavorable evidence.

Now I am reminded of Ernest's comment—as, finally settling to a steady path, he realizes he must make his way by writing—that "there are a lot of things that want saying which no one dares to say, a lot of shams that want attacking, and yet no one attacks them. . . . [I]t is my fate to say them." Overton warns that this is bound to make him unpopular. Ernest replies that that's too bad: "hornets' nests are exactly what I happen to like" (408–409).

Well, even though, like Ernest, I haven't always heeded his advice, I would like to conclude by thanking Edward Overton—who unfortunately is unable to be with us today—for his invaluable help in thinking all this through.

NOTES

1. Francis Bacon, "Of Truth" (1625) in *Francis Bacon's Essays*, ed. Oliphant Smeaton (London: Dent, and New York: Dutton; Everyman's Library, 1906), pp. 1–3. The quotations are from pp. 1 and 2.

2. I have in mind Eliot's *Daniel Deronda* (1878), on the power of ignorance; Lewis's *Arrowsmith* (1925) and Cooper's *The Struggles of Albert Woods* (1952) on the role of personality in science; and Butler's *The Way of All Flesh* (1903) on intellectual integrity— the novel on which I shall focus here.

3. My source is J. Gross, ed., *The Oxford Book of Aphorisms* (Oxford: Oxford University Press, 1988), p. 262.

4. My source for these quotations is the anonymous introduction to Samuel Butler, *The Way of All Flesh* (1903: New York: Random House, Modern Library Paperback edition, 1998), pp. v–vii. All subsequent page references to *The Way of All Flesh* are to this edition.

5. Commentators tell us that Overton represents the mature Butler, reflecting on the life of the young Butler, as represented by Ernest. As Overton remarks, "[e]very man's work . . . is always a portrait of himself. . . . I may very likely be condemning myself, all the time that I am writing this book, for I know that whether I like it or no I am portraying myself more surely than I am portraying any of the characters. . . ." (67).

6. Of course, what Tennyson had written, in *In Memoriam* XXVII, was: "T'is better to have loved and lost/than never to have loved at all."

7. Charles Sanders Peirce, *Collected Papers*, eds. Charles Hartshorne, Paul Weiss, and (vols. 7 and 8) Arthur Burks (Cambridge: Harvard University Press, 1931–58), 1.49. [References are by volume and paragraph number.] Citations to Peirce in the text are from this source.

8. As Peirce observes, "A man cannot startle himself by jumping up with an exclamation of *Boo!*" (5.58).

9. This isn't intended as a complete theory of belief, only as a first step. For a fuller account, see my *Defending Science—Within Reason* (Amherst, NY: Prometheus Books, 2003), pp. 156–61.

10. This isn't intended as a complete theory of truth, only as a first step. For a fuller account, see my "Confessions of an Old-Fashioned Prig," in *Manifesto of a Passionate Moderate* (Chicago: University of Chicago Press, 1998), pp. 7–30, pp. 21ff., and "The Unity of Truth and the Plurality of Truths," pp. 43–60 in the present volume.

11. Peirce again: 1.44.

12. See my "Epistemology Legalized: Or, Truth, Justice, and the American Way," *American Journal of Jurisprudence* 49 (2004): 43–61.

13. I thought I remembered this from Harry Frankfurt, "On Bullshit," in *The Importance of What We Care About* (Cambridge: Cambridge University Press, 1989), pp. 11–33, and subsequently reprinted as a book (!) (Princeton: Princeton University Press, 2005); but this turns out to have been a false memory, and I have not been able to discover the real source.

14. Quoted in Carolyn Eisele, ed., *The New Elements of Mathematics* (The Hague: Mouton, 1976), vol. 4, p. 977.

15. Frege's letter to Russell, dated June 22, 1902, appears in Jean van Heijenoort, ed., *From Frege to Gödel: A Source Book in Mathematical Logic 1879–1931* (Cambridge, MA: Harvard University Press, 1967), pp. 127–28.

16. James D. Watson, *The Double Helix: A Personal Account of the Discovery of DNA* (1967: edited by Gunther Stent, New York: W. W. Norton, 1980), p. 59.

17. See also James Gouinlock, *Eros and the Good* (Amherst, NY: Prometheus Books, 2004), pp. 272ff., on the growth of intellectual independence, and pp. 274ff., on the "scientific ideal."

18. Percy W. Bridgman, "The Struggle for Intellectual Integrity," *Harper's Magazine* (December 1933); reprinted in Bridgman, *Reflections of a Physicist* (New York: Philosophical Library, 1955), pp. 361–79. Page references in the text are to the reprinted version.

19. See my *Defending Science* (n. 9 above), chapters 1 and 4; and "The Integrity of Science: What It Means, Why It Matters," pp. 103–27 in the present volume.

20. See *Defending Science* (n. 9 above); and "Scientific Secrecy and 'Spin,'" pp. 129–45 in the present volume.

21. My source is Gerald Holton, *Einstein, History, and Other Passions: The Rebellion of Science at the End of the Twentieth Century* (1995: New York: Addison Wesley, 1996), p. 31.

22. See "Confessions of an Old-Fashioned Prig" (n. 10 above); and "Staying for an Answer," and "The Unity of Truth and the Plurality of Truths," pp. 25–36 and 43–60 in the present volume.

23. Marvin Frankel, "The Search for Truth: An Umpireal View," *University of Pennsylvania Law Review* 121, no. 5 (1975): 1031–59, p. 1038.

24. On this subject, Thorstein Veblen's *The Higher Learning in America* (1919; Stanford, CA: Academic Reprints, 1954) is classic; and Jacques Barzun, *The American University: How It Runs, Where It Is Going* (1968: second edition, Chicago: University of Chicago Press, 1993) is also essential. See also my "Preposterism and Its Consequences (1996), in *Manifesto of a Passionate Moderate* (n. 10 above), pp. 188–208.

25. Compare this, from Nietzsche's *Daybreak* (1881), aphorism 1: "Reasonableness After the Fact": "all things that live long enough are gradually so soaked through with reason that their origin in unreason comes to seem improbable."

26. The phrase is Richard Rorty's: "you can still find [philosophers] who will solemnly tell you that they are seeking *the truth* . . . lovably old-fashioned prigs." *Essays on Heidegger and Others* (Cambridge: Cambridge University Press, 1991), p. 86.

14

AFTER MY OWN HEART

Dorothy Sayers's Feminism

Lord, teach us to take our hearts and look them in the face, however difficult it may be.[1]

There was a time when, disinclined to mix business with pleasure, I found the very idea of the philosophical novel off-putting. I think it was Alison Lurie's *Imaginary Friends*,[2] a deliciously comic exploration of cognitive dissonance and the pitfalls of social-scientific inquiry, that changed my mind, persuaded me of the merits of mixing pleasure with business, and gave me a great fondness for (not the epistolary but) the epistemological novel.

In this genre, I have a particular admiration for Samuel Butler's reflections on the ubiquitous epistemological vices—self-deception, sham inquiry, hypocrisy—that really are *The Way of All Flesh*;[3] and a special fondness for Dorothy L. Sayers's *Gaudy Night*, a book I discovered only when a graduate student who had heard me give a lecture entitled "Concern for Truth: What It Means, Why It Matters"[4] sent me a copy. She was right on the mark. For the plot of Sayers's story turns precisely on a character's concern for truth, and the disastrous series of reactions it prompts; and an important preoccupation is the relation of epistemological to other values: why is honesty valuable in scientific and other inquiry? is suppressing a fact as bad as telling a lie? what is the relation

---

between epistemological and ethical values? do the obligations of one's job always, or ever, override considerations of personal loyalty?

Sayers's story is set in the imaginary Oxford women's college, Shrewsbury, of which Harriet Vane, professional detective novelist and part-time sleuth, is a graduate. Miss de Vine, Shrewsbury's history don, is "a soldier knowing no personal loyalties, whose sole allegiance [is] to the fact" (18), her devotion to the intellectual life "a powerful spiritual call" (137). In her previous position as provost of Flamborough College she exposed the dishonesty of a professorial candidate who, on finding an old letter that undermined his thesis, purloined and hid the evidence instead of ripping up his dissertation and starting again. The exposure costs him his career and, as he turns to drink and falls into despair, his life. His widow, now using her maiden name of Annie Wilson, has taken a post as scout as Shrewsbury, where she expresses her rage at Miss de Vine and her resentment of women scholars generally in vandalism, poison-pen letters, and even attempted murder.

Significant among Annie's acts of vandalism is the destruction of the college library's copy of C. P. Snow's *The Search* (258).[5] In Snow's novel (loosely based on the early work in X-ray crystallography by W. T. Astbury and his group in textile sciences at Leeds) a young man starting out in science is tempted to destroy the photograph that undermines his beautiful theory, but resists the temptation. Later, however, just as he is about to be appointed to an important post, he finds he has made a careless mistake in his work, the discovery of which costs him the position—after which he decides he doesn't really want to be a scientist after all.

To suppress a truth, avers Miss Edwards, Shrewsbury's biologist, is to publish a falsehood. The bursar wonders aloud what anyone could hope to gain by deliberate falsification, and her colleague Miss Lydgate concurs: "What satisfaction could one possibly get out of a reputation one knew one didn't deserve? It would be horrible" (373). But Miss Hillyard notes that such dishonesty frequently happens, out of ambition, or to get the better of an argument. The dean recalls that at the end of Snow's novel another scientist deliberately falsifies a result, but the man who made the original mistake says nothing, because the culprit is hard up, and has a wife and family to keep. "Of course one couldn't do that," responds Miss Barton, "not for ten wives and fifty children" (374). And then Miss de Vine tells her story of Arthur Robinson and his dishonest Master's thesis.

No less significant among Annie's acts of vandalism are the burning of Miss Barton's book on *The Position of Women in the Modern State*, and the mutilation of the painstakingly corrected proofs of Miss Lydgate's book on prosody, in which the usually mild-mannered and tolerant English don has subjected Mr. Elkbottom's ridiculous theories to harsh criticism. No less significant, because they symbolize Sayers's second theme, intertwining with questions about the relation of the epistemological and the ethical: the place of women in the life of the mind.

When Harriet, with the help of Lord Peter Wimsey, exposes her as the criminal, Annie—the desperately angry Total Woman—is defiant: "Couldn't you leave my man alone? He told a lie about someone who was dead and dust hundreds of years ago. . . . You broke him and killed him—all for nothing. Do you think that's a woman's job?" (485). Annie thinks women should be wives and mothers; these women dons, and the women students for that matter, are unnatural creatures, taking away men's jobs.

Sayers's cast of characters enables her to look at Annie's question from just about every angle. Among the graduates, there's Mary Attwood, née Stokes, who as a student was the charming, polished center of her set, taking the lead in all those late-night discussions of love, art, and religion, but who has by now succumbed to mental stagnation: "one of those small, summery brains that flower early and run to seed" (9); Catherine Freemantle, who took her degree and married a farmer: "all that brilliance, all that trained intelligence, harnessed to a load that any uneducated country girl could have drawn" (47); and Phoebe Tucker, a former history student who now works with her archeologist husband, and whose little boy has recently very carefully and correctly excavated the gardner's rubbish heap. Among the undergraduates, there's Miss Cattermole, who really wants to be a cook or a nurse, but whose parents insisted that she go to college; and Miss Layton, who, when her fiancé shows an interest in the emotionally predatory Miss Flaxman, puts him off by telling him she's a great scholar (she plans, when she herself gets the first-class degree she expects and deserves, to pretend she did it by being fragile and pathetic in the viva). And then there's Beatrice, Annie's small daughter, sketched in a half-dozen vivid lines. What does she want to do when she grows up, Harriet asks; to keep a garage, Beatrice replies. Her mother scolds her: you'll never find a husband if you mess around in a garage getting dirty. Beatrice pouts: "I don't want [a husband]. I'd rather have a motorcycle" (246).

Harriet herself is the most rounded and real of the characters in the book: she is nostalgic for the sheltered academic life, but having made her way in the real world (and survived the scandal of being falsely accused of the murder of her lover) she isn't entirely comfortable back in Oxford; she isn't sure Miss de Vine did the best thing, but she is sure that people like Annie, who make other people their jobs, are dangerous to have around; looking *her* heart in the face, she finally acknowledges her love for Peter Wimsey but fears that to accept the proposal of marriage he makes on special occasions—as a birthday treat, on Guy Fawkes's

Day, and regularly on April Fool's Day—would be fatally to sacrifice her independence. Lord Peter, however, surprises her by acknowledging her right to run her own risks to solve the crimes: "That was an admission of equality. . . . If he conceived of marriage along those lines, then the whole problem would have to be reviewed in a new light." Twice in the course of the book Harriet rejects Peter's proposals ("No, I'm sorry." "No. I can't see my way to it."); but on the last page of the book, when he proposes again (*"placetne, magistra?"*), she accepts (*"placet"*) (501).

One advantage of a novel, as of a Platonic dialogue, is that many different approaches and answers can be presented and explored; one disadvantage of a novel, as of a Platonic dialogue, is that the reader may be left unsure which approach the author takes to be best, which answers she takes to be true. Happily, however, we know how Sayers herself would reply to Annie; for, besides her detective fiction, her translations of the *Chanson de Roland* and of Dante, among her wide-ranging essays (on politics, on Dr. Watson's Christian name, on the richness and flexibility of the English language, etc., etc.), Sayers published a pair of crisp and refreshingly unorthodox papers on feminism.[6] I say "on feminism," though Sayers herself eschews the term, because by my lights she surely *is* a feminist; not, to be sure, a feminist of any of the now-fashionable varieties, but an old-fashioned, humanistic, individualistic feminist: a feminist, in short, after my own heart.

Since, these days, both "humanist" and "individualist," are likely to be misunderstood, I had better explain that "humanist," in this context, means "concerned with what human beings have in common *qua* human beings," and carries no connotation of aggressive atheism. (In fact, Sayers was a devout Anglican—too devout for my taste. Among her works is the famous radio play of the life of Jesus, *The Man Born to Be King*, and a whole corpus of writings on theological matters.) Even more importantly, perhaps, "individualist" here means "valuing the individuality of individual human beings, respecting the differences between you and me," and carries no connotation of every-man-for-himself-ism; it has the sense rather of William James's shrewd essay "On the Importance of the Individual" than of what John Dewey calls "ragged individualism."

Sayers defends two main positive themes: that women are fully human beings, just as men are; and that, like all human beings, women are individuals, each one different. These are so closely interrelated that disentangling them is close to impossible—but probably, as this passage reveals, also undesirable: "'What,' men have distractedly asked from the beginning of time, 'what on earth do women want?' I do not know that women, *as* women, want anything in particular, but as human beings they want, my good men, exactly what you want yourselves: interesting occupation, reasonable freedom for their pleasures, and a sufficient emotional outlet. What form the occupation, the pleasures and the emotion may take, depends entirely upon the individual. You know that this is so with yourselves—why will you not believe that it is so with us?"[7]

Observing that "women are more like men than anything else on earth,"[8] Sayers stresses the needs that all human beings share: meaningful work, and family, friends, someone to love. "A woman is as good as a man"—if it is not to be as meaningless as "an elephant is as good as a racehorse" (as good as a racehorse for what?)—should mean that a woman is just as much an individual human being as a man is.[9] And *qua* individual human being, a woman should be free to do whatever work she is best at. (Like Plato, Sayers seems to assume that if each person does what he or she is best at, each job will be done by the person who does it best. Not so, unfortunately; but I won't pursue the point.) Probably, she thinks, there will always be fewer women mathematicians and composers than men; but what matters is that talented women can become mathematicians or composers if they choose. But what woman, it will be asked, really prefers a job to a home and family? Relatively few, Sayers believes. The unfairness is that a woman who devotes herself to her work is apt to be regarded as a freak, while a man who does the same is seen as dedicated; and—now Sayers sounds a lot like Harriet—that women should so often have to make the choice between work and family, whereas men do not.

Heterodox in her own day, apparently, and even more so in ours, Sayers deliberately plays down the idea of women as a class, category, or group. On some topics, she grants, women are likely to have special knowledge, though even there they will probably disagree among themselves; but on most questions, she insists, there is no "woman's point of view." "Are women really *not human*," she asks, "that they should be expected to toddle along all in a flock like sheep?"[10] Yes, there is a fundamental difference between men and women; but it is not the only fundamental difference in the world. In some ways she has a lot in common with her cleaning lady, but in a discussion of art and literature she would have far more in common with Mr. Bernard Shaw. And her opinions on questions of art or literature, she continues, are just that, *her* opinions: "I am occasionally desired by congenital imbeciles and the editors of magazines to say something about the writing of detective fiction 'from the woman's point of view.' To such demands, one can only say, 'Go away and don't be silly. You might as well ask what is the female angle on an equilateral triangle.'"[11]

Those who opposed admitting women to the universities asked rhetorically, "Why should women want to know about Aristotle?" The answer is not that all women would be the better for knowing about Aristotle, much less that they would be more companionable wives for their husbands if they did; no, "What women want as a class is irrelevant. . . . I, eccentric individual that I am, do want to know about Aristotle, and I submit that there is nothing in my shape or bodily functions that need prevent my knowing about him."[12] Sayers might have chosen literature or logic, archeology or architecture as her example; but her choice of Aristotle has a particular poignancy, for also among her essays is "Aristotle on Detective Fiction," adapting and applying the *Poetics* to a new genre.[13]

Sayers's angle on Aristotle is certainly not the, or even a, "woman's point of view." It is *her* angle, the point of view of a particular person with her own particular interests, her own particular projects. It puts me in mind of the disagreement I once had with Jürgen Habermas: I had argued that the idea that women bring to philosophy the special insight made possible by their oppression "neglects the most important qualities talented women have to offer philosophy: logical acumen, textual sensitivity, creative imagination, analytic rigor, conceptual subtlety and penetration, etc.";[14] Habermas maintained, in the kindest possible way, that his women graduate students *had* brought special insights, pointing out to him that Aristotle's view of women was in some respects unenlightened. No doubt Sayers would have been quick to give the answer I wish I'd given: "*Not good enough!* Each serious woman scholar of Aristotle will have her own contribution to make to our understanding of his work; to expect anything less is condescension." Sayers's angle on Aristotle, I might add, is fresh and illuminating, while the supposed "woman's angle" is by now, surely, more than a little stale.

When Sayers wrote "Are Women Human?" in 1938 the battle for the admission of women to the universities was already won. (Sayers herself earned first-class honors in Medieval and Modern Languages at Oxford in 1915, but received her degrees only at the historic ceremony in 1920 at which the first women graduates were honored.) She would surely have been pleased by the great advances women have made since then, in the life of the mind as elsewhere. But she would not have been pleased to see college becoming less and less an opportunity for those who genuinely delight in building and stretching their intellectual muscles than an exercise in credentialism; nor to see how inhospitable today's academy can be to the genuinely independent thinker, of whatever gender. She would have detested the jargon-choked, muddy blandness of contemporary academic prose. And she would surely have been dismayed to find how influential the idea has become that a woman academic had better take the "woman's point of view," or else be deemed guilty of complicity in sexism.

Doubtless some will see Sayers's whole approach as passé, a holdover from the Dark Ages before second-wave feminism; but I see it as a much-needed antidote to the emphasis on women-as-a-class that predominates in feminism today. A focus on women-as-a-class was the basis of old practices of exclusion, and those who fought to get rid of those practices had no alternative but to focus on women-as-a-class themselves. Now, however, focusing too exclusively on the category, Woman, risks playing into the hands of the oppressors. "It used to be said," Sayers observes, "that women had no *esprit de corps*; we have proved that we have—do not let us run into the opposite error of insisting that there is an aggressively feminist 'point of view' about everything."[15]

A refusal to acknowledge women's full humanity, and a correlative inability to appreciate each woman's full individuality, really is at the very heart of sexism (and, *mutatis mutandis*, of racism). So it is disturbing that many women in the academy today, rather than being unambiguously welcomed as full participants in the life of the mind, find themselves subtly or not-so-subtly encouraged to confine themselves to the pink-collar ghetto of "women's issues" and "feminist approaches," as it is to hear the echoes of old, sexist stereotypes in contemporary feminist philosophy: feminist ethics will focus on caring rather than duty, or on virtue rather than justice; or, logic is a masculinist enterprise; or, feminist epistemology should stress connectedness, community, emotion, trust, the body, etc.

How much better it would be if, instead of casting around for an epistemology that represents "the feminist point of view," we tried, as feminists, finally to get beyond the stereotypes; and, as epistemologists, to develop a true account of knowledge, evidence, warrant, inquiry, and so on. Then we might be readier to acknowledge that any halfway adequate epistemology will need to be at once quasi-logical, personal, and social; concerned with the cognitive capacities and limitations that all human beings share, and with the idiosyncracies, expertise, and imaginative contributions of individuals; looking to the way interactions among individuals may compensate for this individual's perceptual and intellectual defects, while keeping the insights only that individual could contribute.

C. S. Peirce once complained: "There is a kink in my damned brain that prevents me from thinking as other people think";[16] but without that kink, without Peirce's intellectual left-handedness, philosophy would have been poorer by far—as feminist thinking would be the poorer without Sayers's quirky, idiosyncratic, literate intelligence. "Somebody who reads only newspapers and at best books of contemporary authors," Einstein observed, "looks to me like an extremely near-sighted person who scorns eyeglasses. He is completely dependent on the prejudices and fashions of his times, since he never gets to see or hear anything else," when at any given time "there are only a few enlightened people with a lucid mind and style and with good taste."[17] And even fewer, I would add, so wryly witty that it's a pleasure doing business with them.

NOTES

1. Dorothy L. Sayers, *Gaudy Night* (1936: New York: Harper Paperbacks, 1995). The passage quoted is from "the extempore prayer of an incoherent curate," p. 334. All subsequent page references in the text are to this edition.

2. Alison Lurie, *Imaginary Friends* (1967: New York, Owl Books, Henry Holt and Company, 1998).

3. See "The Ideal of Intellectual Integrity, in Life and Literature," pp. 195–208 in the present volume.

4. Haack, "Concern for Truth: What It Means, Why It Matters," in *The Flight from Science and Reason*, eds. Paul R. Gross, Norman Levitt, and Martin W. Lewis, *Annals of the New York Academy of Sciences*, 775 (1996): 57–62; also reprinted in a book of the same title (Baltimore: Johns Hopkins University Press, 1997), pp. 57–62.

5. C. P. Snow, *The Search* (New York: Charles Scribner's Sons, 1934).

6. "Are Women Human?" (1938), and "The Human-Not-Quite-Human" (undated), in Sayers, *Unpopular Opinions: Twenty-One Essays* (New York: Harcourt, Brace and Company, 1947), pp. 129–41 and 142–49.

7. Sayers, "Are Women Human?" (n. 6), pp. 138–39.

8. Sayers, "The Human-Not-Quite-Human" (n. 6), p. 142.

9. "Are Women Human?" (n. 6), p. 129.

10. "Are Women Human?" (n. 6), p. 138.

11. "Are Women Human?" (n. 6), p. 137.

12. "Are Women Human?" (n. 6), p. 131.

13. Sayers, "Aristotle on Detective Fiction," in *Unpopular Opinions* (n. 6 above), pp. 222–36.

14. I was presenting "The Best Man for the Job May Be a Woman . . . and Other Alien Thoughts on Affirmative Action in the Academy," now published in Haack, *Manifesto of a Passionate Moderate: Unfashionable Essays* (Chicago: University of Chicago Press, 1998), pp. 167–87, at New York University Law School, where Habermas was then visiting.

15. "Are Women Human?" (n. 6), p. 141.

16. Reported by E. T. Bell in *The Development of Mathematics* (New York: McGraw-Hill, 1949), p. 519.

17. Albert Einstein, "On Classical Literature" (1952), reprinted in *Ideas and Opinions by Albert Einstein*, ed. Carl Selig, trans. Sonja Bargmann (New York: Crown Publishers, 1954), pp. 64–65.

15

WORTHWHILE LIVES

"**W**hat is the meaning of life?" is a really bad question. Presupposing that there is something—some *one* thing—for the right answer to identify, it invites a religious response in terms of God's plan for us. It encourages us to run together what gives people's lives shape and meaning *for them*, with what makes human life *as such* significant; and which goals, activities, relationships, or ideas people find engaging, with which are really satisfying, and which morally good.

As I struggled to get free of this bad old question and to come to grips with some of the better questions it occludes, that stirring passage from one of Dorothy Sayers's refreshingly unorthodox papers on "the woman question" kept coming back to mind:

> "What," men have distractedly asked from the beginning of time, "what on earth do women want?" I do not know that women, *as* women, want anything in particular, but as human beings they want . . . exactly what you want yourselves: interesting occupation, reasonable freedom for their pleasures, and a sufficient emotional outlet. What form the occupation, the pleasures and the emotion may take, depends entirely upon the individual. You know that this is so with yourselves—why will you not believe that it is so with us?[1]

This is just about exactly right—not only about women, who after all really *are* "more like men than anything else on earth"[2]—but about people generally. We need to combine a sense of what human beings have in common, and an appreciation of the multifarious differences among individuals: of the very human need to feel you matter, which makes so many people ready to believe that we humans are not just remarkable animals, but the chosen creatures; and of the satisfaction almost all of us feel in using our human capacities, and especially our special talents—which enables some people to live satisfying lives without the help of this flattering illusion.

The purposes and projects that give shape to people's lives are as various as people are: a passion for dancing, for making music, for painting, for working or playing with words, for running faster or jumping higher, for playing football or following a team, for gambling, bungee jumping, making money, conquering territory, controlling others; a love of horses or orchids or bugs or gold; devotion to family or friends, to a cause, to God; the hope of discovering how this natural phenomenon works, the cause and cure of this disease, how to turn base metals into gold, or how to build a perpetual-motion machine; satisfaction in craftsmanship, in putting food on the family table, in enduring hardship, in one's enemy's downfall; pride in titles or honors, in one's sexual conquests, in the stylishness or the outlandishness of one's dress. Many people's lives touch only those close to them; but some relationships, enterprises, successes, failures, lifetimes or moments of heroism or self-sacrifice, courage or cowardice, resentment or rage make a person's life significant for many others. Some projects and passions are morally admirable, some morally deplorable, some morally indifferent; and some are genuinely satisfying, while others are not. Sometimes—as with the writer who aspires hopelessly to be Shakespeare when he could have crafted great detective stories—we get diverted into projects and activities that are a poor fit for our particular talents and tastes. And only too often we get diverted into projects and activities that aren't really satisfying for anyone. Trivial tasks and preoccupations take up some of almost everyone's time; but it's a waste of a short life if they take up too much. A life devoted to the service of others may be thoroughly worthwhile, and years devoted to a project not freely chosen but thrust upon you may be very well spent; but an entirely vicarious life, besides imposing a great burden on others, fails to be one's own. A life devoted to the redress of injustice or the mitigation of evil is undeniably worthwhile; but a life colored through and through by resentment of the disadvantages you have suffered excuses in advance a failure to achieve what you might otherwise have been able to do. There is profound satisfaction to be had in tackling difficult tasks, and those who aspire beyond their reach often achieve something worthwhile all the same; but a life consumed by a pointless or impossible project is, once again, a waste.

Human beings are remarkably adaptable and resilient, able to take pride and satisfaction in what they make of the most adverse circumstances—like Rudyard Kipling's galley-slave, reflecting on his last day at the oar:

> The leg-bar chafed our ankle and we gasped for cooler air,
> But no galley on the water with our galley could compare!
>
> . . .
>
> But to-day I leave the galley. Shall I curse her service then?
> God be thanked! Whate'er comes after, I have lived and toiled with men![3]

But we should never forget that, adaptable and resilient as people can be, war, tyranny, cruelty, famine, disease, and disaster can make it hard for any human being to do more than endure; nor that the freedom, and the opportunity, for individuals to follow their own bent in work or play or in relations with others is a precious cultural and social good, by no means achieved always or everywhere.

How might my life have been different had I lived at a time when severe short sight was a real handicap rather than a correctable glitch, or when educational and other opportunities were closed to women? Reading *Middlemarch*,[4] I wonder: had I been born a hundred years earlier, might I have been, not Susan Haack, but Dorothea Brooke, yearning to live the scholar's life vicariously through her sickly, joyless husband, Mr. Casaubon, and his hopeless project, the never-to-be-finished *Key to All Mythologies*?

Even scarier than the thought that I might have been Dorothea, though, is the thought that I might actually *be* Mr. Casaubon!—that the philosophical questions with which I spend so much time wrestling might be meaningless, as the old positivists maintained, or beyond the capacity of human beings to answer, as others have suggested. On a day-to-day basis I worry more about the sad degeneration of the academy generally, and of its philosophical arm in particular; still, when the problem at hand is especially recalcitrant, the old joke describing philosophy as "a blind man in a dark room looking for a black hat that isn't there" is more disturbing than funny. Many questions asked by philosophers have indeed been flawed; but the reason, I believe, is that they rest on false assumptions, and the solution is to identify those false assumptions, and formulate better questions— as I have tried to do with "What Is the Meaning of Life?"

NOTES

1. Dorothy L. Sayers, "Are Women Human?" (1938), in Sayers, *Unpopular Opinions; Twenty-One Essays* (New York: Harcourt, Brace and Company, 1947), pp. 129–41, p. 142. See also "After My Own Heart," pp. 209–16 in this volume.

2. Dorothy L. Sayers, "The Human-Not-Quite-Human," in *Unpopular Opinions* (n. 1), pp. 142–49, p. 142.

3. Rudyard Kipling, "The Galley-Slave," in *Rudyard Kipling's Verse: Inclusive Edition 1885–1926* (Garden City, NY: Doubleday, Doran & Company, Inc., 1931), pp. 82–84.

4. George Eliot, *Middlemarch* (1872; New York: The New American Library of World Literature, Inc., 1964).

16

WHY I AM NOT
AN OXYMORON

I n *Manifesto of a Passionate Moderate* I wrote forthrightly about the "fad, fashion, obfuscation, and fear of offending the influential" now endemic in the academy.[1] So I expected some strong critical responses. One criticism, however, I hadn't anticipated: that my title was oxymoronic. Ouch.

At first I thought these critics had simply misconstrued my title, as if I had styled myself—what, a kindly torturer, perhaps, or an innovative bureaucrat? But of course my point wasn't that I was heatedly lukewarm, or calmly enraged, but that I am passionate about moderation. *Either* you condone the old boy network, it is sometimes said, *or else* you press for preferential hiring of women; *either* science uses a uniquely rational method, *or else* there's nothing to it but power, politics, and rhetoric; *either* Our ways are in every way superior to Theirs, *or else* all standards are culturally relative; *either* Truth is a goddess to be worshipped, *or else* it's just an illusion, and there's no reason to give a damn whether what you believe is true; and so on. Over and over I argued in reply, as carefully as I could, "no; neither of the above." And over and over I insisted, as politely as I could, that it really *matters* that we avoid both faulty extremes.

But maybe the critics understood my title well enough after all; perhaps their point was a different one: that in the nature of the case passion overwhelms careful argument. If the word "passionate" invariably connoted hair-tearing rage

---

or paroxysms of grief (as my translator tells me "apasionada" unavoidably does in Spanish), this would be true; and even if the word can be understood in a less melodramatic, more sober way, is there really any doubt that passion is apt to get in the way of clear thinking?

But now we need to beware of another false dichotomy: *either* Reason must control the Passions, *or else* it's the other way around. No: neither of the above! Strong feelings may cloud your judgment, making you unwilling or unable to look squarely at evidence favoring a view you detest; but when it's a false dichotomy that makes you hopping mad, strong feelings motivate you to look hard at the evidence on both sides. Strong feelings may make you reluctant to look into a touchy question at all; but strong feelings may be just what's needed to get the cognitive juices flowing. Thinking hard is—well, it's *hard*; something has to push you to it. Indignation works for me, and disgust; and that awful suffocating feeling of being trapped in a bad dichotomy, which just about guarantees that I will puzzle, ponder, fiddle, fidget, twist, and turn until I see my way out of the impasse.

Only a few words left: just enough for me to apologize for disappointing any readers who had hoped for revelations about my sex life, or about my love of horses, Handel, or hang-gliding. . . .

NOTE

1. *Manifesto of a Passionate Moderate: Unfashionable Essays* (Chicago: University of Chicago Press, 1998), p. 192.

17

FORMAL PHILOSOPHY?

A Plea for Pluralism

$\mathbf{A}$ s I mulled over the questions put to me, what came first to mind was Frege's illuminating metaphor for the differences between formal and natural languages:

> We build for ourselves artificial hands, tools for particular purposes, which work with more accuracy than the hand can provide. And how is this accuracy possible? Through the very stiffness and inflexibility of parts the lack of which makes the hand so dextrous.[1]

Hot on its heels came this shrewd observation of Nietzsche's:

> In his heart every man knows very well that being unique, he will be in the world only once, and that no imaginable chance will for a second time gather together in a unity so strangely variegated an assortment as he is.[2]

Let me explain.

I was educated, in the late 1960s and early 1970s, first at Oxford and then in Cambridge, largely in the then-dominant linguistic-conceptual-analytical style. Quite early on, someone or something led me to W. V. Quine, who led me to Rudolf Carnap and to C. S. Peirce,[3] who led me to the other classical Pragmatists. Over time, it has been Peirce's work that has come to influence me the most: his formal fluency and logical innovations, of course, but also his distrust of easy dichotomies, his idea of the growth of meaning, his attractively naturalistic theory of inquiry, his constructive reconception of metaphysics and its role—not to mention his penchant for neologisms. William James hasn't been as strong an influence, but his observation that Pragmatism "'unstiffens' our theories" resonates with me;[4] for Pragmatism opened my eyes to a conception of philosophy broader and more flexible than, as Anthony Quinton puts it, the "lexicographical needlework" of pure linguistic analysis.[5]

Over several decades, I have worked in logic and philosophy of logic; in metaphysics, epistemology, and philosophy of science; on questions of culture and society; and most recently on issues at the interface of epistemology and the law of evidence—and, of late, on the epistemological novel. So you shouldn't be surprised to hear that I think of philosophy, not as a sharply delineated and tightly specialized discipline, but as a loose federation of inquiries into a characteristic, though constantly evolving, class of questions—some of which are also of interest to inquirers in other fields. I see, for example, no bright line separating metaphysical questions about the nature, origin, and evolution of physical laws from questions in physical cosmology, or questions in philosophy of logic from questions in semiotics or theoretical linguistics, or questions in epistemology or ethics from questions in the jurisprudence of evidence or of culpability—and so on.[6]

So naturally I think there are many different talents useful to a philosopher, among them "logical acumen, textual sensitivity, creative imagination, analytic rigor, conceptual subtlety and penetration, etc.";[7] and many different legitimate ways of tackling the rich variety of questions within the purview of philosophy. The various members of the loose-knit family of approaches and techniques vaguely indicated by the phrase "formal methods"—which may refer, quite narrowly, to the syntactic methods of formal logic, but may also include Tarskian methods of extensional formal semantics, "Montague grammar," applications of the mathematical calculus of probability, etc., etc.; and which, at its broadest, encompasses any and every use of any and every kind of symbolic apparatus—are just a few among those "many legitimate ways."

Formal methods can be, and sometimes have been, very useful in philosophy; but I don't believe they are the only useful methods, or even that they enjoy any special privilege. Sometimes a formal approach is just what is needed; but sometimes it is inappropriate to the task at hand, sometimes it obliges us artificially to restrict the scope of our questions or the depth of our analysis—and sometimes it is little more than decoration, a superficially mathematical or scientific gloss on weak or woolly thinking (as the statistical apparatus deployed by social scientists sometimes is). Frege had it just about exactly right: for certain purposes the symbolism of modern logic is more powerful and more precise than natural language; but it is also less flexible and less versatile.

These days, however, with philosophy increasingly professionalized, increasingly self-conscious about its status as a discipline, and increasingly splintered into sub-specialisms, it seems that many philosophers seek to define themselves professionally by their allegiance to a specialized sub-field or to a specialized method of philosophizing. Of course, there is quite a long tradition of Continental philosophers scoffing at the persnickety logic-chopping of their analytic counterparts, and analytic philosophers scoffing, in return, at the pretentious vagueness of their Continental colleagues; and now even within neo-analytic philosophy there are internecine disputes about the relative importance of formal-logical tools, of close attention to ordinary language, to conceptual "intuition," or to the findings of this or that area of science. Worse yet, in the culture of boosterism and self-promotion that now pervades the universities, many are tempted to tout whatever philosophical questions most interest them as *the* most important or critical issues, and whatever way of going about philosophy best suits their temperament or talents as *the* most fruitful, *the* most rigorous, *the* most up-to-date, *the* most scientific, etc., method.[8]

If you are inclined, as I am, to a tolerantly expansive (but not boundless) view of the scope of philosophy and a flexibly pluralistic (but not promiscuous) attitude to its "method(s)," this situation seems—well, less than ideal. And since the questions before me seem in part to reflect the present unhappy situation, my responses will in part reflect my unease about it.

1. "Why were you initially drawn to formal methods?"

I have never thought of myself, as this question seems to presuppose, as a "formal philosopher"; but I can say something about how my interest in logic arose.

In my student days it was commonly taken for granted that logic was a *male* thing; women were supposedly more suited to ethics and such. (It is distressing, to say the least, that this idea has since been revived—in the name of feminism, yet!)[9] I suspect that my initial interest in logic may have arisen at least in part from my instinctive resistance to this ubiquitous presumption; at any rate, I still recall my disappointment on discovering that Dana Scott and Hilary Putnam were not, as I had innocently imagined, women. Whatever the initial motivation, though, what came to appeal to me was the rigor and clarity logic made possible, its clean elegance; but also—as, reading Frege and Peirce, I learned more about its history—the sense of modern logic as a remarkable, and still-evolving, intellectual achievement.

Reading in the history of logic taught me to distinguish an older, broader, Aristotelian conception of the subject, and a newer, narrower, Fregean conception. Logic in the broader sense, the theory of whatever is good in the way of reasoning, would include not only systematic, formal representations of deductively valid arguments, and meta-theoretical results about such systems, but also theories of non-deductive reasoning, and theories of the term, of propositions, truth, etc. These days, however—rather as, thanks to the success of particular brands, "Xerox" has become a generic word for photocopying, and "Kleenex" for tissues—"logic" seems usually to refer, quite narrowly, to syntactically characterizable systems of valid reasoning, of which the Frege-Peirce-Russell propositional and predicate calculi would be the paradigm. Dewey's *Logic: The Theory of Inquiry*, for example, though it surely is logic in the older, broader sense, bears little resemblance to logic in the newer, narrower understanding.[10]

I have long—at least since the time of my B.Phil. dissertation on ambiguity and fallacies of equivocation—been interested as much in the messy philosophical issues encompassed in the broader conception of logic as in the elegant formalisms of logic in the narrower sense. Perhaps it is unnecessary for me to say that the fact that my conception of logic is broader than Frege's doesn't mean that I have any sympathy with the virtually vacuous use of "logic" in which philosophers of religion once routinely wrote of "the logic of 'God'" and moral philosophers of "the logic of 'good,'" and in which cultural critics and literary theorists now routinely write of the "logic of capitalism," the "logic of gender," and such.[11] But probably it *is* necessary to say that it doesn't mean, either, that I endorse the idea of "philosophical logic" as conceived by those who take epistemic, deontic, or other intensional logics to be somehow peculiarly philosophical. I don't see epistemic logic as any substitute for substantial epistemology, nor deontic logic for ethics; and I see philosophically interesting questions arising with respect to just about every logical system.

2. "What examples from your work illustrate the role formal methods can play in philosophy?"

Once again, the question makes me uneasy. The best methodological motto for a philosopher, to my mind, is Nike's: "just do it." At any rate, I have always tried to use whatever tools—formal, conceptual, linguistic, phenomenological, etc.— are appropriate to the task at hand. And most to the present point perhaps, though there are numerous illustrations of the role of formal methods to be found in my work, there is also a long-standing preoccupation with questions about the scope and limits of formalism.

In my first book, *Deviant Logic*,[12] I explored various efforts to revise the "classical," Russellian, two-valued propositional and predicate calculi. I proposed a way of distinguishing extensions of classical logic from deviant systems; replied to a range of arguments purporting to show that classical logic was not revisable; assessed proposed interpretations of deviant logics in terms of reference failure, vagueness, future contingents, etc.; and studied many-valued, Intuitionist, free, and quantum logics. In my next book, *Philosophy of Logics*,[13] I explored philosophical issues in the interpretation of formal-logical calculi, including propositions, validity, truth, the semantic paradoxes, modality, etc., and metaphysical and epistemological questions about the logical enterprise, especially those posed by the existence of a plurality of logical systems.

In this second book—the first chapter of which opens with Saul Kripke's observation that "there is no mathematical substitute for philosophy"—the question of the scope of formal methods arose first in the context of Alfred Tarski's pessimism about the applicability of his methods outside well-behaved formal languages—at that time an issue made urgent by the burgeoning "Davidson program," proposing those methods as the basis for a theory of meaning for natural languages. In 1978, I concluded, cautiously, that it could not be said with any confidence that Davidson had succeeded in answering Tarski's reservations. Now, I would say that—impressive as Tarski's achievement undeniably is from a technical point of view—the difficulties in Davidson's (now-abandoned) program suggest that Tarski was right all along about the restricted applicability of his extensional methods.

Writing *Philosophy of Logics* also gave me an opportunity to look at relevance and fuzzy logics, two families of non-classical systems that came to my attention only after *Deviant Logic* was published. Both raised questions about the limits of logic. According to electrical engineer Lotfi Zadeh, the resolution of problems in electrical engineering requiring gradational variables reveals that we stand in need of a radically new, "fuzzy" logic: a logic in which the truth-values are themselves fuzzy, local, and subjective; in which the set of such values is not closed under the usual logical operations, so that "linguistic approximations" like "very true" and "fairly true" are needed to guarantee closure; in which inference is approximate rather than exact, and semantic rather than syntactic; and to which considerations such as consistency and completeness are "peripheral."[14] In short, according to Zadeh "fuzzy logic" refers, not simply to a logic of vagueness, but to a logic that is itself vague. I didn't go quite so far as Dana Scott—who, in a talk entitled "Deviant Logic: Fact or Fiction?" commented that fuzzy logic wasn't just fiction, it was pornography!—but I did argue that fuzzy logic "lack[s] every feature that the pioneers of formal logic wanted logic *for*."[15]

Critics, pointing to the success of fuzzy thermostats, fuzzy dishwashers, the fuzzy braking system in the Tokyo subway, and so forth, replied that fuzzy logic must be right—after all, it *works*.[16] I suspected, but couldn't at that time be sure, that fuzzy technology (though perhaps it used fuzzy set theory) *didn't*, indeed *couldn't*, really depend on the strange, vague pseudo-formal logic Zadeh had described. Eventually, I managed to figured out how fuzzy controllers for air conditioners, cement kilns, and such, work: in effect, by mimicking human operatives' gradual adjustments of temperature; and then it was clear that the success of such devices does not require the adoption of a radically non-classical theory of truth-preserving inferences.[17]

The fact that some relevance logics *both* extend *and* deviate from classical logic revealed hitherto-unsuspected complexities in the apparently simple distinction I had made earlier; and the proliferation of rival formal systems all claiming to correct the classical neglect of relevance suggested that this concept might be far from simple. Alan Ross Anderson and Nuel D. Belnap had referred approvingly to F. C. S. Schiller's complaint that "the central doctrine of the most prevalent logic still consists in a flat denial of Relevance."[18] Noting that Schiller had intended this observation not as a call for formalizing relevance but as a critique of the ambitions of formal logic, I began to suspect that relevance might depend on content rather than form, and thus in principle resist syntactic characterization. Once again, in 1978 I was cautious in my conclusion. And once again, now—with yet more rival systems of "relevance" and "relevant" logic on offer— I would be less tentative: many years of work in epistemology have convinced me that the concept of relevance is not explicable in purely formal terms, but contains ineliminably material elements.

While *Philosophy of Logics* was in press, in the course of the work that was eventually presented in "Fallibilism and Necessity"[19] (hoping to shed light on our susceptibility to error not only in our empirical, but also in our logical and mathematical beliefs), I had initially adopted what seemed to be the obvious strategy of characterizing fallibilism formally, using the language of epistemic logic. But everything I tried turned out, directly or indirectly, to collapse fallibilism into the thesis that some propositions are contingent. Eventually it dawned on me that I would have to go about things differently; and that a real epistemological understanding would require attention not only to the propositions known or believed, but also to knowing subjects and their interactions with the world and each other.[20]

One manifestation of this conception of the way to go about tackling epistemological issues was my decision in *Evidence and Inquiry* (1993) to take as *explicandum* "A is more/less justified, at t, in believing that *p*. "[21] I called the resulting epistemological theory "foundherentism": like coherentism, it allowed the legitimacy of mutual support among a person's beliefs; like foundationalism, it acknowledged the relevance of experience to justification. An analogy with crossword puzzles helped me explore the role of experiential evidence (the analogue of clues), and reasons (the analogue of already completed entries), and to articulate the difference between legitimate mutual support and a vicious circle.

In this context I argued that the structure of evidence isn't linear, like a mathematical or logical proof; rather, reasons ramify, as crossword entries do. And the determinants of evidential quality are multidimensional: supportiveness (analogue: how well a crossword entry fits with its clue and completed intersecting entries); independent security (analogue: how reasonable those other completed entries are, independent of the support of this one); and comprehensiveness (analogue: how much of the crossword has been completed). Moreover, I argued, supportiveness of evidence is not a narrowly logical matter. For one thing, that evidence E deductively implies *p* doesn't make E conclusive with respect to *p*; for inconsistent evidence deductively implies any *p* you like, but it certainly isn't conclusive evidence for anything—let alone for everything! More radically, I suggested that lesser degrees of supportiveness of evidence, though often conceived as the realm of "inductive logic," are not syntactically characterizable; and that it may not be feasible to assign numerical degrees of justification, or even a linear ordering.

At the time, however, though I had come to doubt that the concept of supportiveness can be spelled out in purely formal terms, I still approached it propositionally: so, in the last stage of my account of evidential quality, experiential evidence had to be represented by "A's experiential C-evidence,"[22] a phrase referring to a set of propositions to the effect that A is in such-and-such a perceptual, introspective, or memory state. These propositional proxies for experiential evidence were clumsy; and they apparently encouraged misunderstandings. Some readers thought I was suggesting that experiential events are themselves propositional; and one, Ryszard Wojcicki—despite my explicit and repeated statements to the contrary—misconstrued me as postulating a class of infallible "experiential beliefs."[23] In an equal and opposite confusion, Paul Thagard hoped to "subsume" foundherentism in his coherentist theory, apparently not noticing that his "Principle of Data Priority" ran together experiential *events*, someone's seeing or hearing this or that, with experiential *beliefs*, i.e., the person's beliefs about those experiential events—which I had been at great pains to keep distinct.[24]

A key theme of my next book, *Defending Science—Within Reason* (2003),[25] was that scientific inquiry is continuous with everyday empirical inquiry. All serious empirical inquirers, I argued—historians, detectives, investigative journalists, legal and literary scholars, and so on, as well as scientists—use something like the "hypothetico-deductive method." What is distinctive about inquiry in the sciences is, rather, the vast array of local and evolving "helps" to inquiry that scientists have developed over centuries of work: models and metaphors to aid the imagination, instruments of observation to aid the senses, intellectual tools like numerals, the calculus, statistics, computer programs, etc., to extend reasoning powers, . . . and so on. Moreover, the evidence with respect to scientific claims is continuous with the evidence with respect to ordinary empirical claims, only more so: the experiential evidence is more dependent on instruments; the internal connections of reasons are even denser and more complex; and, almost always, the evidence is a shared resource, pooled within and across generations.

Like ordinary empirical claims, scientific claims need to be anchored in experience. Fortunately, by the time of *Defending Science* I had figured out how to handle experiential evidence without the awkward apparatus of propositional proxies, and could write that "[e]xperiential evidence consists, not of propositions, but of perceptual interactions; and it contributes to warrant, not in virtue of logical relations among propositions, but in virtue of connections between words and world set up in language-learning" (p. 63). However, I argued, the old distinction between ostensive and verbal definitions, consonant with a foundationalist approach, won't do; a better account, in harmony with a foundherentist conception of the structure of evidence, recognizes that the meanings of different words are acquired, in different proportions, partly by ostension and partly verbally. This explains how someone's seeing, hearing, etc., this or that can contribute to the warrant of a claim when key terms are learned by association with these observable circumstances; *and* why sensory evidence contributes more [less] to warrant the more [the less] the meaning of those key terms is exhausted by that association.

This represents a significant simplification and refinement of my earlier account of experiential evidence. But it is much more than that. It is also an expression of a newly articulated, more comprehensive conception of the proper role of logic in epistemology generally, and in philosophy of science in particular—a conception that breaks quite radically with assumptions inherited from the Logical Positivists.

In contradistinction to older-fashioned forms of plain Positivism, "Logical" Positivism was so-called because of its reliance on the remarkable innovations made by Boole, Frege, Peirce, Russell, and others, in formal logic, which seemed the very model of rigor. Repudiating metaphysics, ethics, aesthetics, etc., as meaningless verbiage or at best bad poetry, the Logical Positivists found themselves obliged to reinvent philosophy; and so they did, as "the logic of science." Carnap announced the reinvented philosophical project in these words: "[t]o pursue philosophy can only be to clarify the concepts and sentences of science by logical analysis. The instrument for this is the new logic."[26]

This idea was at the root of the Old Deferentialism in philosophy of science, an approach focused on structure, on method, on logic. Well, actually the Old Deferentialism might be better described as an unruly, squabbling family of approaches; for there were several competing styles of "inductive logic" on offer, while Popper and his followers insisted that the logic of science is exclusively deductive. In due course, the Old Deferentialism was challenged by proponents of a radically different kind of approach, which originated among sociologists of knowledge but by now had more than a foothold in philosophy of science: the New Cynicism, skeptical of the supposed rationality of science, and focused on power, politics, and rhetoric. From the true premise that the scientific enterprise cannot be fully understood in purely formal terms, the New Cynics drew the false conclusion that science isn't a rational enterprise after all. But, just as the Old Deferentialists had, they still took for granted that, if science *were* a rational enterprise, its rationality would be a matter of logic.

The way forward, I realized, was to recognize that this shared assumption is flawed: the rationality of the scientific enterprise cannot be understood in narrowly logical terms. This prompted me to wonder what might be missing *both* from the narrowly logical approach of the Old Deferentialists *and* from the historico-sociologico-rhetorical approach of the New Cynics.[27] Once the question was clear, the answer was obvious: the world, and our interactions with the world. This is why the philosophy of science presented in *Defending Science* is not "word-y," but "worldly."[28] This worldliness is manifested not only in the simplified and refined account of experiential evidence I have described, but also in an amplified account of the role of content in evidential support, an amplified account that suggests a new perspective on the role of conceptual innovation in science.

So far from being, as the New Cynics imagined, an obstacle to the rationality of science, the introduction of a new vocabulary and shifts of meaning in an existing vocabulary can advance the scientific enterprise by gradually developing a terminology that, corresponding more closely to real kinds, enables explanation. Now the reservations I had expressed in *Evidence and Inquiry* about the prospects for "inductive logic" could be grounded. Carnap and Hempel were right, I argued, in assuming that there is such a thing as supportive-but-less-than-conclusive evidence; but Popper, though wrong in denying this, was right that there is no inductive logic. For, as Hempel seemed to be on the brink of acknowledging in his 1964 "Postscript on Confirmation,"[29] the moral of the "grue" paradox is that supportiveness of evidence does not depend on form alone; for "All emeralds are green" and "All emeralds are grue" have the same form, but different content. My account of supportiveness in terms of increment of explanatory integration of evidence with the claim in question led to the same conclusion, that the concept is not susceptible of purely formal treatment; for explanatoriness requires the identification of real kinds of thing or event, and hence is vocabulary-sensitive.

Of course, even while I was working all this out, I was uncomfortably aware that many philosophers of science (and some, though fewer, epistemologists) were cheerfully confident that probability theory could carry the burden of an account of quality of evidence. I had never shared this optimism; but it took a while to articulate why. Obviously, if the concept of warrant is anything like as subtle and complex as my account suggests, the probability calculus (devised originally to represent the mathematics of games of chance) couldn't constitute a complete theory of warrant. And neither, given the comprehensiveness condition, could the calculus of probabilities even be an adequate calculus of degrees of warrant—for the probability of p and the probability of not-p must add up to 1, but if there is insufficient evidence either way, neither a claim nor its negation may be warranted to any degree.[30]

So it was a relief to discover (unfortunately, however, only after the publication of *Defending Science*) that John Maynard Keynes had held that epistemic probabilities may not be susceptible of numerical values: "[s]o far from our being able to measure [the probabilities of arguments], it is not even clear that we are always able to place them in an order of magnitude"; and that Richard von Mises, whose maxim was "FIRST THE COLLECTIVE—THEN THE PROBABILITY," had insisted that the calculus of probabilities applies only where we are dealing with a large class of uniform events, and *not* to epistemic probabilities: "[o]ur probability theory has nothing to do with such questions as: Is there a probability of Germany being at some time in the future involved in a war with Liberia?"[31]

The epistemological picture developed in *Defending Science* goes beyond the narrowly logical in other ways as well, not least in acknowledging the deeply social character of the scientific enterprise. *Evidence and Inquiry* had focused on the individual inquirer; *Defending Science* also aspires to represent the epistemological role of interactions among inquirers. This, however, posed a difficulty: the evidence with respect to scientific claims and theories is almost always a shared resource, pooled within or across generations of scientists; but the evidence with respect to any warranted empirical claim must include experiential evidence, which can be had only by individuals. Noting how different my approach is from Popper's "epistemology without a knowing subject," I handled this tension by taking as my starting point an account of the warrant of a claim for a person at a time, on which I built an account of warrant for a group of persons, and then an account of the warrant of a scientific claim at a time, period. This represented a further move away from the "logic of science" approach, and toward a kind of *rapprochement* of epistemology with sociology of science—and hints at one of the many cross-disciplinary connections that have drawn my interest.

3. "What is the proper role of philosophy in relation to other disciplines?"

Now, however, I am uneasy about the implied conception of philosophy as a clearly distinguishable "discipline" with a unique "proper role" in relation to other disciplines—a conception that seems to me faithful neither to the often vague and permeable boundaries of partially overlapping areas of inquiry, nor to the richness and complexity of the multifarious interrelations of philosophy with other fields. Sometimes, for example, philosophy properly forges ahead into waters as yet uncharted by the sciences; sometimes it properly engages in underlaborer duties after scientific advances. Since it is quite impossible to do justice in a few paragraphs to the rich, complex, and multifarious interrelations of philosophy with other areas of human endeavor, the best I can do is sketch a few examples from my own work of how other disciplines bear on philosophy; of how philosophy bears on other disciplines; and of how philosophy contributes to our understanding of the relations among other disciplines or other human enterprises.

In *Evidence and Inquiry* I urged the merits of a modest naturalism according to which the sciences of cognition—though they cannot replace epistemology—have contributory relevance to epistemological questions. This modest naturalism contrasted both with old, purely a priori conceptions of epistemology, and with new, scientistic forms of naturalism, such as Alvin Goldman's, according to which epistemological questions can be answered by cognitive psychology, or Paul and Patricia Churchland's, according to which epistemological questions are illegitimate, and should be abandoned in favor of neurophysiological ones.[32]

My approach in *Defending Science* remained modestly naturalistic; but in this context I needed to explain how my style of naturalism differed, on the one hand, from Philip Kitcher's suggestion that acknowledgment of the role of the inquiring subject itself constitutes naturalism and, on the other, from Larry Laudan's idea that empirical studies of science suffice to track the evolution of "the scientific method."[33] Writing that "it is not within the competence of the sciences to articulate core epistemological concepts and values," but that "nevertheless, they do have an epistemological contribution to make," I argued that the psychology of cognition has contributory relevance to an understanding of human cognitive capacities and weaknesses: how large is the risk of experimenter bias, for example, and when can giving people additional information actually impair their judgment of evidence? And writing that "rather than a distinctive 'scientific method,' there is only . . . the core epistemological values common to all inquiry, and . . . the myriad local and evolving techniques and helps that make scientific inquiry 'more so'" (p. 309), I argued that the history of science has contributory relevance to an understanding of the interplay between the underlying processes and procedures common to all serious inquiry, and the evolution of those special scientific helps.

In *Defending Science* I also took the opportunity to explore the potential for cooperation between epistemology and sociology of science—a potential that, I argued, had been obscured by a false contrast between the rational and the social taken for granted by Old Deferentialists and New Cynics alike. No epistemological conclusions can be established by sociological investigation alone; but in conjunction with a sound understanding of the role of evidence-sharing in the warrant of theories, and a sound understanding of the determinants of better and worse conducted inquiry, sociological investigation of the peer review system, of the incidence of scientific fraud and plagiarism, of the politics of science funding, of science education, or of litigation-driven science, could illuminate what social factors help, and what hinder, good, honest, thorough, creative scientific work.[34]

Next, some examples of the bearing of philosophy on other disciplines: As the essays in this volume testify, over the past several years I have devoted a good deal of time to applied epistemology—exploring what an account of the determinants of evidential strength and of well-conducted inquiry could contribute to such diverse questions as the feasibility of economics-as-science,[35] the legitimacy of "weight of evidence" methodology in epidemiology,[36] or the benefits and drawbacks of "evidence-based medicine." But I have focused most intensively on the interface between epistemology and the law of evidence. Initially, my interest was piqued by the discovery that the "New Evidence Scholarship" in legal theory (so-called because of its new focus on the structure and content of evidence, rather than exclusively on legal rules of admissibility and burdens and standards of proof) was embroiled in a debate between "fact-based" and "story-based" approaches—i.e., to all intents and purposes, a debate between foundationalism and coherentism. In due course I found myself diagnosing the epistemological confusions at work in the US Supreme Court's rulings on the admissibility of scientific testimony;[37] exploring the tensions between fallibilism and finality and between inquiry and advocacy that underlie the difficulties our legal system has encountered in handling scientific evidence;[38] and submitting arguments for and against adversarialism and exclusionary rules of evidence to epistemological scrutiny.[39]

Chapter 5 of *Defending Science* illustrates another, rather different way in which philosophy bears on other disciplines. The central question here is: what are the metaphysical presuppositions of the scientific enterprise—how must the world be for scientific inquiry to be possible? My argument is, in brief, that science would be impossible—as would everyday empirical inquiry of the most ordinary kind—unless there were particular things and events to which inquirers have some kind of sensory access, and unless those particular things and events were of kinds, and subject to laws. Whether or not my Innocent Realist answer is correct,[40] the question to which it responds identifies the kind of contribution that metaphysics might make to the sciences: not by underpinning this or that specific physical, cosmological, or other scientific theory, but by articulating the preconditions of scientific investigation.

It also falls to philosophy—this is my third theme—to inquire into the relations among other disciplines, or other fields of human endeavor. In chapter 6 of *Defending Science*, for example, the focus is on the similarities and the differences between the social and the natural sciences; in chapter 8, on the similarities and the differences between science and literature; and in chapter 10, on the relations between science and religion.[41] (The concluding chapter, by the way, in line with my early preoccupation with ambiguity, focuses on distinguishing the many different philosophical, socio-historical, and scientific, ideas offered under the equivocal rubric, "the end of science": the threatened epistemological demotion of science; its inherent limits; and the prospect of its annihilation, of its culmination, or of its eventual completion.)

4. "What do you consider the most neglected topics and/or contributions in late twentieth-century philosophy?"

These would be perfectly appropriate questions to put to a natural scientist. Between 1952 and 1963, for example, most molecular biologists would probably have said with some confidence that at least *a* very significant outstanding issue was the "coding problem" for DNA (and by the time of the Cold Spring Harbor symposium for 1966, most of them would have said with some confidence that this problem was almost completely solved).[42] Asked about philosophy, however, these questions suggest an unrealistically "progressivist" picture, as if, like molecular biology, philosophy were on a clear (albeit steep and rocky) path of advance. Not a few problems once regarded as the province of philosophy have evolved into more readily soluble scientific questions; moreover, I believe, there *can* be, and sometimes is, progress in philosophy. Nevertheless, philosophy really *isn't* much like normal science; and neither, I'm afraid, does it presently seem to be on any clear forward path.

Instead, many seem to cling to the flattering and reassuring illusion that the ideas of our time are bound to be an advance over anything that went before, and so miss opportunities to build on earlier insights. Proponents of "radical" theses are rewarded with attention and renown—even, perhaps especially, when those radical theses are radically implausible. Young people who aspire to join the profession are likely to be trained in aggressive but formulaic criticism, or in over-ambitious speculation; urged to browse the *Philosopher's Index* to find a recent article to which they can reply; and pressured, ready or not, to publish *now*. Rarely, however, are they encouraged to develop the patience they would need to work constructively and in detail. No wonder, these days, it often seems that philosophy is going backwards, sideways, or nowhere—any which way but forwards!

As a result of the "chauvinism of the present" characteristic of much recent neo-analytic philosophy, earlier contributions—when they are not neglected outright—are apt to be "co-opted": X, who is no longer alive, or just isn't one of the boys, is given a passing mention as having "anticipated" some contemporary or better-known Y; or an older approach is transmuted and its name adopted for a neo-analytic *ersatz*. The label "Pragmatism," for example, first kidnapped by Rorty and his admirers, is now apparently being adopted by neo-analytic philosophers proffering ideas at best vaguely reminiscent of something in the classical Pragmatist tradition.

Yet Peirce's constructive reconception of metaphysics as, not wholly *a priori*, but in part dependent on experience—on close, "phaneroscopic" attention to aspects of everyday experience ordinarily too commonplace to notice, not on the recherché kinds of observation that can only be made by means of scientific instruments—has been thoroughly neglected in almost a century of neo-Leibnizian, neo-Kantian, or outright scientistic, metaphysics.[43] And Peirce's distinction of existent particulars and real "generals," and its deployment in the resolution of the problem of induction and of cosmological issues about the evolution of laws, has been conspicuous by its absence from (almost all)[44] the recent literature in philosophy of science. Again, George Herbert Mead's remarkably suggestive theorizing about the ways in which the human mind is like animal mentality and the ways in which it is different, and about how our peculiar mental capacities might have arisen,[45] gets barely a mention despite the oceans of ink expended on philosophy of mind in the late twentieth century.

Another example: in all the excitement over "minimalism," "deflationism," "disquotationalism," etc., in the theory of truth, neither Alfred Tarski nor Frank Ramsey are always given their due. Granted, Tarski's semantic theory, Ramsey's laconicist theory, and contemporary minimalism, deflationism, and other views, are all in intent or in effect attempts to articulate Aristotle's dictum that "to say of what is that it is, or of what is not that it is not, is true" in a completely generalized way; but they differ very significantly among themselves. Yet Quine suggests that Tarski may be classified as a disquotationalist[46]—even though Tarski himself had insisted that the enclosed expression in a quotation-mark name is not semantically a part of the name; which was precisely why he believed it was impossible to generalize his T-schema along the lines of "(p) ('p' is true iff p)." The editors of Ramsey's papers on truth observe that it is "remarkable how close [he] came to anticipating Tarski"[47]—even though Tarski himself says emphatically that his T-schema is not, and cannot be turned into, a definition of truth, while Ramsey had written that "*[my] definition of truth* is that a belief is true if it is 'a belief that p' and p, but false if it is 'a belief that p' and -p" (my italics). Scott Soames writes that Tarski's semantic conception is "the most famous and influential version of deflationism"—leaving it a mystery why Tarski himself took a hundred or so pages *beyond* the T-schema to articulate his definition of truth.[48] And so on.[49]

5. "What are the most important open problems in philosophy, and what are the prospects for progress?"

For reasons that should by now be too obvious to bear repeating, I am unwilling to be drawn into trying to identify "*the* most neglected topics" or "*the* most important open problems" in philosophy today. I am drawn instead to a passage in which, commenting on the "puny, rickety, and scrofulous" state of metaphysics in his time, Peirce proceeds "to set down almost at random a small specimen of the questions of metaphysics which press . . . for industrious and solid investigation":

> Whether or no there be any real indefiniteness, or real possibility and impossibility? Whether there be any strictly individual existence? Whether there is any distinction . . . between fact and fancy? Or between the external and the internal worlds? What general . . . account can be given of the different qualities of feeling . . . ? Do all possible qualities of sensation . . . form one continuous

system . . . ? . . . Is Time a real thing . . . ? How about Space . . . ? Is hylozoism an option, actual or conceivable, rather than a senseless vocable . . . ? . . . What is consciousness or mind like . . . ?[50]

So here, set down almost at random (and following Peirce's agreeably antique style of punctuation), is *my* "small specimen of philosophical questions which press for industrious and solid investigation": Whether the grounds of validity of the laws of logic are to be found in language, in conceptual structures, in the nature of representation, in the world, or where? Whether Peirce's idea of necessary reasoning as essentially diagrammatic is defensible, or Russell's distinction of logical and grammatical form? How Aristotle's dictum could best be generalized to arrive at a satisfactory definition of truth? How, if this will require propositional quantifiers, these can be interpreted without using "true"? Whether a unified interpretation of quantifiers is possible, and if so in what terms? Whether the semantic paradoxes are a sign of deep incoherence in the ordinary truth-concept, or a trivial verbal trick? Whether these paradoxes must be avoided by recourse to an artificial language in which they cannot be expressed, or resolved by probing the ordinary, informal concept of truth? Whether Tarski's definition really advances our understanding of truth beyond Ramsey's simple formula, and if so, how? . . . How we are to understand the relation between the neurophysiological realization of a belief and its content? How belief-contents are best represented? How they should be individuated? How degrees of belief affect degrees of justification? How to articulate the desirable kind of interlocking or consilience that gives some congeries of evidence greater strength than any of their components? How to assess the weight of shared evidence when there is disagreement within a group, or when members give shared reasons different degrees of credence? What the proper relation is between belief and the will? What the mechanisms are of self-deception and of wishful and fearful thinking? . . . How to understand "real," as applied to particulars? to kinds? to laws? to the world? Whether "real" has the same meaning as applied to social as to natural kinds and laws? How to distinguish the cosmological role of historical singularities and of laws? How to understand the evolution of laws? . . . How works of imaginative literature can convey truths they do not state? Whether vagueness is always undesirable, or sometimes benign or even useful? How the precision sought by a logician differs from that sought by a novelist or a poet? . . .

Though I don't doubt that formal methods will play a part, I anticipate that the means of resolving such questions will prove as various as the questions themselves.

NOTES

1. Gottlob Frege, "On the Scientific Justification of a Conceptual Notation" (1882), trans. Terrell Ward Bynum, in Bynum, ed., *Conceptual Notation and Related Articles* (Oxford: Clarendon Press, 1972), pp. 83–89, p. 86.

2. Friedrich Nietzsche, "Schopenhauer as Educator" (1874), in *Untimely Meditations*, trans. R. J. Hollingdale (Cambridge: Cambridge University Press, 1983), pp. 125–94, p. 127.

3. To Carnap by way of "Epistemology Naturalized," in *Ontological Relativity and Other Essays* (New York: Columbia University Press, 1969), pp. 69–90; to Peirce by way of chapter 1 of *Word and Object* (Cambridge: MIT Press, 1960).

4. William James, *Pragmatism* (1907), Frederick H. Burkhardt, Fredson Bowers, and Ignas Skrupskelis, eds. (Cambridge: Harvard University Press, 1975), p. 43. James notes that he borrowed "unstiffens" from the young Italian pragmatist Giovanni Papini.

5. Anthony Quinton, "Character and Will in Modern Ethics," in Quinton, *From Wodehouse to Wittgenstein* (Manchester, UK: Carcanet Press, 1998), pp. 39–55, p. 39.

6. See also Susan Haack, "Not Cynicism, but Synechism: Lessons from Classical Pragmatism," pp. 79–94 in this volume.

7. Here I am quoting myself, from "The Best Man for the Job May Be a Woman . . . and Other Alien Thoughts on Affirmative Action in the Academy," in Susan Haack, *Manifesto of a Passionate Moderate: Unfashionable Essays* (Chicago: University of Chicago Press, 1998), pp. 167–87, p. 175.

8. See Haack, "Preposterism and Its Consequences," in *Manifesto of a Passionate Moderate* (n. 7), pp. 188–208.

9. See e.g. Andrea Nye, *Words of Power* (London: Routledge, 1990).

10. John Dewey, *Logic: The Theory of Inquiry* (New York: Henry Holt and Co., 1938).

11. See e.g., Frederic Jameson, *Postmodernism, or, the Cultural Logic of Late Capitalism* (Durham, NC: Duke University Press, 1991); Marjorie Garber, "The Logic of the Transvestite: *The Roaring Girl* (1608)," in *Staging the Renaissance: Reinterpretations of Elizabethan and Jacobean Drama*, ed. David Scott Kastan and Peter Stallybras (New York: Routledge, 1991), pp. 221–34.

12. Susan Haack, *Deviant Logic* (Cambridge: Cambridge University Press, 1974).

13. Susan Haack, *Philosophy of Logics* (Cambridge: Cambridge University Press, 1978).

14. Lotfi Zadeh, "Fuzzy Logic and Approximate Reasoning," *Synthese* 30 (1975): 407–25.

15. Haack, *Philosophy of Logics* (n. 13), pp. 162–69; "Do We Need 'Fuzzy Logic'?" (1979), in Susan Haack, *Deviant Logic, Fuzzy Logic: Beyond the Formalism* (Chicago: University of Chicago Press, 1996), pp. 232–22 (the quotation in the text is from p. 237); "Is Truth Flat or Bumpy?" (1980), in *Deviant Logic, Fuzzy Logic*, pp. 243–58.

16. See e.g., J. Fox, "Towards a Reconciliation of Fuzzy Logic and Standard Logic," *International Journal of Man-Machine Studies* 15 (1981): 213–20.

17. Haack, *Deviant Logic, Fuzzy Logic* (n. 15), pp. 230–31.

18. Alan Ross Anderson and Nuel D. Belnap, *Entailment* (Princeton, NJ: Princeton University Press, 1975), p. 30, citing F. C. S. Schiller, *Logic for Use* (New York: Harcourt, Brace, 1930), p. 75.

19. Haack, "Fallibilism and Necessity," *Synthese* 41 (1979): 37–63.

20. An idea expressed, in what now seems to me a somewhat fumbling form, in Haack, "Epistemology *With* a Knowing Subject," *Review of Metaphysics* XXXIII.2.130 (1979): 309–35.

21. Susan Haack, *Evidence and Inquiry: Towards Reconstruction in Epistemology* (Oxford: Blackwell, 1993; 2nd ed., Amherst, NY: Prometheus Books, forthcoming 2009); see especially chapter 4. See also Susan Haack, "A Foundherentist Theory of Empirical Justification" (1998), in Ernest Sosa and Jaegwon Kim, eds., *Epistemology: An Anthology* (Oxford: Blackwell, 2000), pp. 226–36; in Michael Huemer, ed., *Epistemology: Contemporary Readings* (New York: Routledge, 2002), pp. 417–34; and in Steven Luper, ed., *Essential Knowledge* (New York: Longman's, 2004), pp. 157–67.

22. Throughout *Evidence and Inquiry* I relied on a distinction between belief-states ("S-beliefs") and belief-contents ("C-beliefs") and, correspondingly, between S- and C-evidence.

23. See Ryszard Wojcicki, "Foundationalism, Coherentism and Foundherentism," in Cornelis de Waal, ed., *Susan Haack: A Lady of Distinctions* (Amherst, NY: Prometheus Books, 2007), pp. 57–68, and my reply, "Of Chopin and Sycamores: Response to Ryszard Wojcicki," pp. 69–72 in the same volume.

24. Paul Thagard, *Coherence in Thought and Action* (Cambridge: Bradford Books, MIT Press, 2000), pp. 41ff., and "Critique of Emotional Reason," in de Waal, ed. *Susan Haack: A Lady of Distinctions* (n. 23), pp. 283–93. See also Susan Haack, "Once More, With Feeling: Response to Paul Thagard," pp. 294–97 in the same volume.

25. Susan Haack, *Defending Science—Within Reason: Between Scientism and Cynicism* (Amherst, NY: Prometheus Books, 2003).

26. Rudolf Carnap, "The Old and the New Logic" (1931); English translation by Isaac Levi, in A. J. Ayer, ed., *Logical Positivism* (Glencoe, IL: Free Press, 1959), pp. 133–46, p. 145.

27. And to recall a particularly shrewd observation of J. L. Austin's, that in every important thinker "there's the part where he says it and the part where he takes it back."

28. "Worldly" was my word (*Defending Science* [n. 25], p. 52); the contrast with "word-y" I owe to A. Philip Dawid.

29. Carl G. Hempel, "Postscript (1964) on Confirmation," in Hempel, *Aspects of Scientific Explanation* (New York: Free Press, 1965), pp. 47–51.

30. Haack, *Defending Science* (n. 25), pp. 78–79.

31. I learned this early in 2004, when I read Donald Gillies' *Philosophical Theories of Probability* (London: Routledge, 2000), which quotes Keynes, *A Treatise on Probability* (London: MacMillan, 1921), pp. 27–28, on p. 34, and von Mises, *Probability, Statistics, and Truth* (London: Allen and Unwin, 2nd. revised English edition, 1928), pp. 18 and 9, on p. 97.

32. *Evidence and Inquiry* (n. 21): chapter 6 disambiguates Quine's "Epistemology Naturalized" (n. 3), and offers a preliminary statement of my modest aposteriorist naturalism, chapter 7 articulates the flaws in Alvin Goldman's reformist scientistic naturalism, and chapter 8 the flaws in the Churchlands' revolutionary scientistic naturalism.

33. *Defending Science* (n. 25), pp. 306–10. The weaker idea is suggested by Philip Kitcher in *The Advancement of Science: Science Without Legend, Objectivity Without Illusions* (New York: Oxford University Press, 1993), p. 9; the stronger is suggested by Larry Laudan in "Progress or Rationality? The Prospects for Normative Naturalism" (1987), in Laudan, *Beyond Positivism and Relativism: Theory, Method, and Evidence* (Boulder, CO: Westview Press, 1996), pp. 125–41.

34. Haack, *Defending Science* (n. 25), pp. 194ff. See also "The Integrity of Science: What It Means, Why It Matters," pp. 103–27 in this volume, and "Scientific Secrecy and 'Spin': The Sad, Sleazy Saga of the Trials of Remune" pp. 129–45 in this volume.

35. See "Science, Economics, 'Vision,'" pp. 95–102 in this volume.

36. See "An Epistemologist Among the Epidemiologists," pp. 179–82 in this volume.

37. See Haack, *Defending Science* (n. 25), chapter 9; "Trial and Error: The Supreme Court's Philosophy of Science," pp. 161–77 in this volume.

38. Haack, "Truth and Justice, Inquiry and Advocacy, Science and Law," pp. 147–60 in this volume.

39. Haack, "Epistemology Legalized: Or, Truth, Justice, and the American Way," *American Journal of Jurisprudence* 49 (2004): 43–61.

40. On Innocent Realism, see Haack, "Reflections on Relativism: From Momentous Tautology to Seductive Contradiction" (1996), in Haack, *Manifesto of a Passionate Moderate* (n. 7), 149–66; and Haack, "Realisms and Their Rivals: Recovering Our Innocence," *Facta Philosophica* 4 (2002): 67–88.

41. See also "Fallibilism and Faith, Naturalism and the Supernatural, Science and Religion," pp. 183–94 in this volume.

42. Horace Freeland Judson, *The Eighth Day of Creation: Makers of the Revolution in Biology* (New York: Simon and Schuster, 1979), p. 488.

43. See Haack, "The Legitimacy of Metaphysics: Kant's Legacy to Peirce, and Peirce's to Philosophy Today," in Hans Lenk, ed., *Kant Today* (Münster, Germany: LIT Verlag, 2006), pp. 312–27, and in *Polish Journal of Philosophy* 1 (2007): 29–43.

44. But not from chapter 5 of my *Defending Science* (n. 25).

45. George Herbert Mead, *Mind, Self and Society* (Chicago: University of Chicago Press, 1934).

46. W. V. Quine, *Quiddities* (Cambridge: Harvard University Press, 1987), p. 213. However, in *Mathematical Logic* (1940; New York: Harper Torchbooks, 1962) Quine himself had endorsed the view that the expression enclosed in quotation marks is not a semantical part of the whole quotation-mark name.

47. Nicholas Rescher and Ulrich Majer, eds., *On Truth: Original Manuscript Materials (1927–29) from the Ramsey Collection* (Dordrecht, the Netherlands: Kluwer, 1992), p. xiv.

48. Scott Soames, *Understanding Truth* (New York: Oxford University Press, 1999), p. 238.

49. See also "The Unity of Truth and the Plurality of Truths," pp. 43–60 in this volume.

50. Charles Sanders Peirce, *Collected Papers*, eds. Charles Hartshorne, Paul Weiss, and (vols. 7 and 8) Arthur Burks (Cambridge: Harvard University Press, 1931–58), 6.6, c.1903. [References by volume and paragraph number.] "Hylozoism" refers to a doctrine from early Greek philosophy to the effect that all matter has life (a doctrine to which Peirce's "Objective Idealism" has some, albeit distant, affinity. See also Haack, "Not Cynicism, but Synechism" (n. 6).

INDEX